AFRICAN ISSUES

Inside Mining Capitalism

AFRICAN ISSUES

Disability Rights and Inclusiveness in Africa JEFF D. GRISCHOW & MAGNUS MFOAFO-M'CARTHY (EDS)*
Inside Mining Capitalism BENJAMIN RUBBERS (ED)
Women & Peacebuilding in Africa LADAN AFFI, LIV TØNNESSEN & AILI TRIPP (EDS)
Land, Investment & Politics JEREMY LIND, DORIS OKENWA & IAN SCOONES (EDS)
Electricity in Africa CHRISTOPHER D. GORE
Volunteer Economies RUTH PRINCE & HANNAH BROWN (EDS)
Africa's Land Rush RUTH HALL, IAN SCOONES & DZODZI TSIKATA (EDS)
The Development State MAIA GREEN
Africa Rising? IAN TAYLOR
Losing Your Land AN ANSOMS AND THEA HILHORST
China's Aid & Soft Power in Africa KENNETH KING
South Africa's Gold Mines & the Politics of Silicosis JOCK McCULLOCH
From the Pit to the Market DIANE FROST
Sudan Looks East DANIEL LARGE & LUKE A. PATEY (EDS)
The Front Line Runs Through Every Woman ELEANOR O'GORMAN
The Root Causes of Sudan's Civil Wars DOUGLAS H. JOHNSON
Zimbabwe's Land Reform IAN SCOONES, NELSON MARONGWE, BLASIO MAVEDZENGE, JACOB B. MAHENEHENE, FELIX MURIMBARIMBA & CHRISPEN SUKUME
Identity Economics KATE MEAGHER
The Ethiopian Red Terror Trials KJETIL TRONVOLL, CHARLES SCHAEFER & GIRMACHEW ALEMU ANEME (EDS)
Diamonds, Dispossession & Democracy in Botswana KENNETH GOOD
Peace without Profit JOSEPH HANLON
The Lie of the Land MELISSA LEACH & ROBIN MEARNS (EDS)
Fighting for the Rainforest PAUL RICHARDS

Published in the US & Canada by Indiana University Press
Gender & Genocide in Burundi PATRICIA O. DALEY
Guns & Governance in the Rift Valley KENNEDY MKUTU
Becoming Somaliland MARK BRADBURY
Undermining Development SARAH MICHAEL
'Letting them Die' CATHERINE CAMPBELL
Somalia: Economy Without State PETER D. LITTLE
Asbestos Blues JOCK McCULLOCH
Killing for Conservation ROSALEEN DUFFY
Mozambique & the Great Flood of 2000 FRANCES CHRISTIE & JOSEPH HANLON
Angola: Anatomy of an Oil State TONY HODGES
Congo-Paris JANET MACGAFFEY & REMY BAZENGUISSA-GANGA
Africa Works PATRICK CHABAL & JEAN-PASCAL DALOZ
The Criminalization of the State in Africa JEAN-FRANÇOIS BAYART, STEPHEN ELLIS & BEATRICE HIBOU
Famine Crimes ALEX DE WAAL

*forthcoming

AFRICAN ISSUES

Inside Mining Capitalism

The Micropolitics of Work on the Congolese and Zambian Copperbelts

Edited by

Benjamin Rubbers

James Currey
is an imprint of
Boydell & Brewer Ltd
PO Box 9, Woodbridge
Suffolk IP12 3DF (GB)
www.jamescurrey.com
and of
Boydell & Brewer Inc.
668 Mt Hope Avenue
Rochester, NY 14620–2731 (US)
www.boydellandbrewer.com

First published 2021

This book was written as part of the WORKinMINING project at the University of Liège, Belgium. The project received funding from the European Research Council (ERC) under the European Union's Horizon 2020 research and innovation programme (grant agreement n° 646802). The ideas developed in this work reflect the authors' views alone. The ERC is not responsible for any use that may be made of the information it contains

A catalogue record for this book is available on request from the British Library

ISBN 978-1-84701-286-9 (James Currey paperback)

This publication is printed on acid-free paper

CONTENTS

MAPS

Full credit details are provided in the captions to the images in the text. The editor, contributors and publisher are grateful to all the institutions and persons for permission to reproduce the materials in which they hold copyright. Every effort has been made to trace the copyright holders; apologies are offered for any omission, and the publisher will be pleased to add any necessary acknowledgement in subsequent editions.

NOTES ON CONTRIBUTORS

Kristien Geenen is a research associate at the University of Liège. She holds a PhD in Social and Cultural Anthropology from the University of Leuven. She has long-standing fieldwork experience in urban Congo, particularly in the cities of Kinshasa, Butembo and Kolwezi. In 2015–16, she was a postdoctoral researcher at Ghent University, examining social life in hospitals in Kinshasa and Mbandaka. From 2017 until June 2020, she was affiliated with Université de Liège as a postdoctoral researcher, examining trade unions in the mining industry in the Congolese copperbelt, as part of the WORKinMINING research project. Besides urban anthropology, she has a keen interest in history and photography.

Emma Lochery is a postdoctoral researcher at the University of Liège. As part of the WORKinMINING project, she researched the regulation and management of employment in Zambia's copper mines. She holds a doctorate in politics from the University of Oxford and worked as a postdoctoral researcher in the Group for Research on Ethnic Relations, Migration and Equality at the Université Libre de Bruxelles. Her work has also examined the politics of infrastructure in post-conflict Somaliland, the governance of citizenship in Kenya, and mobility and trade between eastern Africa and China.

Thomas McNamara is a lecturer in Development Studies at La Trobe University and the Deputy Director of La Trobe's Master in International Development. As part of the WORKinMINING project, he studied the role of trade unions in the mining industry in Zambia. His key research interest is how Global South economies are shaped by and guide affective relationships and moral norms, especially norms and narratives relating to 'development'. He has a PhD from the University of Melbourne and has conducted fieldwork in Zambia and Malawi.

James Musonda received an MA degree in Labour Policy and Globalisation from the University of Witwatersrand in 2016. His MA thesis was concerned with the ways in which mineworkers living in the communities around a mine experience and respond to the pollution caused by the company which is also their employer. James is currently a doctoral student at University of Liège. As part of the WORKinMINING project, he investigated the changes brought about by new mining investments to the organisation of work, and on gender and intergenerational relationships within mineworkers' families in Zambia. His previous experience as a trade union leader in the Zambian mining sector, and his close links with mineworkers and trade unions, was important to carrying out his research.

Francesca Pugliese is currently working in the WORKinMINING project as a PhD candidate in Social Anthropology at the University of Liège and in History at Leiden University. Her research within the project focused on mineworkers in the Congolese copperbelt. After obtaining her BA and MRes degrees in Ethnology and Cultural Anthropology at Sapienza, University of Rome, she received an MA in African Studies from the University of Leiden. Her master's thesis explored issues linked to land tenure, land grabbing and corporate social responsibility of oil and gas companies in Western Ghana. Before starting her PhD project, she worked for two years on a European project dealing with gender inequalities in the workplace and women's difficulties maintaining a work–life balance.

Benjamin Rubbers, the book editor and the principal investigator of the WORKinMINING project, received his PhD degree in Social Anthropology from the Université Libre de Bruxelles and the École des Hautes Études en Sciences Sociales in 2006. After a postdoctoral fellowship at the University of Oxford, he was appointed Full Professor at the Université de Liège and part-time Lecturer at the Université Libre de Bruxelles. In 2015, he was invited to become Research Associate at the Society, Work, and Development Institute of the University of Witwatersrand. His research focuses on social changes in the Congolese copperbelt, where he has conducted research since 2000.

ACKNOWLEDGEMENTS

This book is the result of the collective research project 'Reinventing paternalism. The micropolitics of work in the mining companies of Central Africa' (WORKinMINING) at the University of Liège, Belgium. Generous funding of the European Research Council (ERC) through a Consolidator Grant in 2014 gave us, the contributors to this book, the opportunity to carry out multiple research stays in the mining sites and towns described in the book, as well as sufficient time to reflect on what we had learned. As the project's principal investigator and the editor of this book, I also received a professorship from the Francqui Foundation, which allowed me to devote myself to the research from 2015 to 2018.

This research would not have been possible without the support of the University of Lubumbashi (UNILU) in the Democratic Republic of Congo, and the Copperbelt University (CBU) in Zambia. Professors Donatien Dibwe, from UNILU, and John Lungu, from CBU, in particular, provided intellectual inspiration as giants in the study of mining in the two copperbelts and spared no effort to help us obtain the necessary authorisations, get our research started, and organise research seminars in Congo and Zambia. We express here our thanks to both of them as well as to Professor Owen Sichone at CBU for their hospitality, support and guidance. In both countries, we owe a great debt of gratitude to those who enabled us to conduct research internships in different trade unions and mining companies, which we cannot name here for confidentiality reasons. We also thank all those who welcomed us to seminars, events and trainings that further enriched our knowledge of the mining sector.

More than 600 people in Congo and Zambia participated in this research, making it impossible to name them all here, even aside from our funder's confidentiality requirements. We would like to thank the many people who welcomed us into their workplaces, homes and social spaces and took the time to answer our questions with great patience. Above and below ground, mineworkers, safety officers, trade unionists, managers, and so many others helped guide our understandings of the micropolitics of work. We would also like to thank those whose knowledge of the mining sector, friendship, and help with introductions encouraged us to ask new questions and re-engage long-standing debates: in particular, Jerry Kalonji, Jean-Paul Lokadja, Luc Mukendi, Paul Mpoyo, Vicky Mukews, Pascal Tshibamb and Bourgeois Tshibangu in Congo; and in Zambia, John Bwalya, Hikabwa Chipande, Marja Hinfelaar, Wisdom Kaleng'a, Robby Kapesa, Yewa Kumwenda, Charles Muchimba, and Limbisani Tembo. We also thank the trade unionists, HR managers, scholars and others who attended our seminars in Kitwe and Lumbumbashi. Their critiques and questions pushed us to improve our arguments and refine our writing.

Besides residents of Congo and Zambia, we benefited from the assistance of other scholars doing research in the Central African Copperbelt. Most of them are members of the Copperbelt research network launched at the beginning of the project; our thanks go to Patience Mususa for organising the initial workshop that brought so many of us together. We thank Miles Larmer, who started a complementary research project on the two copperbelts at the same time; he has been a generous colleague and a linchpin in the Copperbelt network. We are also grateful to Stephanie Laemmert, Sarah Katz-Lavigne, Duncan Money, and Iva Pesa. Finally, our deep gratitude goes to Michel Naepels, our project's ethics advisor, for his sincere and benevolent interest in our research. We also warmly thank the two reviewers for their attentive reading of the first version of this manuscript. Their relevant and constructive critiques and suggestions enabled us to improve the quality of the book.

ABBREVIATIONS

CNMC	Chinese Non-Ferrous Metals Company
CREG	China Railway Group
CSR	Corporate Social Responsibility
FDI	Foreign Direct Investment
GDP	Gross Domestic Product
Gécamines	Générale des Carrières et des Mines
HR	Human Resource
ICMM	International Council on Mining and Metals
MMD	Movement for Multiparty Democracy
MP	Member of Parliament
MUZ	Mineworkers' Union of Zambia
NRMWU	Northern Rhodesia Mine Workers' Union
NUM	National Union of Mineworkers (South Africa)
NUMAW	National Union of Mine and Allied Workers
ODO	Organisational Development Officer
PPE	Personal Protective Equipment
RAA	Rhodesian (later Zambian) Anglo American
RST	Rhodesian (from 1964, Roan) Selection Trust
Sicomines	Sino-Congolaise des Mines
SOE	State-Owned Enterprise
UMHK	Union Minière du Haut-Katanga
UMUZ	United Mineworkers Union of Zambia
UNTZ	Union Nationale des Travailleurs Zaïrois
ZCCM	Zambian Consolidated Copper Mines
ZCCM-IH	Zambian Consolidated Copper Mines Investment Holdings
ZCTU	Zambian Congress of Trade Unions
ZIHRM	Zambian Institute of Human Resource Management

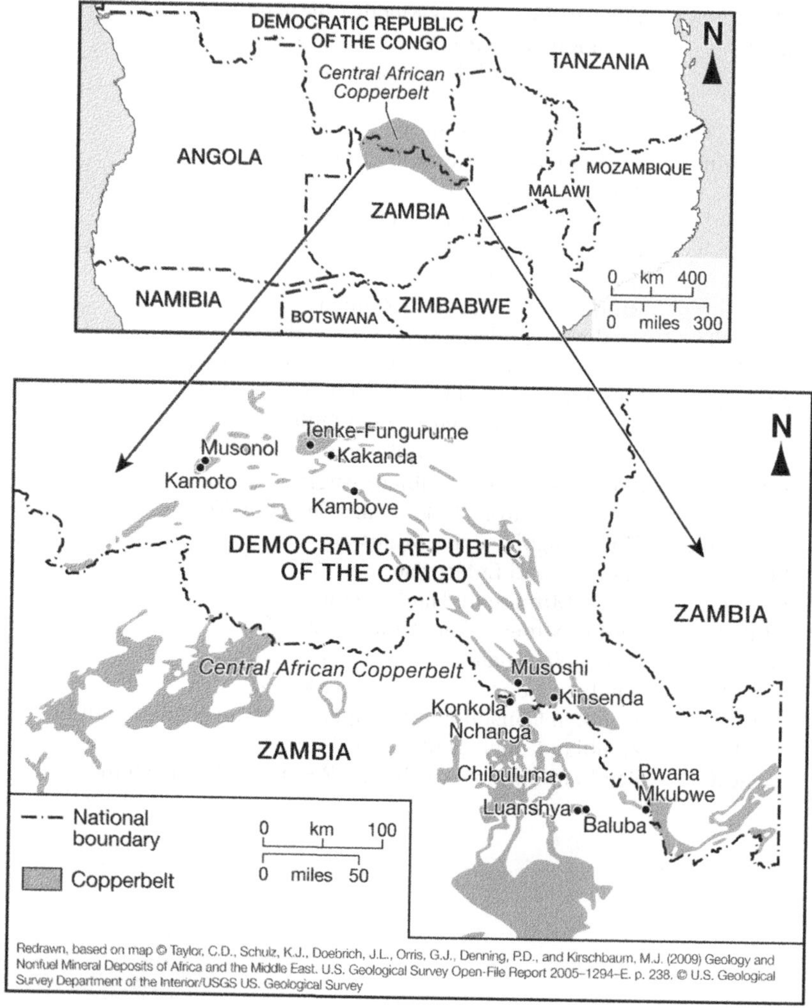

Map 1. Geological Map of the Central African Copperbelt. Based on map © Taylor, C.D., Schulz, K.J., Doebrich, J.L., Orris, G.J., Denning, P.D., and Kirschbaum, M.J. (2009) Geology and Nonfuel Mineral Deposits of Africa and the Middle East. U.S. Geological Survey Open-File Report 2005–1294–E. p. 238. © U.S. Geological Survey Department of the Interior/USGS US. Geological Survey.

Introduction: Mining Capitalism from Below

BENJAMIN RUBBERS

As you read these lines, you are probably using copper in one way or another. Do you know how it has been produced? The general aim of this book is to enhance our knowledge of the working conditions in which this metal is extracted in one of the world's major copper-producing regions: the Central African Copperbelt. In following the everyday life of mineworkers, union leaders and human resource (HR) managers, it seeks to shed some light on the 'hidden abode of production' of one of the most basic commodities of the contemporary world (Marx 1867; see Fraser 2014). Although used every day, copper is generally hidden from view, in wire sheaths or appliance cases, and most people do not know much about how it was extracted and processed before arriving in their house, their car or their computer. Used as a basic material in the construction sector, the automobile industry and the manufacture of household appliances, copper is at the same time ubiquitous and largely invisible.

Abundant in the earth's crust, malleable and resistant to corrosion, copper was the first metal worked by men and women to make jewellery, tools and coins. It was only after its electrical conductivity was discovered in the nineteenth century, however, that it began to be extracted on a large scale to manufacture the cables and wires necessary for the extension of the power grid all over the world. With world population growth, urban development and the ever-increasing number of household appliances, demand for copper has risen steadily ever since. The 'red metal' is everywhere; it is an essential component of modernisation projects, from the electrification of nations in the late nineteenth century to the information and communication technology revolution of the twenty-first.

To some extent, this growing significance of copper in the global world has been eclipsed by oil, to which the media, the arts and the social sciences have often conferred a 'demiurgic power' in the making of modernity (Appel, Mason and Watts 2015). Whether in the news, in literature, or in the social sciences, discourses about oil often take on a mythical dimension. Oil is imagined ambiguously, as a miracle resource that brings wealth and development or as a cursed resource engendering poverty, disorder and conflict. While a similar process of reification occurs for other precious materials such as gold or diamonds, it is rarely the case for copper. It has largely remained discreet, a base metal, one that does not arouse much public interest. Yet the global race for copper preceded the oil era and will certainly survive it. The rapid development of new technologies, renewable energies and electric vehicles will increase demand. If the energy transition from fossil fuels to renewables is to take place, it will depend on the availability of low-cost copper.[1]

To meet the ever-increasing demand for copper, the mining industry has had to extract ore from deposits with ever lower copper grades and/or located further from the main consumer markets (Schmitz 2000; Evans and Saunders 2015). The global centre of gravity of copper mining has consequently shifted several times since the nineteenth century. Long established in Europe (United Kingdom, Spain), it migrated to North America (United States, Canada) in the early nineteenth century before gradually moving to South America (Chile, Peru). In this shifting global geography, the Central African Copperbelt (straddling the north of Zambia and the south of the Democratic Republic of Congo), which is the concern of this book, emerged as an important secondary mining centre from the 1930s onwards. Notwithstanding the highs and lows of their copper production, Zambia and Congo have been among the world's ten leading copper producers ever since.

Over the course of the 2000s, demand from China and other emerging economies led to a surge in copper prices, which triggered a boom of foreign direct investment (FDI) in the copper mining sector. Independently of the rise of Chinese demand, this increase of FDI in copper mining must be understood as the result of several processes, including the gradual depletion of copper deposits in the Americas since the 1950s, the reforms undertaken by most resource-rich countries in the Global South since the 1980s to liberalise their mining sector and attract foreign investors on favourable terms, and the availability of capital on the financial markets in the late 1990s and early 2000s.

Since then, world copper production has virtually doubled, from 11 billion metric tonnes in 2000 to 21 billion metric tonnes in 2018 (ICSG 2018). This boom has not fundamentally altered the topography of copper mining in the world as the bulk of financial flows have been directed towards traditional copper-mining countries such as Chile, the United States, Australia, Zambia and Congo. What is new in this boom is that it led to a diversification of the sector globally, with new actors investing in copper mining and processing overseas. These include Swiss commodity trading companies; American, Canadian, South African or Australian exploration companies; Chinese, Polish or Kazakh state-owned enterprises

[1] The same could be said for cobalt, of which the Congolese copperbelt is the world's main producer. From 2016 to 2018, speculation on the growth of the market for electric cars led to a surge in the price of this metal due to its use in manufacturing rechargeable batteries. As had occurred in the past, this sudden rise in cobalt prices was a welcome boost for mining companies at a time of declining copper prices. Since then, however, the price has collapsed: the demand for electric vehicles has been slower to materialise than expected, and cobalt stocks on the world market are in surplus.

(SOEs) and so forth. The development of new mining projects has also been accompanied by the dissemination of new excavation, processing and labour management techniques, enabling companies to produce more at lower cost. Although the adoption of these techniques has been far from uniform or systematic, it has had multifaceted consequences for the relationships that foreign companies have with various categories of people in the countries where they start new mining projects, beginning with the workers themselves.

Dealing with the Legacy of Paternalism

This book focuses on the power relations implicated in the implementation of new labour management strategies by foreign companies that have developed new copper-mining projects in Congo and Zambia in the period between 2000 and 2018. Its aim is to study how the workforce management practices of these companies are negotiated by various categories of local actors. The Central African Copperbelt is a particularly interesting research site from which to address this question, for two main reasons.

On the one hand, the mining sector on both sides of the border between Congo and Zambia border was long dominated by large companies that put in place a paternalistic labour regime (see Chapter 1 of this book). From the 1930s, they built housing estates and social infrastructure allowing them to take charge of, and control, the lives of their workers and their families. This regime was continued into the 1980s when the Zambian Consolidated Copper Mines (ZCCM) in Zambia and the Générale des Carrières et des Mines (Gécamines) in Congo – the two SOEs that resulted from the merger and nationalisation of colonial mining companies after independence in the 1960s – began to decline.

On the other hand, the liberalisation of the mining sector has attracted foreign companies of various sizes and origins in both countries. In the late 1990s and early 2000s, the Zambian and Congolese governments were under pressure from the World Bank to dismantle their mining SOEs and to take measures to attract foreign investors in the mining sector. The two countries then witnessed an influx of companies of all kinds: American majors, Canadian juniors, South African and Australian exploration companies, Chinese SOEs, and businessmen from Belgium, India, or Israel – in short, all the actors of the global copper-mining sector. They were competing to take over the most promising assets of ZCCM and Gécamines at low cost and/or to obtain rights over untouched world-class deposits.

Unsurprisingly both the Congolese and the Zambian mining sectors have been the theatre of numerous mergers and acquisitions since the early 2000s. Despite this eventful history, almost thirty mining projects – including a dozen large or mid-sized projects – have now entered the production phase. Together these projects produced two million tonnes of copper in 2018, that is, eight times more than ZCCM and Gécamines at their record low in 2000. Once the dozen mining projects still in the development phase start production, the Central African Copperbelt may well become one of the world's most important centres of copper mining.

By examining the power relations involved in the implementation of new labour management strategies by new mining companies, the broader ambition behind this book is to understand how new labour management practices are built from the ruins of twentieth-century paternalism. To what extent do these new labour practices break with those of ZCCM and Gécamines in the past? Our hypothesis is that new mining projects should not be exclusively conceived as the result of external forces, but as the outcome of a 'formation' process involving various categories of actors both inside and outside corporations (on the concept of formation, see Berman and Lonsdale 1992; Bayart 1993). This is especially the case since mining projects have become very capital-intensive. To make their investment secure and profitable, foreign companies have to cope with the pressures exerted by political leaders, the laws enforced by state officials, and the demands made by trade unions and the workers – a set of rules, norms and expectations that are, in the cases of Congo and Zambia, profoundly marked by the paternalistic model inherited from Gécamines and ZCCM.

Putting in place a particular labour management strategy does not fall within the perfectly controlled implementation of a rational plan: it is a complex process of improvisation and adaptation, giving rise to various forms of mobilisation, translation and resistance (Akrich, Callon and Latour 2002a, 2002b; see also, in the anthropology of development, Olivier de Sardan 2005; Mosse 2005; Lavigne-Delville 2012). Our aim is accordingly to understand how a range of actors involved in the domain of work in Congo and Zambia understand and transform mining companies' labour management practices. Far from colonising a *terra nullius*, these companies are caught in various constellations of power which influence how their projects are carried out. This approach 'from below' is not meant to underestimate the power of foreign corporations but to reposition their projects within the complex power relationships that mediate them locally, and to capture the distinctive dynamics created by these interactions. It also involves paying particular attention to the historicity of practices and discourses relating to work in the mining sector. Because of the century-old inclusion of the mining industry in the social fabric of both copperbelts, the expectations and conflicts aroused by the arrival of new companies cannot be adequately understood independently of the model provided by ZCCM and Gécamines in the past. From this perspective, the recent boom in foreign investments in Central Africa is not viewed simply as a form of 'dispossession' by a new form of imperialism (Harvey 2003; see also Li 2009, 2011, 2017), but as a more complex 'grafting' process (Bayart 1994, 1996), through which mining capitalism becomes entangled in the historical trajectories of the two copperbelts in new ways.

The Micropolitics of Work

Capitalism is simply defined here as a mode of production based on private property and wage labour, oriented towards the accumulation of profit and capital. As such, it is associated with corporate business organisation and the use of machines in the production process. Accordingly, the concept of mining capitalism refers to the activities of companies which hire wage workers to operate mines by mechanical means. It differs in this respect from artisanal mining, where miners are neither owners of the mine, nor the employees of a company, and use simple hand tools to extract and process the ore. While artisanal mining is integrated into the global commodity market, it is not a capitalist mode of production. This book does not deal with the complex articulations existing between these two modes of production (see Rubbers 2019a). Its aim is more precisely to contribute to our understanding of the relationship between capital and labour in the mining industry.

This relationship is a long-standing area of research in the literature on mining since the 1950s (Epstein 1958; Nash 1993 [1979]; Parpart 1983; Moodie 1994; Kublock 1998; Finn 1998; see Rubbers forthcoming). The main focus of this body of literature has been the ability of workers to create a world of their own in the mines, and the development of a militant working-class consciousness. Special attention has historically been paid to their social and cultural life, to strikes and other forms of resistance, and to the dynamics of trade unionism. For various reasons, this interest in class politics has tended to fade into the background in the literature on the most recent mining boom, in which a new generation of mining projects use excavation and processing techniques that enable them to mine large deposits with fewer workers than in the past. At the same time, because these projects have a shorter lifespan than those that came before them, their impact on the environment is more visible and impressive. Today, mining companies dig, in a few years, holes wider and deeper than those their predecessors made in almost a century.

In this context, researchers' attention has been largely concentrated on the new type of relationships that mining companies develop with local communities in the Global South: the protest actions of local communities against mining corporations (Bebbington and Bury 2013; Kirsch 2014; Golub 2014; Sawyer and Gomez 2014; Li 2015; Filer and Le Meur 2017); the tendency of mining projects to operate inside securitised enclaves isolating them from this potentially hostile environment (Ferguson 2005, 2006; Hönke 2009, 2010; Appel 2012; Côte and Korf 2018; Pijpers 2019); the implementation of corporate social responsibility (CSR) programmes to win some support in the local communities (Hilson 2012; Szablowski 2007; Dashwood 2012; Rajak 2011; Welker 2014); and the broker role played by local elites, especially customary chiefs, in these politics of contention and patronage (Manson and Mbenga 2003; Negi 2010; Geenen and Claessens 2013; Capps and

Sonwabile 2016; Smith 2018). Labour is not absent from these studies on the relationship between companies and communities, but tends to be reduced to the issue of access to jobs, and to be exclusively understood in terms of compensation (Filer and Le Meur 2017: 17). As a result, the social condition of mineworkers, and the politics of production more generally, is only discussed briefly and marginally in this body of literature, when it is not discarded outright as being of secondary importance.

If industrial mineworkers are no longer centre stage in the literature on mining, several social scientists have nevertheless sought to understand how they have been affected by the transformations undergone by the global mining industry since the 1990s: the rise of subcontracting, the promotion of a safety culture, the adoption of 12-hours shifts, the development of fly-in fly-out operations, the provision of credit facilities, and/or the co-optation of trade unions as corporate partners (Rolston 2010, 2013, 2014; Donham 2011; Bezuidenhout and Buhlungu 2011; Rajak 2012, 2016; James and Rajak 2014; Moodie and Von Holdt 2015; Capps 2016; Kesküla 2016, 2018; Botiveau 2017; Keskula and Sanchez 2019; Phakathi 2018).[2] In contrast to studies on mineworkers in the twentieth century, these authors do not seek to depict class cultures. Distancing themselves from a research agenda in terms of class making, they focus on how workers cope with new labour management techniques.

Even if mineworkers are now fewer in number and politically weaker than in the past, these studies show the insights that can be gained from taking work as a lens to study the transformations of the mining industry in the twenty-first century. This book follows this line of enquiry by focusing on the 'micropolitics' of work. This concept of 'micropolitics' is of relatively common use in the social sciences, including mining studies (e.g. Negi 2011; Rubbers 2013; Pijpers 2018). Although the meaning conferred to it in these studies is presumably close to the one we give to it below, what it is supposed to highlight, or the type of approach it calls forth, remains unclear or indefinite. Below the concept of 'micropolitics' is elaborated in more detail as a heuristic tool to explore the power relations that come into play in the domain of work. Its aim is to make operational the approach of the mining boom from below advocated above.

[2] This is particularly the case in South Africa, where researchers have continued to investigate the social world of miners from different perspectives. The Marikana massacre, in which thirty-four miners were killed during a strike in 2012, sparked an avalanche of analyses about the changing nature of work in the mining industry, the new face of trade union politics and state violence in post-apartheid South Africa (see, e.g., Alexander 2013; Chinguno 2013; Stewart 2013; Moodie 2016).

The Co-production of Capitalism

Focusing on the micropolitics of work enables a better understanding of how the development of mining projects is supported, constrained and shaped by workers, trade unionists, labour inspectors, customary chiefs and so on. In this perspective, mining companies are not viewed as external monolithic institutions that enter into relationships with local communities while developing new extractive projects, an implicit view in most of the literature. Instead, extractive projects are studied as being themselves co-produced by various actors both inside and outside mining companies, from the very first steps that foreign investors take in the country.

In contrast to recent scholarship in mining studies (O'Neill and Gibson-Graham 1999; Welker 2014; Golub 2014), the purpose of this approach is not so much to dissolve the representation of the mining corporation by showing how it is enacted as an ideational macro-actor in different ways depending on circumstances than to bring to light the material, social and symbolic work necessary for developing mining projects in a given context. Building on recent scholarship in the anthropology of capitalism, we seek to understand how these extractive projects are generated out of the social networks, life projects and ethics of various local actors (see Yanagisako 2002; Ho 2009; Shever 2012; Bear 2015; Bear *et al.*, 2015; Tsing 2015). The various forms of disposition and capital that these people bring into mining projects can be viewed as productive powers essential to the expansion of mining capitalism in different parts of the world.

Since it focuses on everyday practices, this anthropological approach runs the risk of disintegrating mining projects into a multitude of practices and discourses and, in so doing, of putting too much emphasis on the contingency of their operations, the uncertainties with which they are confronted, the very fragility of their existence. This is a pitfall that would make it difficult to account for the development of capitalism in the longer term. Yet, as we have seen above, the history of copper-mining capitalism since the nineteenth century shows certain regular tendencies, which derive principally from the continued increase of demand for copper, the inexorable depletion of copper deposits, and the price inelasticity of both supply and demand in the copper market. From these basic tendencies result – among other things – the expansion of copper-mining capitalism on a global scale, the increasing mechanisation of production, the escalating capital intensity of the industry, the growing importance of financial actors, and the booms and busts of investments. As the literature on mining reviewed above suggests, these general trends have had far-reaching consequences on workers globally.

The challenge for the social sciences is to relate the contingent practices that enable the accumulation of capital on a day-to-day basis to the longer-term tendencies that characterise the history of capitalism (Sewell 2008).

To make this connection, we propose to include in the analysis of the micropolitics of work the government techniques that mining companies, but also trade unions, state administrations and other institutional bodies, use to organise their activities and structure work practices in the mining sector: these include safety rules, industrial relations procedures, labour laws, etc. Although these government techniques do not come from the same source of power and are used for different purposes, they contribute to making the work environment in which mining companies operate more stable and predictable, two fundamental conditions for the development of modern capitalism according to Max Weber. This is, I would add, *a fortiori* the case for industrial mining projects. While they are confronted with strong uncertainties of various sorts, the importance of their capitalisation calls forth a long-term amortisation plan – a necessity which is often overlooked by the media when dealing with mining investments in Africa.

In the context of the recent boom, the global mining sector has witnessed the diffusion of new labour management techniques in the form of more or less standardised models (management software, surveillance devices, lean management solutions, participative methods, etc.). This diffusion accounts for the apparent resemblances in the organisation of work between numerous mining projects around the world. These management techniques have nevertheless been appropriated selectively by the different companies that participated in the boom. In each of these, some new techniques coexist with older techniques (recruitment methods, collective agreements, personnel archives, welfare programmes, etc.).

Drawing inspiration from Foucault, the mining corporation can be seen as an assemblage of multiple 'government techniques' whose implementation involves complex 'power games' – the *micropolitics of work* of this study – and which contribute to establish more or less stable 'states of domination', and which we term 'labour regimes' in the next chapter. Focusing on corporate government techniques is not new in mining studies. Whether they explicitly build on the work of Foucault or not, several social scientists in the past twenty years have studied some of the government techniques that mining companies put in place, especially the securitised enclave and CSR programmes. These studies examine in great detail the power games involved in the implementation of such techniques as well as their power effects. As they focus on a single government technique, however, they miss a key point of Foucault's approach, that of taking into consideration the variety of government techniques, which often have distinctive backgrounds and involve different power games (Rubbers 2020; see Lascoumes 2004; Lascoumes and LeGalès 2005; Rose, O'Maley and Valverde 2006). Once examined through these government techniques, mining companies – and mining capitalism more generally – appear caught in different power constellations and timescapes (Bear 2015; Bear *et al.* 2015).

Changing Power Constellations

Taking the micropolitics of work as an analytical lens then entails turning the question around to ask how the various actors involved in the transformation of working conditions in the mining sector contribute, by doing so, to the transformation of broader power constellations in the social spaces where mining projects are established. A focus on work is warranted for studying these broader dynamics in the Central African Copperbelt. For more than a century, living in the urban centres of this region has been closely associated with the opportunity to find a job, and especially a job in the mining industry. From a more general point of view, it is difficult to understand the political struggles and the dynamics of inequality that have marked the history of both copperbelts without paying special attention to the role of mineworkers. As explained above, the hypothesis behind this book is that new mining investors cannot leave this past behind them. The micropolitics of work involved in the development of new mining projects can therefore provide an interesting angle from which to analyse the broader changes that they engender in various power constellations.

The first power constellation to take into consideration is, of course, the *union field*.[3] In both copperbelts, the mining boom was accompanied by a revitalisation of union activities, with trade unions entering into a fierce competition to represent workers in the new mining companies. Their introduction into these companies has confronted the unions with new challenges that have profoundly affected their strategies and the meanings unionists give to their action. However, far from being limited to the union field, the study of the micropolitics of work can also shed new light on conflicts in *political arenas*.[4] In a context where well-paid jobs are few, the competition in the labour market is strong. Far from becoming a secondary issue, access to employment is high on the list of demands made to mining companies, and various political actors try to act as labour brokers between the local communities and the mining companies. In both countries, chiefs, ethnic associations and local political authorities do not hesitate to recommend people to mining companies, to exert pressure on their local content policy, and to intervene in labour disputes.[5] Finally, it

3 In the sociology of Bourdieu, the field is a relatively autonomous space of confrontation organised around specific issues or resources, and structured by specific institutions, rules, and cultural dispositions (see Hilgers and Mangez 2014).

4 Like the power field, the concept of political arena refers to a space of confrontation organised around specific issues or resources (Bierschenk 1988; Bierschenk and Olivier de Sardan 1998). In contrast to the power field, however, this space is thought of as relatively localised, unstructured and heterogeneous. In other words, the political arena is not organised by specific institutions, rules and cultural dispositions.

5 The term 'local content policy' refers to all the measures taken by mining companies to contribute to local economic development. These measures mostly focus on increasing local employment, procurement, and subcontracting.

is possible to study the micropolitics of work from the various categories of state and non-state actors involved in the implementation of labour policies (political leaders, senior officials in national ministries, labour officers, labour consultants, union representatives, HR managers, etc.). These actors are not viewed in this perspective as competitors striving for specific resources in a power field or in a political arena, but as translators along *chains of political action* (see Pressman and Wildavsky 1973; Lascoumes and Le Galès 2012).

No matter which power constellation is taken into consideration, special attention must be paid to the scale at which it comes into play. Indeed, the micropolitics of work is not confined to the local level. Workers' claims during a strike, for instance, are likely to be instrumentalised by actors in the union field, the political arena, or even along the public action chain at the local, regional, national, or international levels. In doing so, claims are subjected to a complex work of selection and translation which allows strikers to win supporters and opponents outside the workplace. In return, this process can affect the way workers perceive the situation and interact with their employer.

Beyond these political constellations, which feature various forms of institutionalised power, a micropolitical approach involves exploring the broader social inequalities that the boom in mining investments has contributed to generate or exacerbate: the recreation of the colour bar, gender and generational dynamics, or new patterns of social mobility and inequality. Among these forms of inequality, gender receives special attention in this book (see Chapter 3).

As part of their paternalistic policies, colonial mining companies established in the Central African Copperbelt sought to impose monogamy, domesticity, and the model of the patriarchal nuclear family upon their workers (Parpart 1986a, 1986b; Dibwe 2001; Rubbers 2015). Although few workers achieved this model, it nevertheless provided them with a set of norms by which to consider their marital lives, the education of their children, or their relationships with kin. Within the companies' housing estates, the patriarchal family model gave rise to a new economy of social distinction, with the practices and symbols associated with 'modern' family life being used by men and women to claim moral credit and social superiority. From the 1970s onwards, however, the decline in workers' remuneration gradually undermined men's authority over their wives and children as they found themselves unable to meet their households' needs. To supplement their revenues, their wives and children developed their own economic activities and gained more autonomy within the family. In these circumstances, the norms and hierarchies constitutive of the patriarchal family model were increasingly subjected to resistance and arguments.

As new mining companies hire mostly men, they contribute to reproducing the mine as a masculine space and to restore the authority of male mineworkers within the family. On the other hand, some companies have developed gender equality programmes and a small number of women have been appointed to positions that were once exclusively occupied by men, such as geologists, electricians, or loader drivers. Moreover, most workers now belong to a generation that has been in contact with new models of love, family life and social success. It can be assumed, therefore, that they do not simply reproduce their parents' family ideals and norms, but 'regenerate' them in new ways; they come into 'fresh contact' with the legacy of patriarchal family and paternalism (Cole and Durham 2006). To understand how work in the mining sector contributes to generating new gender dynamics, Francesca Pugliese and James Musonda focus, in Chapter 3, on the everyday life of female mineworkers in the workplace and at home, and reflect on the historical significance of their experience.

At the societal level, many studies focus on the dispossession of local people by foreign companies and conclude that their new mining projects only benefit the few (shareholders, political leaders and a minority of workers).[6] If this analysis – that the contribution of mining investments to local development is limited – is not wrong, it is also far too simplistic, as it leads to a stark opposition between a minority of winners and a majority of losers. A focus on the micropolitics of work provides a better starting point to study the class inequalities generated by the mining boom. As Wright (1997; see also Rubbers 2019a, 2019b) reminds us, the analysis of labour relations is key to making sense of the dynamics of class divisions caused by the development of capitalism, in this case, mining capitalism. Such an approach provides a more complex picture of these dynamics than an approach exclusively focusing on the property of the means of production.

Methodology

In short, to study the changes caused by new mining projects in the Central Africa Copperbelt, this book foregrounds an approach from below, centred on the micropolitics of work. This approach aims to understand how actors within and outside companies shape the implementation of mining projects and how, in doing so, they participate in the transformation of various power configurations in Congo and Zambia.

To study the micropolitics of work in the mining sector, a team comprising six researchers including myself carried out extended fieldwork in Zambia and Congo from 2016 to 2019.[7] During this period, we interviewed or had

[6] This critical line of analysis can be found in most studies on mine-affected communities cited above as well as in a multitude of reports on the social impact of mining investments by non-governmental organisations.

[7] This book is the result of the WORKinMINING project at the University of Liège, Belgium (see www.workinmining.ulg.ac.be). The research project was funded by the European Research Council (ERC) Consolidator Grant programme (ID 646802).

in-depth informal conversations with more than 600 people involved in the mining industry, principally workers, managers, subcontractors, trade unionists, labour officials and political authorities at different levels. In addition to these interviews, we carried out participant observation both inside and outside mining companies: James Musonda spent nine months doing participant observation in a mining company in Zambia, including six months helping workers to carry out various tasks in an underground mine; Francesca Pugliese and Benjamin Rubbers completed one-month internships in the HR departments of three different mining companies in Congo; Thomas McNamara was granted a desk at the head office of the main mining union in Zambia, which allowed him to follow trade union representatives in their everyday activities during the entire period of his fieldwork; and Kristien Geenen and Emma Lochery had, respectively, the opportunity to follow a strike in a Chinese company in Congo and to attend professional training sessions for HR managers in Zambia. To varying extents, all team members also participated in the social life of research participants at home, in bars, at church, etc. Finally, the team did research in the archives and collected various types of documents from mining companies, labour courts and state administrations.

Our research was organised around three complementary subprojects, each carried out by two researchers, one in Congo and the other in Zambia.

The first subproject dealt with the multiple dimensions of the work experience in mining companies. Drawing inspiration from classical ethnographies of mining work cultures (Gordon 1977; Nash 1993 [1979]; Moodie 1994; Finn 1998), two doctoral students (Pugliese in Congo and Musonda in Zambia) studied the everyday life of various categories of mine employees at work, in the family, and during leisure activities. Their research focused on three main themes: workers' tactics, that is, the multiple means through which they appropriate, change or undermine the social order of mining corporations; their moral economy, or the values that they use to evaluate their working conditions; and the gender and generational dynamics in which mineworkers take part. In developing these lines of analysis, their aim has been to understand how mining companies' labour management techniques contribute to organising workers' subjectivities, and to develop a broader reflection on the social and cultural changes that the mining boom has generated in both copperbelts.

Carried out by two postdoctoral researchers (Geenen in Congo and McNamara in Zambia), the second subproject focused on the dynamics of the trade union power field. As elsewhere, the existing scholarship on trade unions in Africa has long focused on their role in social and political emancipation movements. Distancing themselves from this tradition, Geenen and McNamara sought inspiration from ethnographies investigating the ordinary work of trade unionists and the dilemmas they face in dealing with employers and workers (Lubeck 1986; Von Holdt 2003; Werbner 2014; Botiveau 2017; Lazar 2017; see Rubbers and Roy 2017). Building on this body of literature, they paid special attention to everyday union activities in the workplace, the internal functioning of union organisations, and the competition between unions in the mining sector. This ethnographic approach allowed them not only to produce a 'thick description' of the critical moments of trade union life, such as union elections and strikes, but also to reflect more broadly on the role of trade unions in the emergence of a new labour regime.

Within the framework of the third subproject about the regulation of work, a postdoctoral researcher and the principal investigator of the research project (Lochery in Zambia and Rubbers in Congo, respectively) interviewed HR managers, labour officials and political authorities at different levels, from customary chiefs to national politicians. By including all the actors involved in the regulation of work in the mining sector, their ambition was to develop an understanding of industrial relations from below. Drawing inspiration from the literature on middle managers (Dalton 1959; Jackall 1988; Kunda 1992; Watson 1994; Mills 2002; Hassard, McCann and Morris 2007; Whyte 2013), they focused on the role of HR managers in the implementation of mining companies' labour management strategies at the interface between expatriate executives, trade unions and state representatives. To study how labour inspectors, judges, or senior officials influence the organisation of work in mining companies, they built on recent ethnographies of the state in Africa (Blundo and Olivier de Sardan 2006; Bierschenk and Olivier de Sardan 2014; de Herdt and Olivier de Sardan 2015) while giving special consideration to the way in which state officials understand and use the law (see Rubbers and Gallez 2015; Andreetta 2018).

The strength of this teamwork method is that it provides the opportunity to develop a comprehensive analysis of the micropolitics of work in both countries. For all the innovations brought to ethnographic fieldwork in the twentieth century, it has largely remained an individual activity. When embarking on a collective research agenda, this typically takes the form of individual research projects conducted separately in different places. Few anthropologists have followed the example of the Rhodes Livingstone Institute (RLI) research team of the 1950s in uniting their efforts to study the various dynamics constitutive of one macro-process, in the same area (Gluckman 1945, 1961; Schumaker 2001). This is the type of collaboration that we attempted to create. Since our research dealt with people in relation with each other, it provided the opportunity to enrich the three subprojects reciprocally (research on corporations, workers, trade unions and state representatives is complementary) and to avoid treating mining companies, the state or trade unions as monolithic institutions. In line with an anthropological perspective, their practices and discourses were studied at ground level, from the everyday work of the people acting as their spokespersons.

This teamwork method also allowed methodologically consistent comparisons to be made between our case studies. While team members had a great deal of freedom in conducting their respective research projects, they were asked, for each subproject, to answer the same limited set of questions, to share their data and to develop a coherent theoretical argument together on the basis of the comparison between their respective case studies in the Congolese and Zambian copperbelts. What is interesting in the comparison between Zambia and Congo is that, since the 2000s, they have witnessed a boom in foreign investment which has led to the development of new mining projects both in traditional mining areas and in remote rural areas. Although to varying degrees depending on their location, these mining projects – which, in some cases, have the same parent company – have to deal with the legacy of paternalism left by ZCCM and Gécamines.

In comparing our data, inspiration also came from the work of the RLI (Gluckman 1940a, 1940b, 1961; Mitchell 1956, 1983; Van Velsen 1967). Gluckman and his colleagues were among the first anthropologists to integrate a comparative approach into the research design itself; to take as units of comparison not cultures, but social processes; to replace these social processes within a wider power field and to analyse them in a historical perspective; and to conceive of the comparative approach not as a means of illustrating universal theories, but as a methodological device whose principal aim is to further explore, and better discriminate, the factors involved in the social processes under study (see Kapferer 2006). Indeed, the main difficulty with the comparison of social processes is to discriminate factors that may account for their similarities and differences as they change over time, involve different domains of practice, and contribute to changes at different scales (Moore 2005). As we will see in the next section, it is however possible, in the case of our research, to identify some of the factors or processes that are likely to affect the micropolitics of work.

Comparing from Below

Although the following chapters are based on specific case studies, our ambition is to shed comparative light on the micropolitics of work among the companies that have developed new mining projects in the Central African Copperbelt in the last twenty years. Taking a geological formation – the Central African Copperbelt – straddling two countries as the setting of the research can lead to confusion since 'Copperbelt' is also the name given to a province in Zambia – the most prominent mining and industrial province of the country since the 1930s (see Map 1). However, in Zambia, the geological formation also stretches into the North-Western Province, where new mines were opened in Solwezi District in the 2000s. Speculation over North-Western's future led the then Zambian president to hail the province as the 'New Copperbelt', a label still used to evoke its emergence as a new mining frontier (Negi 2009: 30). In Congo, people do not have a specific name for the copper veins that run through their country along the border with Zambia, from Kolwezi to Sakania; the term 'Congolese copperbelt' is used by geologists and academics. From an administrative point of view, the copperbelt in Congo was long located in the south of Katanga province. Following the division of Katanga into four smaller provinces in 2015, it is now found in the provinces of Haut-Katanga and Lualaba. For reasons of convenience, we use the terms Congolese and Zambian copperbelts to refer to the two sections of the geological formation on either of the border, and Copperbelt Province for the Zambian province.

In comparing the micropolitics of work in this space, the most obvious factors derive from the distinctive features of the historical formation of the mining industry, the state, the union power field and the working class, in both countries. These processes, which provide the background of the research results presented in Chapters 2 to 6, will be discussed in more detail in the next chapter. The risk of a comparison between two countries, however, is to presume that they exhibit fundamental differences that need to be expounded in the analysis. After all, the idea that Congo and Zambia have completely different political cultures was taken for granted by many of our respondents during the research; it was also expressed in some conversations with other Africanist scholars. The aim of this book is not to add weight to this line of thought, but to highlight the different factors involved in the micropolitics of work and the power constellations in which they take part. Far from exclusively pointing to national differences, these factors also include determinants associated with geology, infrastructural geography, or power struggles at play at other levels such as those between financial markets and mining companies.

Following the ontological turn in the social sciences, several authors in geography and anthropology have highlighted the importance of geological constraints in the power dynamics around mining projects (Bridge 2000; Bakker and Bridge 2006; Bebbington and Bury 2013; Luning and Pijpers 2017). Each deposit has geological characteristics that require the use of specific extraction, processing and transport techniques, and consequently have effects on the conflicts around mining projects and the political regulation of the industry. Accordingly, the micropolitics of work in the mining sector of the Central African Copperbelt must be first understood from the constraints imposed by the geology of the mines: whether the mine is opencast or underground, whether the water table is high or low, whether copper grades are high or low, whether there are other minerals present or not: parameters that impact on the excavation and processing techniques used, the workers recruited, the labour management policy made possible, the profit margins achieved and, consequently, on the micropolitics of work.

To the constraints deriving from the nature of the subsoil, it is necessary to add those arising from the built environment on the surface (Rubbers 2019b). It is usual practice in the literature on extractive industries to make a distinction between 'brownfield' and 'greenfield' projects, both of which are found in both the Congolese and Zambian copperbelts. Whether the project is located near old mining towns or in a remote rural area has an effect not only on how workers are housed, the amount and type of benefits they receive, and their interactions with each other on a day-to-day basis, but also on the influence of trade unions, the role of local political elites, and the importance of divisions based on autochthony within the workforce. Having said this, it is also possible to find intermediate cases, such as mining projects in rural areas which are close to a former workers' camp, or are near a relatively important town which lacks a mining past. Beyond the stark opposition between brownfield and greenfield projects, other essential factors are the development of infrastructures, the presence of industrial workers, and the political trajectory of the area where they are established.

If, in Montesquieu's words, 'the empire of climate [what we could call today the material environment] is the first of all empires', it is certainly not the only one to take into consideration when comparing the power constellations that develop around work in the mining sector. The pressures that financial institutions such as banks and funds exert on mining projects are at least as important. In her book on Zambia, Lee (2017) highlights in a subtle way what distinguishes the labour management policies of mining projects funded by Chinese state capital and by global private capital. In contrast to multinationals, she explains, the presence of a Chinese SOE in the Zambian mining sector is not exclusively driven by the pursuit of profit, but also by strategic and diplomatic considerations. This 'encompassing imperative of accumulation' pushes it to prioritise long-term production over short-term profits and, if under strong political pressure (as it has been the case in Zambia since 2000), to make concessions to workers. This process may explain why, although wages in the Chinese SOE remain low, it provides more stable jobs than global private companies.

All these factors come into play in the comparison of the micropolitics of work between Congo and Zambia, independently of any consideration of these countries' political cultures. Ore bodies in Congo, for instance, usually contain cobalt in addition to copper and have higher-grade copper than those in Zambia. In addition, many in Congo lie nearer to the surface, which is not the case on the other side of the border. These geological characteristics gave some mining companies in Congo – though not all – the opportunity to produce more rapidly and at lower cost when copper prices soared in the second half of the 2000s and, when the price of cobalt rose in 2017–2018, to offset low copper prices by selling a metal long considered a secondary product. This opportunity to make higher profits arguably gave mining companies in Congo more leeway in their negotiations with workers and trade unions than in Zambia.

In including these factors in the analysis, the challenge is not only to avoid the pitfalls of culturalism or methodological nationalism, but also to give room to the variety of mining projects to which the boom of foreign investments gave rise. Too often the attention of researchers has concentrated on a single mining project, most often a greenfield project by a multinational mining corporation. To compare mining projects from below, through a focus on the micropolitics of work, should make it possible to take into account the diversity of mining projects by type of mine, location, and the origins of capital and, in doing so, to develop a more complex understanding of the labour regime that is emerging in the twenty-first century.

Structure of the Book

The aim of this book is not to present all the findings of our research – many of which have already appeared in journal articles – but to answer a set of questions that allow for comparisons between the two copperbelts. These are the questions the authors try to answer in the chapters below. Rather than writing separate chapters on Congo and Zambia, as is usually the case in edited volumes, they co-authored chapters discussing the similarities and differences between two cases – one in Congo, the other in Zambia – in a consistent way. To my knowledge, this is a form of comparative writing that remains rare in the social sciences.

As our hypothesis is that new mining projects are caught in various power constellations with specific historical dynamics, it is important to place the changes that they have brought to labour in Congo and Zambia in a longer-term perspective. To do so, the first chapter, co-authored by Benjamin Rubbers and Emma Lochery, builds on the existing literature to propose a historical comparison of labour regimes in the Congolese and Zambian mining sectors from the 1920s to the present day. This broad historical picture provides the necessary background for the following chapters, which study the labour regime that is currently emerging in more detail and from different angles.

The next two chapters, by Francesca Pugliese and James Musonda, emerge from the subproject on mineworkers. Chapter 2 deals with one of the most striking aspects of new mining projects, the importance given to safety. Although a concern with safety is omnipresent on mine sites, it has been largely neglected in the recent literature on mining. On the basis of two contrasting case studies, an open-pit mine in Congo and an underground mine in Zambia, the chapter identifies the measures taken by employers to make the work environment safer before focusing on how workers deal with safety rules and regulations in everyday life. This investigation leads the authors to reflect on the contradictions between these safety devices and the increasingly precarious nature of work in the mining sector.

Chapter 3 studies the changes in gender dynamics caused by the mining boom from the perspective of women working in mining companies: their hopes and motivations, the challenges with which they are confronted in and outside the workplace, and the strategies they put in place to overcome them. This category of women workers is neglected in the literature on both copperbelts, which focus exclusively on workers' wives – the women targeted by the family policies of mining companies. Although female workers remain few in number, they provide an original angle from which to reflect on gender dynamics in the mining sector.

Chapters 4 and 5 are co-authored by Kristien Geenen and Thomas McNamara, who propose to compare the dynamics of the union power field in Congo and Zambia at two critical moments in the life of these organisations, union elections and strike actions. The study of union elections in Chapter 4 allows a better understanding of union politics in the workplace (workers' motivations to engage in union activities, their electoral strategies, and their frustrations) in a context of strong dependence on employers. This dependence, the authors argue, lead union representatives to reflect on what it means to be a responsible trade unionist. This is an old question in both copperbelts, but one which takes on a new meaning in a political economy marked by repeated mass layoffs and the rise of subcontracting.

Chapter 5 compares the unfolding of two wildcat strikes in Chinese mining companies in Congo and Zambia. In doing so, it brings an additional perspective to the ambiguous relationship that trade unions have with workers and employers: in both countries, strikes are generally organised by workers without the support of trade unions. The two case studies also highlight the role that political leaders can play in labour disputes, and the special place that is given to Chinese firms in the political arena. By shedding light on the constraints faced by trade unionists in the workplace, and by replacing their ambiguous role in the historical trajectories of trade unionism in both countries, the chapters together provide a nuanced and comprehensive analysis of their actions that contrasts with the more militant approach usually found in the literature (see Rubbers and Roy 2017; McNamara and Spyridakis 2020).

The last chapter, co-authored by Lochery and Rubbers, closes these exploratory investigations into the micropolitics of work in the mining sector by focusing on HR managers. In both countries, HR managers are of Congolese or Zambian nationality, but work in the interests of foreign companies' managers and shareholders. After examining their career paths and the multiple skills that they must develop as part of their job, the authors study how HR managers represent management's interest vis-a-vis the workers and, outside the firm, state administrations and political leaders. Special attention is paid to the room they have to manoeuvre in implementing HR policies, and the multiple pressures they face in a context where jobs are few and precarious.

The Conclusion, written by Rubbers, attempts to outline the answers provided by the different chapters to the questions raised in this introduction: what are the labour practices of new investors? How far do they break with the paternalism of ZCCM and Gécamines? How are they negotiated by local actors? Which broader social and political dynamics do they contribute to generating? These lines of analysis conclude with some reflections on our research participants' request for recommendations on improving the conditions of employment in the mining sector in Central Africa.

Bibliography

Akrich, M., Callon, M. and Latour, B. (2002a). The Key to Success in Innovation Part 1: The Art of Interessement. *International Journal of Innovation Management* 6(2): 187–206

Akrich, M., Callon, M. and Latour, B. (2002b). The Key to Success in Innovation Part 2: The Art of Choosing Good Spokespersons. *International Journal of Innovation Management* 6(2): 207–25

Alexander, P. (2013). Marikana, Turning Point in South African History. *Review of African Political Economy* 40(138): 605–19

Andreetta, S. (2018). *'Saisir l'Etat'. Les conflits d'héritage, la justice et la place du droit à Cotonou.* Paris: L'Harmattan

Appel, H. (2012). Walls and White Elephants: Oil Extraction, Responsibility, and Infrastructural Violence in Equatorial Guinea. *Ethnography* 13(4): 439–65

Appel, H., Mason, A. and Watts, M. (2015). Introduction: Oil Talk. In Appel, H., Mason, A. and Watts, M., eds, *Subterranean Estates. Life Worlds of Oil and Gas.* Ithaca, NY: University of Cornell Press, pp. 1–26

Bakker, K. and Bridge, G. (2006). Material Worlds? Resource Geographies and the 'Matter of Nature'. *Progress in Human Geography* 30(1): 5–27

Bayart, J.-F. (1993). *The State in Africa. The Politics of the Belly.* London: Longman

Bayart, J.-F. (1994). L'invention paradoxale de la modernité économique. In Bayart, J.-F., ed., *La réinvention du capitalisme.* Paris: Karthala, pp. 9–43

Bayart J.-F. (1996). L'historicité de l'Etat importé. In Bayart, J.-F., ed., *La greffe de l'Etat.* Paris: Karthala, pp. 11–39

Bear L. (2015). *Navigating Austerity: Currents of Debt along a South Asian River.* Stanford, CA: Stanford University Press

Bear, L. *et al.* (2015). Gens: A Feminist Manifesto for the Study of Capitalism. Theorizing the Contemporary. In *Fieldsights.* Available at: https://culanth.org/fieldsights/gens-a-feminist-manifesto-for-the-study-of-capitalism (accessed 19 February 2021)

Bebbington, A. and Bury, J., eds (2013). *Subterranean Struggles. New Dynamics of Mining, Oil, and Gas in Latin America.* Austin: University of Texas Press

Berman, B. and Lonsdale, J. (1992). *Unhappy Valley: Conflict in Kenya and Africa.* London: James Currey

Bezuidenhout, A. and Buhlungu, S. (2011). From Compounded to Fragmented Labour: Mineworkers and the Demise of Compounds in South Africa. *Antipode* 43(2): 237–63

Bierschenk T. (1988). Development Projects as Arenas of Negotiation for Strategic Groups. *Sociologia Ruralis* 28(2–3): 146–60

Bierschenk, T. and Olivier de Sardan, J.-P., eds (1998). *Les pouvoirs au village. Le Bénin rural entre démocratisation et décentralisation.* Paris: Karthala

Bierschenk, T. and Olivier de Sardan, J.-P., eds (2014). *States at Work: Dynamics of African Bureaucracies.* Leiden: Brill

Blundo, G. and Olivier de Sardan, J.-P. (2006). *Everyday Corruption and the State in Africa.* London: Zed Books

Botiveau, R. (2017). *Organise or Die? Democracy and Leadership in South Africa's National Union of Mineworkers.* Johannesburg: Wits University Press

Bridge, G. (2000). The Social Regulation of Resource Access and Environmental Impact: Production, Nature and Contradiction in the US Copper Industry. *Geoforum* 31(2): 237–56

Capps, G. (2016). Labour in the Time of Platinum. *Review of African Political Economy* 42(146): 497–507

Capps, G. and Sonwabile, M. (2016). Claims from Below: Platinum and the Politics of Land in the Bakgatla-ba-Kgafela Traditional Authority Area. *Review of African Political Economy* 42(146): 606–24

Chinguno, C. (2013). Marikana and the Post-Apartheid Workplace Order. Society, Work and Development Institute Working Paper 1. Available at: www.swop.org.za/working-papers (accessed 19 February 2021)

Cole, J. and Durham, D. (2006). Introduction. Age, Regeneration and the Intimate Politics of Globalization. In Cole, J. and Durham, D., eds, *Generations and Globalization: Youth, Age, and Family in the New World Economy*. Bloomington: Indiana University Press, pp. 1–28

Côte, M. and Korf, B. (2018). Making Concessions: Extractive Enclaves, Entangled Capitalism and Regulative Pluralism at the Gold Mining Frontier in Burkina Faso. *World Development* 101: 466–76

Dalton, M. (1959). *Men Who Manage. Fusions of Feeling and Theory in Administration*. New York: Wiley and Sons.

Dashwood, H.S. (2012). *The Rise of Global Corporate Social Responsibility. Mining and the Spread of Global Norms*. Cambridge: Cambridge University Press

De Herdt, T. and Olivier de Sardan, J.-P. (2015). *Real Governance and Practical Norms in Sub-Saharan Africa: The Game of the Rules*. London: Routledge

Dibwe dia Mwembu, D. (2001). *Bana Shaba abandonnés par leur père: structures de l'autorité et histoire sociale de la famille ouvrière au Katanga. 1910–1997*. Paris: L'Harmattan

Donham, D. (2011). *Violence in a Time of Liberation: Murder and Ethnicity at a South African Gold Mine, 1994*. Durham, NC: Duke University Press

Epstein, A.L. (1958). *Politics in an Urban African Community*. Manchester: Manchester University Press

Evans, C. and Saunders, O. (2015). A World of Copper: Globalizing the Industrial Revolution, 1830–70. *Journal of Global History* 10(1): 3–26

Ferguson, J. (2005). Seeing Like an Oil Company: Space, Security, and Global Capital in Neoliberal Africa. *American Ethnologist* 107(3): 377–82

Ferguson, J. (2006). *Global Shadows: African in the Neoliberal World Order*. Durham, NC: Duke University Press

Filer, C. and Le Meur, P.-Y., eds (2017). *Large-Scale Mines and Local-Level Politics. Between New Caledonia and Papua New Guinea*. Acton: Australian National University Press

Finn, J. (1998) *Tracing the Veins. Of Copper, Culture and Community from Butte to Chuquicamata*. Berkeley: University of California Press

Fraser, N. (2014). Behind Marx's Hidden Abode. For an Expanded Conception of Capitalism. *New Left Review* 86: 55–72

Geenen, S. and Claessens, K. (2013). Disputed Access to the Gold Sites in Luhwindja, Eastern DRC. *Journal of Modern African Studies* 51(1): 85–108

Gluckman, M. (1940a). Analysis of a Social Situation in Modern Zululand. A. The Social Organization of Modern Zululand. *Bantu Studies* 14: 1–29

Gluckman, M. (1940b). Analysis of a Social Situation in Modern Zululand. B. Social Change in Zululand. *Bantu Studies* 14: 147–74

Gluckman, M. (1945). The Seven Year Research Plan of the Rhodes-Livingstone Institute, Human Problems in British Central Africa. *Rhodes-Livingstone Journal* (December): 1–32

Gluckman, M. (1961). Ethnographic Data in British Social Anthropology. *The Sociological Review* 9(1): 5–17

Golub, A. (2014). *Leviathans at the Gold Mine. Creating Indigenous and Corporate Actors in Papua New Guinea*. Durham, NC: Duke University Press

Gordon, R.J. (1977). *Mines, Masters and Migrants. Life in a Namibian Mine Compound*. Johannesburg: Ravan Press

Harvey, D. (2003). *The New Imperialism*. Oxford: Oxford University Press

Hassard, J., McCann, L. and Morris, J. (2007). At the Sharp End of New Organizational Ideologies. Ethnography and the Study of Multinationals. *Ethnography* 8(3): 324–44

Hilgers, M. and Mangez, E. (2014). Introduction to Pierre Bourdieu's Theory of Social Fields. In Hilgers, M. and Mangez, E., eds, *Bourdieu's Theory of Social Fields. Concepts and Applications*. London: Routledge, pp. 1–36

Hilson, G. (2012). Corporate Social Responsibility in the Extractive Industries: Experiences from the Developing Countries. *Resources Policy* 37(2): 131–37

Ho, K. (2009). *Liquidated. An Ethnography of Wall Street*. Durham, NC: Duke University Press

Hönke, J. (2009). Transnational Pockets of Territoriality. Governing the Security of Extraction in Katanga (DRC). Working Paper series of the Graduate Centre Humanities and Social Sciences of the Research Academy Leipzig 2. Available at: https://home.uni-leipzig.de/~gsgas/fileadmin/Working_Papers/WP_2_Hoenke.pdf (accessed 19 February 2021)

Hönke, J. (2010). New Political Topographies. Mining Companies and Indirect Discharge in Southern Katanga (DRC). *Politique africaine* 4(120): 105–27

ICSG (2018). World Copper FactBook 2018. Report for the International Copper Study Group

Jackall, R. (1988). *Moral Mazes: The World of Corporate Managers*. New York: Oxford University Press

James, D. and Rajak, D. (2014). Credit Apartheid, Migrants, Mines and Money. *African Studies* 73(3): 455–76

Kapferer, B. (2006). Situations, Crisis, and the Anthropology of the Concrete. The Contribution of Max Gluckman. In Evens, T.M. and Handelman, D., eds, *The Manchester School. Practice and Ethnographic Praxis in Anthropology*. Oxford: Berghahn, pp. 118–39

Kesküla, E. (2016). Temporalities, Time and the Everyday: New Technology as a Marker of Change in an Estonian Mine. *History and Anthropology* 27(5): 521–35

Kesküla, E. (2018). Risky Encounters: The Ritual Prevention of Accidents in the Coal Mines of Kazakhstan. In Pijpers, J. and Eriksen, T.H., eds, *Mining Encounters. Extractive Industries in an Overheated World*. London: Pluto Press, pp. 156–73

Kesküla, E. and Sanchez, A. (2019). Everyday Barricades: Bureaucracy and the Affect of Struggle in Trade Unions. *Dialectical Anthropology* 43: 109–25

Kirsch, S. (2014). *Mining Capitalism. The Relationship between Corporations and their Critics*. Oakland: University of California Press

Kublock, T.M. (1998). *Contested Communities. Class, Gender, and Politics in Chile's El Teniente Copper Mine, 1904–1951*. Durham, NC: Duke University Press

Kunda, G. (1992). *Engineering Culture: Control and Commitment in a High-Tech Corporation*. Philadelphia, PA: Temple University Press

Lascoumes, P. (2004). La gouvernementalité: de la critique de l'Etat aux technologies de pouvoir. *Le portique* 13–14: 1–13

Lascoumes, P. and LeGalès, P. (2005). Introduction: L'action publique saisie par ses instruments. In Lascoumes, P. and LeGalès, P., eds, *Gouverner par les instruments*. Paris: Presses de Sciences Po, pp. 11–44

Lascoumes, P. and LeGalès, P. (2012). *Sociologie de l'action publique*. Paris: Armand Colin

Lavigne-Delville, P. (2012). Affronter l'incertitude? Les projets de développement à contre-courant de la 'révolution du management de projet'. *Revue Tiers-Monde* 3: 153–68

Lazar, S. (2017). *The Social Life of Politics: Ethics, Kinship and Union Activism in Argentina*. Redwood, CA: Stanford University Press

Lee, C.K. (2017). *The Spectre of Global China. Politics, Labor, and Foreign Investment in Africa*. Chicago, IL: University of Chicago Press

Li, F. (2015). *Unearthing Conflict. Corporate Mining, Activism, and Expertise in Peru*. Durham, NC: Duke University Press

Li, T.M. (2009). To Make Live or Let Die? Rural Dispossession and the Protection of Surplus Populations. *Antipode* 41(1): 66–93

Li, T.M. (2011). Centering Labor in the Land Grab Debate. *Journal of Peasant Studies* 38(2): 281–98

Li, T.M. (2017). After Development: Surplus Population and the Politics of Entitlement. *Development and Change* 48(6): 1247–61

Lubeck, P. (1986). *Islam and Urban Labor in Northern Nigeria: The Making of a Muslim Working Class*. Cambridge: Cambridge University Press

Luning, S. and Pijpers, R. (2017). Governing Access to Gold in Ghana: In-Depth Geopolitics on Mining Concessions. *Africa* 87(4): 758–79

Manson, A. and Mbenga, B. (2003). 'The Richest Tribe in Africa': Platinum-Mining and the Bafokeng in South Africa's North West Province, 1965–1999. *Journal of Southern African Studies* 29(1): 25–47

Marx, K. (1867). *Capital. Critique of Political Economy. Book 1: The Process of Production of Capital*. Moscow: Progress Publishers

McNamara, T. and Syridakis, M. (2020). Introduction. Trade Unions in Times of Austerity and Development. *Dialectical Anthropology* 44: 109–19

Mills, C.W. (2002). *White Collar: The American Middle Classes*. Oxford: Oxford University Press

Mitchell, J.C. (1956). *The Kalela Dance. Aspects of Social Relations among Urban Africans in Northern Rhodesia*. Manchester: Manchester University Press

Mitchell, J.C. (1983). Case and Situation Analysis. *The Sociological Review* 31(2): 187–211

Moodie D.T. (in collaboration with V. Ndatshe) (1994). *Going for Gold: Men, Mines, and Migration*. Berkeley: University of California Press

Moodie, T.D. and Von Holdt, K. (2015). Introduction to the Special Issue: New Frontiers of Mining in South Africa. *Labour, Capital and Society* 48(1–2): 2–9

Moodie, T.D. (2016). Making Mincemeat out of Mutton-Eaters: Social Origins of the NUM Decline on Platinum. *Journal of Southern African Studies* 42(5): 841–56

Moore, S.F. (2005). Comparisons: Possible and Impossible. *Annual Review of Anthropology* 34: 1–11

Mosse, D. (2005). *Cultivating Development: An Ethnography of Aid Policy and Practice*. London: Pluto Press

Nash, J. (1993 [1979]). *We Eat the Mines and the Mines Eat Us. Dependency and Exploitation in Bolivian Tin Mines*. New York: Columbia University Press

Negi, R. (2009). Copper Capitalism Today: Space, State and Development in North Western Zambia. PhD thesis, Ohio State University. Available at: https://etd.ohiolink.edu/apexprod/rws_olink/r/1501/10?p10_etd_subid=69258&clear=10#abstract-files (accessed 19 February 2021)

Negi, R. (2010). The Mining Boom, Capital, and Chiefs in the 'New Copperbelt'. In Fraser, A. and Larmer, M., eds, *Zambia, Mining and Neoliberalism. Boom and Bust on the Globalized Copperbelt.* New York: Palgrave Macmillan, pp. 209–36

Negi, R. (2011). The Micropolitics of Mining and Development in Zambia: Insights from the Northwestern Province. *African Studies Quarterly* 12(2): 27–43

Olivier de Sardan, J.-P. (2005). *Anthropology and Development. Understanding Contemporary Social Change.* London: Zed Books

O'Neill, P. and Gibson-Graham, J.K. (1999). Enterprise Discourse and Executive Talk: Stories that Destabilize the Company. *Transactions of the Institute of British Geographers* 24(1): 11–22

Parpart, J. (1983). *Labor and Capital on the African Copperbelt.* Philadelphia, PA: Temple University Press

Parpart, J.L. (1986a). Class and Gender on the Copperbelt: Women in Northern Rhodesian Copper Mining Communities, 1926–1964. In Robertson, C. and Berger, I., eds, *Women and Class in Africa.* New York: Africana Publishing, pp. 141–60

Parpart, J.L. (1986b). The Household and the Mine Shaft. Gender and Class Struggles on the Zambian Copperbelt, 1926–1964. *Journal of Southern African Studies* 13(1): 36–56

Phakathi, S. (2018). *Production, Safety and Teamwork in a Deep-Level Mining Workplace. Perspectives from the Rock-Face.* Bingley: Emerald Insight

Pijpers, R. (2018). Navigating Uncertainty. Large-Scale Mining and Micro-Politics in Sierra Leone. Unpublished PhD thesis, University of Oslo

Pijpers, R. (2019). Territories of Contestation: Negotiating Mining Concessions in Sierra Leone. In Pijpers, R. and Eriksen, T.H., eds, *Mining Encounters. Extractive Industries in an Overheated World.* London: Pluto Press, pp. 78–96

Pressman, J. and Wildavsky, A. (1973). *Implementation. How Great Expectations in Washington are Dashed in Oakland.* Berkeley: University of California Press

Rajak, D. (2011). *In Good Company. An Anatomy of Corporate Social Responsibility.* Stanford, CA: Stanford University Press

Rajak, D. (2012). Platinum City and the New South African Dream. *Africa* 82(2): 252–71

Rajak, D. (2016). Hope and Betrayal on the Platinum Belt: Responsibility, Violence and Corporate Power in South Africa. *Journal of Southern African Studies* 42(5): 929–46

Rolston, J.S. (2010). Risky Business: Neoliberalism and Workplace Safety in Wyoming Coal Mines. *Human Organization* 69(4): 331–42

Rolston, J.S. (2013). The Politics of Pits and the Materiality of Mine Labor: Making Natural Resources in the American West. *American Anthropologist* 115(4): 582–94

Rolston, J.S. (2014). *Mining Coal and Undermining Gender: Rhythms of Work and Family in the American West.* New Brunswick, NJ: Rutgers University Press

Rose, N., O'Maley, P. and Valverde, M. (2006). Governmentality. *Annual Review of Law and Social Science* 2: 83–104

Rubbers, B. (2013). Introduction au thème. Les sociétés africaines face aux investissements miniers. *Politique africaine* 131: 5–25

Rubbers, B. (2015). When Women Support the Patriarchal Family. The Dynamics of Marriage in a Gécamines Mining Camp (Katanga Province, DR Congo). *Journal of Historical Sociology* 28(2): 213–34

Rubbers, B. (2019a). Mining Boom, Labour Market Segmentation and Social Inequality in the Congolese Copperbelt. *Development and Change* 51(6): 1555–78

Rubbers, B. (2019b). Mining Towns, Enclaves and Spaces: A Genealogy of Worker Camps in the Congolese Copperbelt. *Geoforum* 98: 88–96

Rubbers, B. (2020). Governing New Mining Projects. The View from the HR Department of a Chinese Company in the Congolese Copperbelt. *Extractive Industries and Society* 7(1): 191–98

Rubbers, B. (Forthcoming). Mineworkers. In Pijpers, R. and D'Angelo, L., eds, *The Anthropology of Resource Extraction*. London: Routledge

Rubbers, B. and Gallez, E. (2015). Beyond Corruption. The Everyday Life of a Justice of the Peace Court in the Democratic Republic of Congo. In De Herdt, T. and Olivier de Sardan, J.-P., eds, *Real Governance and Practical Norms in Sub-Saharan Africa. The Games of the Rule*. London: Routledge, pp. 245–62

Rubbers, B. and Roy, A. (2017). Entre opposition et participation. Les syndicats face aux réformes en Afrique. *Revue Tiers-Monde* 224: 1–16

Sawyer, S. and Gomez, E., eds (2014). *The Politics of Resource Extraction. Indigenous People, Multinational Corporations, and the State*. New York: Palgrave Macmillan

Schmitz, C. (2000). The World Copper Industry: Geology, Mining Techniques and Corporate Growth, 1870–1939. *Journal of European Economic History* 29(1): 77–105

Schumaker, L. (2001). *Africanizing Anthropology. Fieldwork, Networks and the Making of Cultural Knowledge in Central Africa*. Durham, NC: Duke University Press

Sewell, W.H. (2008). The Temporalities of Capitalism. *Socio-Economic Review* 6(3): 517–37

Shever, E. (2012). *Resources for Reform. Oil and Neoliberalism in Argentina*. Stanford, CA: Stanford University Press

Smith, J. (2018). Colonizing Banro: Kingship, Temporality, and Mining of Futures in the Goldfields of South Kivu, DRC. In Comaroff, J. and Comaroff, J., eds, *The Politics of Custom. Chiefship, Capital, and the State in Contemporary Africa*. Chicago, IL: University of Chicago Press, pp. 279–304

Stewart, P.F. (2013). Kings of the Mine: Rock Drill Operators and the 2012 Strike Wave on South African Mines. *South African Review of Sociology* 44(3): 42–63

Szablowski, D. (2007). *Transnational Law and Local Struggles: Mining Communities and the World Bank*. Portland, OR: Hart Publishing

Tsing, A. (2015). *The Mushroom at the End of the World. On the Possibility of Life in Capitalist Ruins*. Princeton, NJ: Princeton University Press

Van Velsen, J. (1967). The Extended-Case Method and Situational Analysis. In Epstein, A.L., ed., *The Craft of Social Anthropology*. London: Social Science Paperbacks, pp. 29–53

Von Holdt, K. (2003). *Transition from Below. Forging Trade Unionism and Workplace Change in South Africa*. Scottville: University of Natal Press

Watson, T. (1994). *In Search of Management. Culture, Chaos and Control in Managerial Work*. London: Routledge

Werbner, P. (2014). *The Making of an African Working Class. Politics, Law, and Cultural Protest in the Manual Workers' Union of Botswana*. London: Pluto Press

Welker, M. (2014). *Enacting the Corporation. An American Mining Firm in Post-Authoritarian Indonesia*. Berkeley: University of California Press

Whyte, W.H. (2013). *The Organization Man*. Philadelphia, PA: University of Pennsylvania Press

Wright, E.O. (1997). *Class Counts. Comparative Studies in Class Analysis*. Cambridge: Cambridge University Press

Yanagisako, S.J. (2002). *Producing Culture and Capital. Family Firms in Italy*. Princeton, NJ: Princeton University Press

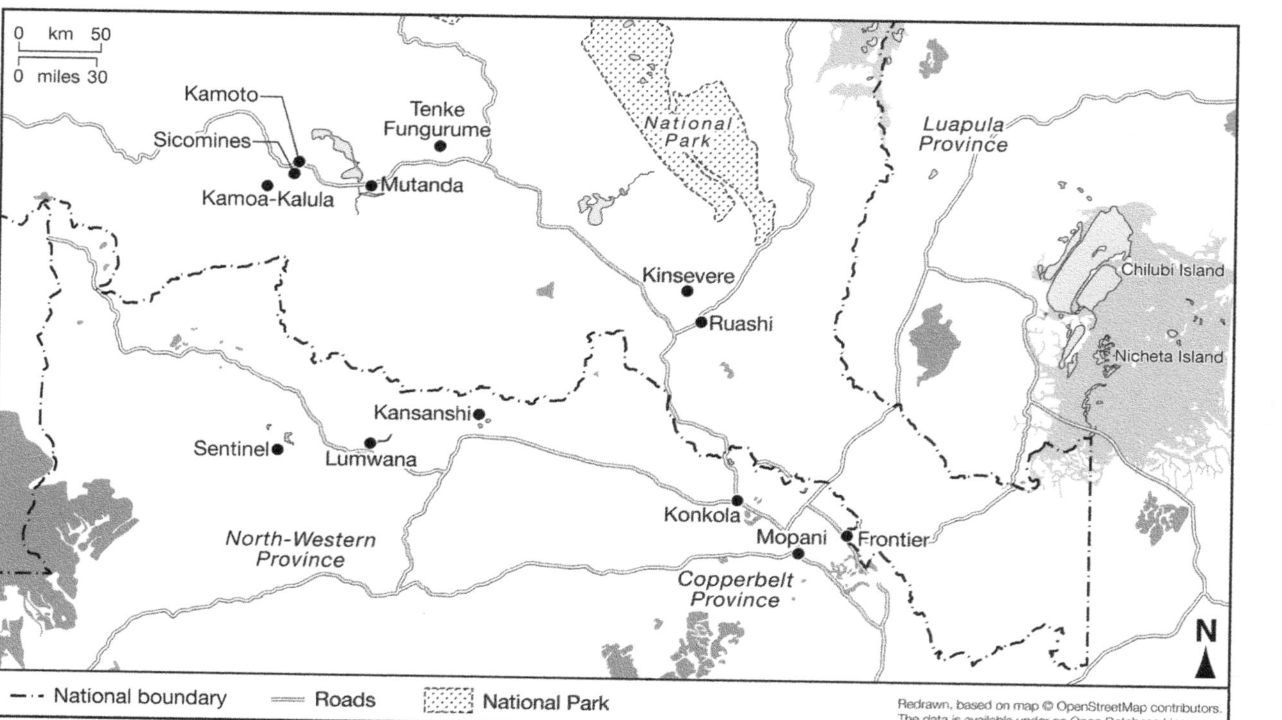

Map 2. Main Mining Projects in the Central African Copperbelt (2018). Based on map © OpenStreetMap contributors. The data is available under an Open Database Licence.

1

Labour Regimes: A Comparative History

BENJAMIN RUBBERS AND EMMA LOCHERY

The history of labour in the mines of Congo and Zambia has been told many times before. A large number of publications have reviewed the development of the mining industry and the making of an African working class during the colonial period (see Epstein 1958; Powdermaker 1962; Henderson 1972; Perrings 1979; Parpart 1983; Higginson 1989; Dibwe 2001; Frederiksen 2010; Money 2016).[1] The literature on the postcolonial period is much less extensive (Henk 1988; Ferguson 1999; Larmer 2007; Rubbers 2013; Mususa 2014), though the rise in foreign investment since the early 2000s has sparked a renewed interest in this topic (Negi 2009; Haglund 2010; Fraser and Larmer 2010; Cuvelier 2011; Lee 2017; Katz-Lavigne 2020). Amongst these publications, a number deal with the interconnections across the border between the Congolese and Zambian copperbelts, generally for a specific historical period (Perrings 1979; Siegel 1989; Musambachime 1989, 1990; White 2000; Hughes 2003). Only recently, however, have these transborder connections been examined over the *longue durée* from the nineteenth century to the present (Guene 2017; Larmer 2017).

Building on this body of literature, this chapter aims to develop a comparative study of labour in the mining sectors of Congo and Zambia since the 1920s. To do so, we will use the concept of *labour regime*. First coined by Burawoy (1985), this concept has been further elaborated in African studies by labour scholars (Andrae and Beckman 1998; Beckman and Sachikonye 2001; Von Holdt 2003; Bezuidenhout 2004; Von Holdt and Webster 2005).[2] In a nutshell, a labour regime is a relatively stable power

1 An ERC-funded collective and comparative research project complementary to the WORKinMINING project has recently been led by historian Miles Larmer at the University of Oxford. This aims to fill the gaps in our knowledge of this period, with a special interest in culture and politics (see https://copperbelt.history.ox.ac.uk).

2 These authors are principally interested in Burawoy's (1985) concept of (post-) colonial labour regime and contribute to making this theoretical framework clearer and more operational. Indeed, Burawoy attempts to define universal labour regimes from a detailed study of very localised case studies; the result is a confusing conceptual framework, that does not hold very well together as a whole (see Greenberg 1986). Sociologists working on Africa are more

configuration of actors and institutions that regulates the labour process over a certain period of time. At the core of a labour regime are, on the one hand, capital's labour requirements and, on the other, workers' responses to the labour practices of capital. However, this relation between capital and labour is mediated by various power institutions, including trade unions, the state and international organisations.

The advantage of this approach is that it does not focus on the history of a single category of actors or type of institution: workers, mining companies, trade unions, or the state. It seeks to grasp more broadly the relationships between various actors in a given period to enable comparisons across historical periods and with other parts of the world. Such an approach is particularly well-suited for highlighting how the nature and politics of labour in the mines across the two copperbelts has changed since the early twentieth century.

The approach developed by Burawoy, Beckman, von Holdt and others can however be criticised for making sweeping generalisations about labour regimes. Attentive to the need to move beyond the economic determinism of orthodox Marxism, these authors put political institutions, and more especially the state, at the centre of their analysis of labour regimes. This state-centred approach, it could be argued, is what leads them to propose that the defining feature of a labour regime is considered *a priori* to be the nature of the political regime broadly speaking. From the study of a single firm or industry, labour regimes are extrapolated to entire countries (e.g. the post-apartheid labour regime) or even to groups of countries with the same type of power regime (e.g. a postcolonial labour regime). Such an approach pays insufficient attention to variations between economic sectors and their specific labour dynamics: obviously, the relationship between capital and labour is not the same across the mining, construction and transport sectors, and in any given sector, this relationship generally exhibits more parallels than differences across countries.

The labour regimes described by authors following Burawoy (e.g. the existence of a postcolonial labour regime) are thus too broad to allow for an examination of a century's worth of changes to labour dynamics in the mining sectors of Congo and Zambia. Therefore, we use the concept of labour regime in a different way from its original promoters. In what follows, we have attempted to define labour regimes more prudently than the existing literature by giving more weight to capital's labour

cautious in their characterisation of labour regimes, as they limit the scope of their analysis to one country or, at most, to Sub-Saharan Africa. In addition, Burawoy's classification of labour regimes is based on Gramsci's distinction between hegemony (consent) and despotism (violence). Dissatisfied with this simplistic opposition, the scholars who have developed his approach on the African continent define labour regimes more precisely, taking as a point of departure the division of labour, the structure of the labour market, the dynamics of industrial relations, and so forth. These authors, however, can be criticised for reproducing Burawoy's focus on political regimes broadly speaking, which leads them to neglect the differences between economic sectors.

requirements. Rather than basing our categories on the type of political regime, we differentiate between labour regimes based on the type of labour policy implemented by mining companies.[3] The result is a succession of four labour regimes from the 1920s to the present day: the migrant labour system (1900–25), industrial paternalism (1925–65), state paternalism (1965–2000), and what we provisionally call the neoliberal labour regime (2000–present). In doing so, the emphasis is put on the similarities between the two countries although, as we will see in each section, these similarities can hide important differences.

Industrial Paternalism (1925–65)

The mining industry in the Belgian Congo was dominated by the Union Minière du Haut-Katanga (UMHK), which was founded by an alliance of Belgian and British capital in 1906 (UMHK 1956; Brion and Moreau 2006). On the other side of the border, copper deposits were discovered at an early stage, but the copper content of the oxide ore on the surface was low in comparison to that found in Congolese mines. Although a few companies developed mines in Northern Rhodesia before the 1920s, production was fitful due to technical challenges and high costs (Bancroft 1961; Gann 1969; Henderson 1972; Cunningham 1981; Frederiksen 2010). It was not until the 1920s when substantial exploration took place and sulphide reserves were discovered in Northern Rhodesia, attracting South African, American and, to a lesser extent, British capital and expertise. Subsequently, from 1930 into the 1960s, the emerging copper-mining industry in Northern Rhodesia was controlled by two large groups: Rhodesian (from 1964, Roan) Selection Trust (RST), largely backed by the American Metal Corporation and Rhodesian (later Zambian) Anglo American (RAA), the majority shareholder in the operating company, Rhokana Corporation.[4]

At first, UMHK and the small mines that emerged in Northern Rhodesia before the First World War drew inspiration from South African mining and established a migrant labour system to recruit African workers (Henderson 1972; Perrings 1979; Kayamba 1986; Higginson 1989; Seibert 2011). By the early 1920s, however, it became clear to UMHK that migrant labour was incompatible with its industrial development plans. While these plans required a larger and more disciplined workforce, the

3 The labour regimes identified in this chapter can be conceived of as ideal types. For Max Weber, an ideal type (from the German *idealtypus*) is an abstract category corresponding to a set of characteristic features common to most cases of the social phenomena under study. It is a methodological tool built by the researcher for the purpose of comparing different, but analogous, social processes. Weber uses this tool to distinguish between different forms of action and domination, but also to analyse various forms of social organisation such as bureaucracy or capitalism.

4 See Cunningham (1981: 80) or Roberts (1982: 349) for diagrams of the relationships between mining firms in Northern Rhodesia during this period.

company was confronted with a severe labour shortage because of the growing competition from other colonial companies in both the Belgian Congo and Northern Rhodesia. It is in these circumstances that UMHK launched a policy aimed at 'stabilising' its workforce near production sites in the copperbelt. This policy led to the company's withdrawal from the migrant labour regime characteristic of the early twentieth century and to the formation of a new labour regime.

To overcome the labour shortage, UMHK was authorised by the Belgian colonial administration to organise its own recruitment missions in other provinces of the Belgian Congo and Ruanda-Urundi and to extend work contracts to three years (Van Nitsen 1933; Bakajika 1993). At the same time, it encouraged workers to come to the mines with their wives and children (Dibwe 2001). It was expected that the presence of their families would encourage workers to stay for longer periods, while also enabling the company to supervise the growth and education of their offspring. In worker camps, brick houses were built for married workers and collective facilities such as nurseries, canteens and schools were created to take care of children. The management of these facilities, and the moral guidance of workers' families more generally, was entrusted to Belgian Catholic orders, which came to play a key role in the daily social life of camps. In the aftermath of the Great Depression, the stabilisation policy came to be viewed as a success (Mottoulle 1946; Toussaint 1956). The challenge from UMHK's perspective was no longer an issue of increasing the workforce but of making it stronger, more disciplined and 'civilised'.

To name the labour regime that UMHK gradually set up from the 1920s onwards, we can use the concept of *industrial paternalism*, a term coined by historians to characterise the type of social policy that large firms in various sectors – but especially in mining and metallurgy – developed during 1870–1940 (Reid 1985; Noiriel 1988; Zahavi 1988; Tone 1997; see Rubbers 2013). The social policy of UMHK shows the main features of industrial paternalism:

1. UMHK built workers' camps equipped with family homes and social infrastructure that enabled the employer to take responsibility for, and at the same time control, nearly all aspects of workers' lives. The built environment of these camps – their division into different areas, the design of the houses, the creation of gardens, the importance given to light and air in the workplace, etc. – was designed with the aim of reforming workers' behaviour. Industrial paternalism was underpinned by the aim of taking total control of the workers, and the organisation of space played a key role in this endeavour.

2. UMHK actively encouraged workers to marry and promoted the model of the modern industrial family: a monogamous nuclear family with a strictly gendered division of work, with the man as breadwinner and the woman as housewife. In this model, the authority of the worker as husband and father within the family is dependent on his wage and, thus, on his own subordination to the employer.

Industrial paternalism is based on a patriarchal cosmology which it seeks to disseminate through various power devices including for example religion or domesticity.

3. The company developed a complex social bureaucracy composed of various professional bodies (doctors, missionaries, social workers, etc.). It also created rites, symbols and communication tools with the aim of making workers participate in a new imagined community, the 'family of Union Minière'. In comparison to face-to-face paternalism (a type of paternalism characteristic of family businesses), industrial paternalism implies a change in scale: the employer has no longer a direct, personal, relationship with workers; the employment relationship is mediated by professional bodies, invented traditions and various media.

4. UMHK's paternalism benefited, in descending order, white employees, African skilled workers and unskilled labour. The stabilisation policy principally aimed at producing an intermediate layer of skilled, experienced and loyal African workers. Besides this core of stabilised workers, the company continued to hire unskilled workers who did not benefit from the same working conditions. Far from making the workforce a homogeneous group, industrial paternalism involved creating a hierarchy of privileges and benefits according to workers' rank, seniority, family size, or perceived degree of 'civilisation'.

The conditions that led to the emergence of this labour regime in the Congo were similar to those characterising the origin of industrial paternalism in Europe and North America. First, it was a response to a shortage of labour in a period marked by the modernisation of technology, the mechanisation of production, the construction of new processing plants, and the expansion of the company's activities. UMHK went through two such periods, in the 1920s and after the Second World War (UMHK 1956; Vellut 1981; Brion and Moreau 2006). Each time, industrial development programmes required a larger and better trained workforce.

At the same time, UMHK's paternalism was also a response to workers' actions and demands. In 1919–20, white English-speaking workers went on strike to claim higher wages, job reservation for whites, and recognition of white workers' unions (Poupart 1960). The company immediately responded by not renewing strikers' contracts, and replacing them either with fresh recruits from Belgium or experienced African workers. One year after this strike, UMHK established its first vocational school for Africans (Mottoulle 1934). From a more general perspective, the stabilisation programme was envisaged as a means to replace white English-speaking workers with Africans in both unskilled and semi-skilled positions. Such a policy allowed the company to save costs, undermine white unionism, and draw attention to its contribution to the colony's civilising mission.[5]

[5] Although white workers, who were mostly Belgian by that time, succeeded in establishing a trade union during the Second World War, the strike actions they

Although stabilisation gave African workers new advancement opportunities to the detriment of white unskilled and semi-skilled workers, they did not earn the right to strike or unionise. In 1941 the most important strike in UMHK history took place (Perrings 1979; Higginson 1989; Dibwe 2001; Seibert 2013). The African workers demanding a raise were immediately successful, but the strike ended with the shooting of at least twenty workers by soldiers during a rally. This massacre seems to have discouraged the Congolese workforce from taking further action for fear of repression; unions for African workers were not introduced at UMHK until after Congo's independence in 1960. In 1946, however, a legislative ordinance from the Belgian colonial administration forced UMHK to create *Conseils indigènes d'entreprise*, that is, bodies representing African workers (Dibwe 2001: 67–85). Its members, elected by the workers, could express grievances that the employer would take into consideration if they were deemed reasonable. These councils were at the root of several improvements in workers' living conditions, even though the company would later claim credit for these improvements as products of its own social policy.

Finally, UMHK's industrial paternalism was a response to the colonial state's social policies. In the aftermath of the Second World War, laws regulating workers' rights, family life and urban planning multiplied, and the colonial administration conceived a ten-year development plan that involved the building of new houses, hospitals, schools and community centres (Vanthemsche 1994). As part of these developments, UMHK not only complied with new social regulations, but sought to remain a step ahead of colonial policy by creating new social infrastructures in the camps or by funding large community development programmes. Its ambition was to create model company towns to win the sympathy of the public and prevent further state interference.

The concept of industrial paternalism can also be used to characterise the labour regime put in place by mining companies in Northern Rhodesia, though its introduction was more halting and reluctant. In several respects, the description Powdermaker (1962: 5–6) gives of Luanshya's RST mine township in 1953–54 could be that of a UMHK camp at the same period. At the entrance to the camp were the township offices. Behind were rows of rectangular white houses. The most common type of house comprised two rooms with a small adjoining kitchen, but there was also a growing number of larger houses with indoor sanitation, electricity and a flower garden, for senior employees. Each section of the township was equipped with public latrines, shower stalls and a washhouse where women gathered to do the laundry. Finally, the township was equipped with various facilities such as a hospital, schools, an open-air market, a sports ground, a welfare centre and a

organised were systematically repressed by layoffs and convictions of leaders (Corneille 1945).

cinema. From the outset, however, a number of differences also appear from the UMHK model. Powdermaker mentions the presence of various churches and large union meetings at the theatre, which UMHK would not have tolerated in its own workers' camps.

To study these similarities and differences in more detail, it is necessary to return to the conditions that prevailed during the emergence of the mining industry in Northern Rhodesia. In the 1920s, going to work in the Belgian Congo, Southern Rhodesia, or South Africa was already common practice among the people of Northern Rhodesia, so they could compare the conditions of employment in these different colonial territories. The main competitor of the Northern Rhodesian mining companies at the time was UMHK, which was experimenting with its new stabilisation programme. Faced with a shortage of labour, RST and RAA were thus forced to offer African workers in Northern Rhodesia similar conditions in order to attract them – that is, to pay more or less equivalent wages to those offered by UMHK, to allow them to come with their wives and children, and to build family homes to house them (Henderson 1972; Parpart 1983). One can see in these measures the sketch of a stabilisation policy that breaks with the migrant labour system characteristic of southern Africa. However, the implementation of such policies was more hesitant in Northern Rhodesia than in the Belgian Congo.

Although mining companies in the Northern Rhodesian copperbelt faced labour shortages in the late 1920s, these were soon eased by wider economic changes. Though the Northern Rhodesian government was reluctant to place strict controls on foreign labour recruitment within the territory, as UMHK looked elsewhere for its labour, recruitment in Northern Rhodesia for the Katangese mines ceased in 1931 (Parpart 1983: 32–4; Perrings 1979: 90–8). The Great Depression and fall in the copper price caused an avalanche of layoffs on both sides of the border and a sharp reduction in employment opportunities for African workers. Thus, as production began in the Northern Rhodesian copperbelt in the 1930s, the mining companies had little difficulty finding experienced workers. Now in a strong position, they could hire migrant workers and limit their efforts to improve living conditions in the mining townships. Under these conditions, the companies' preferred option was to employ cheap migrant labour and to transfer the cost of its social reproduction onto the rural areas (Henderson 1972; Parpart 1983).

Moreover, unlike UMHK, companies in Northern Rhodesia predominantly operated underground mines, which required more labour than open pit mines. To make profits, they had to keep an eye on labour costs (Perrings 1979). It was only after the copper price rose again in the late 1930s that mining companies increased spending on workers. There were also differences between the two groups. RAA controlled the Rhokana Corporation, whose directors had made their careers in the South African mines and were slower to move away from a migrant labour model. The directors of RST, meanwhile, were predominantly American and were more inclined to continue with the limited stabilisation policy initiated before the 1930 crisis, also because the geology of the orebody required more skilled labour (Parpart 1983: 35; Perrings 1979: 111).

The political context in Northern Rhodesia also meant that, unlike UMHK, RST and RAA failed to prevent the rise of white mineworkers' power. The Northern Rhodesia Mine Workers' Union (NRMWU) was created in 1936 and successfully lobbied London to instruct the mining companies to recognise it (Money 2016: 85–87). During the Second World War, the union managed to convince the companies to introduce a *de facto* colour bar, achieved by the requirement in the union recognition agreement that 'daily-paid employees had to be union members' and that 'union membership was restricted to Europeans' (Money 2016: 129). Because of this closed shop, the companies were unable to promote a policy of African advancement following the example of UMHK until the late 1950s.

Finally, although the British colonial administration took some measures to create a migrant labour market for mining companies in Northern Rhodesia, it was less favourable to stabilisation than the Belgian colonial administration. The brief existence of mining projects before the First World War, followed by mass layoffs in the aftermath of the Great Depression, had shown that employment in the mines was by definition unstable (MacMillan 2012). Under such conditions, the colonial administration feared that a stabilisation policy would generate a large 'detribalised' population in mining towns, both cut from its rural roots and dependent on wage work: if copper prices fell, this proletariat would be unemployed, and the situation in mining towns would become explosive.[6] Colonial officials and white settlers considered it wiser to continue the migrant labour system.

For these reasons, and for a long time, the length of service at RST and RAA was shorter, and the percentage of married workers lower, than at UMHK (Parpart 1983; Henderson 1972; Perrings 1979; Juif and Frankema 2018). The situation gradually changed from the end of the 1930s when the Northern Rhodesian companies increased production, which required a larger and more experienced workforce, but the commitment of companies to investment in the infrastructure needed for their stabilisation policy was limited (Parpart 1983; Kalusa 1993). It was really only in the aftermath of the Second World War that their labour policies converged with that of UMHK to take the form of a paternalistic labour regime – at a time when UMHK itself was focusing on further mechanisation and stabilisation tactics.

[6] It was to address these fears of detribalisation and disorder that the RLI was created in 1937 (Crehan 1997; Schumaker 2001). However, although they continued to take the idea that Africans in rural areas belonged to 'tribes', Gluckman and his colleagues questioned the assumption that they lost this 'tribal' identity by migrating to colonial towns. Their work argued, on the contrary, that tribal identities were reinvented in urban situations (Mitchell 1956; Epstein 1958; Gluckman 1960).

In contrast to the Belgian Congo, repeated strike and protest action by African workers played a significant role in the emergence of industrial paternalism in Northern Rhodesia. African workers called a strike in 1935 and then again, in a more organised fashion, in 1940. This won them concessions in some mines but in the end was brutally repressed. After the war, the British colonial administration decided – like the Belgian administration – to authorise the creation of trade unions for African workers (Berger 1974). Unlike in the Belgian Congo, however, this decision was followed by concrete measures, and in 1949 the African Mineworkers' Union was founded. It quickly gained a large base of support among workers and organised several protest actions demanding wage increases and improvements to the mine townships. The rise of union activism encouraged mining companies to develop a paternalistic labour policy similar to that of UMHK on the other side of the border (Parpart 1983: chap. 7): an end to job reservation for Whites to allow the advancement of skilled African workers; new, larger houses in the townships; ambitious welfare programmes; finally, they tightened control over workers by controlling access to the townships and paying company spies among the inhabitants. The companies aimed to increase, for the workers, both the benefits of being loyal and the cost of being critical.

Thus, despite a late convergence, industrial paternalism provides a useful conceptual frame through which to understand the labour regime that mining companies in both copperbelts established between 1925 and 1965. As we have seen, the conditions in which this labour regime was formed differed on both sides of the border. In the 1950s, it was commonplace in British colonial policy circles to say that UMHK had implemented a policy of stabilisation while RST and RAA had opted for stabilisation without urbanisation (see, for instance, Prain 1956). However, although mining companies in Northern Rhodesia were more reluctant to stabilise their workforce, this distinction is based on a misunderstanding of UMHK's labour policy, which never aimed to cut its workforce from their rural roots. On the contrary, UMHK took measures to encourage workers to stay in contact with their rural kin and to retire to their villages at the end of their working lives.

What distinguished UMHK from RST and RAA is the amount of money that it invested in its stabilisation policy and the degree of support it received from the colonial administration and the Catholic missions (Vellut 1983). In comparison, the mining companies of Northern Rhodesia not only exerted less control over their workers (whether for marriage, religious practices, or forming associations),[7] they were also unable to stifle the rise of first white, and then black, trade unionism with the same force and intransigence.

7 This contrast is also reflected in the wages of African mineworkers (Juif and Frankema 2018). While wages rose in parallel in both copperbelts – in the late colonial period they were the best-paid workers in Africa – RST and RAA paid a larger portion in cash relative to UMHK, which provided a larger portion as benefits in kind.

State Paternalism (1965–2000)

In 1964, Northern Rhodesia gained independence as Zambia, while in the newly independent Congo, the UMHK-supported Katangese secession was violently suppressed (on the relationship between the two processes, see Hughes 2003; Kennes and Larmer 2017; Guene 2017). Control of the mining industry immediately became a priority for the two new national governments. They had ambitious economic and social development plans, and copper was their main source of revenue and foreign exchange. Mining companies on both sides of the border were either totally or partially nationalised in the second half of the 1960s. In 1967, UMHK and its subsidiaries were entirely taken over by the Zairian state and, after several name changes, renamed Générale des Carrières et des Mines (Gécamines). In 1969, RST and Anglo American were forced to cede 51 per cent of their shares to the Zambian state in exchange for bonds guaranteed by the government, but maintained exclusive management contracts. In 1973, the Zambian government paid off the bonds and broke off the service contracts, claiming managerial control of the two state-controlled companies, Nchanga Consolidated Copper Mines and Roan Consolidated Mines (Stoever 1981; Cunningham 1985). In both countries, private shareholders were generously compensated for the loss of their colonial assets, and continued to sell mining companies' production on international markets until the early 1970s, when the Zambian and Zairian governments created their own commodity trading firms.

This nationalisation of colonial mining companies led to the emergence of a new labour regime that we will call 'state paternalism'.[8] This labour regime kept some of the characteristic features of industrial paternalism in the colonial era:

1. Mining companies on both sides of the border continued to maintain, modernise and extend the workers' housing estates inherited from the colonial period. Besides their cash wages, workers continued to receive a large range of benefits in kind: food rations, free housing, access to company schools, hospitals, sport facilities and so forth.

2. This labour policy continued to rest on a certain conception of the family, the patriarchal nuclear family. Even though there was some publicity about a growing number of female workers, in reality they were very few. Jobs in mining companies remained largely the prerogative of men, who had to register their wives and children to include them in the calculation of their wages and social benefits. The members of the 'extended' family who lived with the workers were not included in this calculation.

[8] State paternalism is to be distinguished from the social or welfare state in that the social benefits are reserved for the employees of state-owned enterprises; they are not part of a social security system extended to all citizens. Enjoying such benefits depends on having a job in such enterprises, not on obtaining citizenship.

3. From the 1970s onwards, the population of copperbelt towns grew, and became increasingly poor. It was no longer necessary for mining companies to mobilise the workers around corporate values: they were already aware that they belonged to a particularly privileged social category. Mining companies nevertheless continued to cultivate workers' feeling of belonging to the same community through sports, media and other rites and symbols.

4. Finally, although personnel nationalisation policies allowed African workers to climb up the hierarchy of jobs in the mines, they did not necessarily reduce inequalities amongst the mining company staff. For one, these policies did not immediately abolish the colour bar. The number of white managers and technicians who, as expatriates, continued to enjoy much higher pay, dropped only gradually. Additionally, another divide deepened: that between African managers and workers. Africans who climbed the job ladder into management not only received higher wages in cash, they were also granted access to houses and infrastructure (schools, hospitals, sport facilities, etc.) previously reserved for whites (Henk 1988; Larmer 2005; Rubbers 2013; Mususa 2014). The social world of mining companies remained hierarchical, with the categorisation of workers largely the same as it had been during the colonial era.

What distinguishes state paternalism from industrial paternalism is less the takeover of production by the state than the enlarged role of the state in industrial relations and the management of mineworkers.[9] In 1967, the Congolese government merged existing trade unions in the mining sector into the overarching Union Nationale des Travailleurs Zaïrois (UNTZ), which became a fully fledged body of the Mobutu regime. In Zambia, meanwhile, the newly independent government created the Zambian Congress of Trade Unions (ZCTU), which, after some resistance, the Zambian Mineworkers' Union joined in 1966. The government then oversaw the creation of the new Mineworkers' Union of Zambia (MUZ) in 1967 and, with the passage of the 1971 Industrial Relations Act, sought greater control over unions through ZCTU (Larmer 2005). Despite the different political trajectories and differing intensity of control, the role assigned to unions was to serve as channels of communication and support for government policies: unions were supposed to communicate workers' demands during official negotiations, and defend them in individual labour disputes; in return, they were expected to prevent wildcat strikes by explaining to workers the decisions taken by the company and the state for their well-being and the development of the nation. In other words, trade unionists were enjoined to act 'responsibly' by 'educating' workers on both industrial and party discipline, which constituted altogether a single national imperative.

9 Management decisions regarding mining and processing operations remained in the hands of expatriate executives until the early 1980s.

In both countries, the control exercised on workers through trade unions was supplemented by the introduction of various political bodies in mining companies. After Congo became independent the surveillance regime that UMHK had put in place in workers' camps had relaxed: no more curfews at night, no more guards at the entrance of camps, no more company spies, and no more inspection visits to workers' houses by social workers. Congolese workers were free to go in town at night, to have extramarital relationships, and to house relatives at home. With the rise of the Mobutu regime, however, the state began exerting tighter control over workers. A new administrative structure and political bodies were established in the camps to monitor and mobilise the workers. This control was aimed less at imposing a certain family model, or at isolating workers from the rest of society, than at creating a climate of suspicion, denunciation and fear. The establishment of this regime contributed to silencing workers' critiques and nipping wildcat strikes in the bud. The workers who were too vocal in their criticism of the company were quickly denounced, surveilled and repressed by security forces (Dibwe 2001: 108).

In comparison, the power exerted by the Kaunda regime in Zambia was less total, arbitrary and brutal. The government co-opted national-level union leaders, most particularly those of MUZ, *de facto* banned strikes, and sanctioned or arrested workers who organised protest actions. Although such measures led to a marked decline in strike action, they did not succeed in breaking mineworkers' militancy (Rakner 1992; Larmer 2007). Workers and their families continued to attend mass meetings organised by the union in mine townships to express their demands and covertly organised localised strikes. When mineworkers' real wages began to decline in the late 1970s, union leaders became more critical of the government and in 1981, strikes occurred at an industry-wide level (Larmer 2006). Over time, trade union leaders, most especially of ZCTU, became *de facto* opposition leaders with strong support in Copperbelt Province. Support from mineworkers was critical for the rise of the multi-party movement which brought the Movement for Multiparty Democracy (MMD) to power in 1991, when trade unionist Frederick Chiluba became president. In contrast to the situation in Congo, the mining industry and the state in Zambia did not succeed in containing workers' militancy.

Under the control of the postcolonial state, mining companies' paternalism was generally more marked by the new political leaders' nationalist projects. The first measure Mobutu and Kaunda took after nationalising the mines was to proceed with nationalising their executive employees. Long-term programmes were adopted to hire and promote national workers in supervisory positions and gradually replace the expatriate staff. Although these programmes took centre stage in the communication of mining companies, in practice their implementation was slow. From 1969 to 1976, the proportion of 'Europeans' in the total workforce only decreased from 5.9 (1,458/24,416) to 3.5 per cent (1,270/35,489) in Gécamines (Gécamines 1969–99), and from 10.8 (4,727/43,500) to 7.6 per cent (4,060/53,082) in the Zambian mining industry (Money 2016: 368–9). Some Zairian and Zambian engineers were appointed to top managerial positions in the 1970s, but they were surrounded by experienced expatriate technicians who were responsible for production. It was not until the 1980s that national managers were granted access to strategic positions in production and the Africanisation of the executive personnel speeded up.

Independent of the nationalisation of executive personnel, the mining companies' labour policy as a whole was justified by the greater interest taken by the new nation-states. In the second half of the 1960s, the mining industry in both countries was portrayed as spearheading national development. To increase production and turn the former colonies into modern nations, the two governments claimed to give particular importance to the human factor, that is, the advancement and the well-being of African workers, and characterised strikes as a form of betrayal. Henceforth, the rites and symbols organised by mining companies were to arouse workers' attachment not only to the corporate community, but more broadly to the nation and the charismatic figure of its leader, the president of the republic. This nationalist discourse was used to impose sacrifices onto the workers and crush wildcat strikes as seditious acts.

The newly independent states of the Democratic Republic of Congo (known as Zaire between 1971 and 1997) and Zambia benefited from high copper prices between 1965 and 1974. In this context, the recently nationalised mining companies did not encounter too many difficulties in pursuing and extending the paternalistic policy inherited from the colonial era and, at the same time, meeting workers' new expectations for advancement and improved living conditions. Under pressure from governments, the companies also had to take charge of public infrastructure and finance national development programmes. From 1974, however, the mining industry was faced with a series of challenges that would eventually lead to bankruptcies. In 1973, the oil shock caused an increase in production costs, a decline in copper prices, and a shortage of foreign exchange. From 1973 to 1978, the border was closed between Zambia and Rhodesia, blocking the main route through which Zambia's imports and exports were transported, and in 1975, the start of the Angolan civil war closed the railway to Lobito, the main route for copper exports to Europe and North America. In 1977 and 1978, the wars of Shaba 1 and 2 disrupted Gécamines' development plan for the mining and industrial complex of Kolwezi. Then, in 1979, the United States Federal Reserve decided to raise interest rates and therefore the price of the dollar. For the mining companies of the Central African Copperbelt, and the economy of Zambia and Zaire more generally, this resulted in increasing import costs and an uncontrollable surge of debt taken on to finance national development plans.

To overcome the situation, the World Bank and the International Monetary Fund imposed structural adjustment plans which involved restructuring the mining industry. In Zambia, the two mining companies merged into Zambia Consolidated Copper Mines (ZCCM) in 1982. In

Zaire, Gécamines was reorganised into a large holding company. The aim of these organisational reforms was to increase production, cut costs, and reduce the misappropriation and misuse of mining revenues by the regimes. Their effects were nevertheless limited: measures taken by the Zambian government to cut labour costs came up against the resistance of mineworkers, and borrowing by ZCCM funded non-mining-related projects and political expenses (Larmer 2006). Meanwhile, the appointment of expatriates to head Gécamines on the advice of the World Bank did not prevent Mobutu from embezzling money from the State-Owned Enterprise (SOE). As the copper price on international markets continued to fall, the financial situation of the mining industry became increasingly desperate.

This series of adverse economic conditions progressively undermined the paternalistic labour policies that the Zambian and Zairian mining SOEs had developed in the late 1960s and early 1970s. From 1974 to 1989, mineworkers on both sides of the border faced a continuous decline in real wages, which pushed families, and most particularly women, to develop various informal activities. In comparison to the rest of the population, however, they remained a relatively protected social category as they continued to receive various social benefits, including a house, free access to school and hospitals and, more and more importantly, food. In Zambia, ZCCM sold mealie meal (maize flour) to its workers at a subsidised price. In Congo, managers could buy subsidised food while workers received family food rations every month. So, even though it was less and less generous, the paternalism of mining SOEs helped to protect their workers from some of the consequences of the crisis in the 1970s and structural adjustment programmes in the 1980s (Mususa 2014).

In the early 1990s, under pressure from opposition movements which had steadily developed in the 1980s, the two regimes resolved to open Zambia and Congo to multipartyism. Contrary to expectations, this political opening did not inaugurate a new period of prosperity. In both countries, the 1990s were marked by new austerity measures, rampant inflation, and a chronic shortage of staple food. A severe drought in 1991 to 1992 severely worsened existing food shortages in Zambia (Mulwanda 1995). In Zaire, meanwhile, the political situation rapidly became chaotic: there was large-scale urban looting in 1991 and 1993, xenophobic violence in Katanga in 1992–93, and an armed rebellion in 1996–97. Supported by Rwanda and Uganda, this rebellion resulted in Laurent-Désiré Kabila's rise to power in 1997, and a regional war which began in 1998 and continued until 2002.

To revive the economy in both countries, international financial institutions recommended privatising SOEs and creating favourable conditions for attracting foreign investors. Mining companies, which were running large deficits at that time, were particular targets of this development strategy (Serageldin 1992). Fearing to see their mining resources sold off to foreign interests, political leaders in both countries hesitated to follow this recommendation. In Zambia, it was not until 1997 that the government decided to dismantle ZCCM and to sell its assets to foreign investors; the controversial process took another three years to come to an end. Seven asset packages were created, with the government only retaining small minority interests (10–20 per cent) in companies through ZCCM-Investment Holdings (ZCCM-IH) (Craig 2001; Fraser and Lungu 2007).

In Zaire, although the first partnership agreements that Gécamines signed with foreign investors date back to 1994–96, most were renegotiated by the new Kabila regime in 1997 before being suspended by foreign investors at the start of the 1998–2002 war. During this war, the Kabila government signed new agreements with white businessmen close to Zimbabwean President Mugabe in exchange for military support from Zimbabwe. But these agreements covered nothing more than operating Gécamines' mines and plants. It was only after the World Bank returned to the country in the early 2000s that a new mining code aiming at liberalising the mining sector and attracting foreign investors was promulgated.

Contrary to what happened in Zambia, however, the reform of the Congolese mining sector did not involve the demise of Gécamines. A recovery plan refocusing on a limited number of mining and industrial assets and making cuts to the workforce was adopted (Rubbers 2013; Carter Center 2017). To facilitate this plan, the 2002 mining code allowed Gécamines to keep rights over its assets and to decide whether it would operate them, sell them, or transfer them to joint ventures with foreign investors. This arrangement was instrumentalised by the ruling elite to make Gécamines a gatekeeper of Congolese mining resources and thereby acquire personal advantage from contracts signed with foreign investors. Gécamines' most promising assets were sold to foreign investors for developing joint venture projects with the SOE as a minority shareholder. As a result, although Gécamines has not disappeared, it is less and less a mining company strictly speaking; independent of the projects in which it is involved as a partner, it produces less than 20,000 tonnes of copper per annum. It has become more like a chartered company, a sovereign instrument that the ruling elite uses to extract revenues from foreign investors in the mining sector.

The mineworkers of ZCCM and Gécamines were the first victims of the restructuring of the mining sector. In the early 1990s, they faced rapid deterioration in their living conditions due to rising consumer prices, disruptions in food supplies and the withdrawal of food subsidies. As their wages had become insufficient, workers and their families relied increasingly on informal economic activities to make ends meet (Dibwe 2001; Rubbers 2013; Mususa 2014). The first waves of mass layoffs came at this time. In 1991, the Zambian government adopted a redundancy programme to reduce ZCCM's workforce from 56,000 to 31,000 workers by 1997. Another third of the workforce was retrenched during and after the privatisation process, bringing employment down to 19,145 in 2001

(Fraser and Lungu 2007: 21). During this process, the government could not afford to pay most workers their terminal benefits; company houses were sold to their existing tenants at reduced rates as one way to cover some of what was owed to former ZCCM employees.

In Congo, the process was longer and more chaotic. In 1992–93, a popular movement to expel people originating from the Kasai region resulted in the departure of 9,000 Kasaian workers from Gécamines, reducing its staff from 32,000 to 23,000 (Dibwe 2001). In 2003–04, the World Bank organised a 'voluntary departure programme' within the framework of its recovery plan, reducing Gécamines personnel from 24,000 to 14,000 workers.[10] In 2017, the staff was further reduced from 12,000 to 8,500 workers through a retirement plan. In addition to these organised departures, hundreds of Gécamines workers were transferred to joint venture projects through an employer substitution procedure.[11]

Today, however, Gécamines remains the largest employer in the Congolese copper-mining sector. While its staff is a quarter of what it was in the early 1990s, it has still 8,500 direct workers out of approximatively 40,000 employed by the sector as a whole. These workers are the last remaining under the 'state paternalism' labour regime, even though the benefits they receive today are much less generous than in the past. Compared to those in new mining projects, these workers enjoy greater job security and benefits, including family housing and free company schools for their children. On the other hand, their wages are much lower than those paid by the large private mining companies and, until recently, they suffered several months of wage arrears. For these reasons, those who are offered the opportunity leave Gécamines for the new joint venture projects without hesitation.

A Neoliberal Labour Regime (2000–)

The influx of foreign investors into the Central African Copperbelt was driven by two principal factors. On the one hand, both Congo and Zambia offered deposits with relatively high copper grades and attractive fiscal incentives. On the other hand, copper prices on international markets rose from below US$ 2,000 per tonne in 2002 to over US$ 10,000 per tonne in 2011. In the case of Congo, an additional attraction was the presence of the world's largest reserves of cobalt – a metal essential for the making of lithium batteries. Due to the growth in the market for electronic devices, and speculation about an expected boom in electric cars, the price of this commodity also rose in 2005–08 and 2016–18.

[10] On the conditions in which this redundancy programme was implemented, and the protest movement it gave rise to among the workers, see Rubbers (2010).

[11] This procedure is generally activated with the consent of the private partner when Gécamines staff are assigned to the mine or plant that is the object of the joint-venture agreement.

As mentioned in the introduction of this book, this boom in the Central African Copperbelt was characterised by the diversity of investors developing new mining projects. Far from being limited to industry majors, they included juniors, former commodity trading companies, SOEs and even family firms, from all continents. Moreover, since the early 2000s, the mining and industrial projects that these investors bought and developed have changed hands several times. In Zambia, many changes occurred between 2000 and 2005, before the start of the boom, and continue to occur at regular intervals (Gewald and Soeters 2010). In Congo, merger and acquisition operations have been more numerous in the last decade following the financial crisis of 2008 and the decline of copper prices in 2011–16, leading to the rise of Chinese capital.

In 2018, the most important industrial mining projects were Kansanshi (First Quantum), Sentinel (First Quantum), Lumwana (Barrick), Konkola (Vedanta) and Mopani (Glencore) in Zambia, and Tenke Fungurume (China Molybdenum), Mutanda (Glencore), Kamoto (Glencore) and Sicomines (China Railway, Sinohydro and Huayou) in Congo (see Map 2). In addition to these relatively large projects are a number of small and midsized mining projects: about five in Zambia and more than a dozen in Congo. Finally, Congo hosts a dozen smelters, or hydrometallurgical plants, that exclusively process the ore (malachite or heterogenite) produced by artisanal miners. In total, in 2018, Congo produced more than 1.2 million tonnes of copper and Zambia about 860,000 tonnes. This gap between the two countries may grow even wider in the forthcoming years when new mining projects in Congo enter the production phase. This is particularly the case with the Kamoa-Kalula project, whose investors (Ivanhoe and Zijin) announced a projected production of 740,000 tonnes of copper per year. Such a production level would make Kamoa-Kalula the second largest mining project in the world.

At the beginning of the mining boom, economic liberalisation in both countries gave mining companies ample room to negotiate highly favourable contracts. Under pressure from international financial institutions, the Congolese and Zambian governments had implemented legal and tax reforms to provide attractive conditions to foreign investors and revitalise the mining sector. In Zambia, important changes were also made to labour legislation, allowing mining companies to implement labour policies that suit their needs. These changes included a reduction of employers' obligations (for example, to provide housing for workers), the introduction of shorter casual contracts, and a shift of collective bargaining from the industry to the enterprise level. Finally, the one-union system was replaced with a situation where several union organisations compete for the representation of workers in mining companies, reducing and fragmenting union power (Rakner 2003; see this book's Chapter 4).

In addition, before the rise of copper prices, foreign investors were in a strong position to negotiate the rights over Gécamines and ZCCM's mining and industrial assets. However, as these agreements granted considerable advantages to foreign companies and were at first not made public, strong suspicions of corruption arose regarding the way they were concluded (Fraser and Lungu 2007; Commission de revisitation des contrats miniers 2007). Moreover, not content with these tax exemptions and contractual advantages, mining companies developed various tax evasion strategies which enabled them to reach a tax rate close to zero (Marysse and Tshimanga 2012; Das and Rose 2014; Readhead 2016). As a result, when copper prices suddenly soared in 2004, it appeared that the Congolese and Zambian governments would not benefit from the mining boom but that all the profits would flow to the shareholders of the various foreign companies.

Since then, the two governments have taken different measures to try and amplify state power vis-a-vis foreign investors and mining companies and to increase mining revenues.[12] In Zambia, the legal and tax regime for the mining industry was amended in 2008, 2012, 2015 and 2016 (Manley 2013, 2015; Lundstol and Isaksen 2018). Then, in 2018, following an audit of the mining industry, the government decided to take several mining companies to court for tax fraud and announced a new tax increase. In May 2019, these steps led the government to seize control of Konkola, claiming that Vedanta (which controlled 79.4 per cent of Konkola, with the rest owned by ZCCM-IH) had breached the terms of their mining licence. In April 2020, it was the turn of Mopani, a subsidiary of Glencore (73 per cent), to face the threat of having its mining licence revoked for not giving enough notice before suspending operations due to the coronavirus pandemic. By early 2021, the Zambian government declared its investment holding company ZCCM-IH would buy back Glencore's shares in Mopani, with a US$ 1.5 billion loan from Glencore subsidiary Carlisa Investments, to be paid off from future sales and profits. The government announced plans to find another investor, emphasising they had acted to save thousands of jobs at the company. Finally, the Zambian government enacted piecemeal reforms to labour laws in response to public anger over casualisation before producing a unified code, the Employment Code Act of 2019, in an effort to strengthen a limited number of worker protections, including lump-sum payouts for employees on fixed-term contracts.

In Congo, between 2007 and 2010, the government renegotiated all partnership agreements between Gécamines and foreign investors. Following its transformation from an SOE into a commercial company in 2011, Gécamines continued to put pressure on its most important foreign partners to have greater control over mining projects in joint ventures and to demand its share of the profits by taking legal action against them and negotiating new agreements. In 2011, a long and laborious process of consultation with the various parties involved was initiated to revise the mining code of

[12] As the Africa Mining Vision initiative shows, this evolution is far from being limited to the Central African Copperbelt (Coderre *et al.* 2020).

2002. It resulted in the adoption of a new mining code in 2018, which has considerably changed the power balance between mining companies and the Congolese state. This new code involves a significant increase in taxes on the mining industry, the obligation for mining companies to repatriate more than half of their export earnings, and greater state participation in mining projects (Lassourd 2018; Custers 2019; Unceta 2020).

The impacts of these reforms remain to be seen. In both countries, the attempts to regain control over the mining sector have at times enabled governments to increase revenues and invest in infrastructure projects. Having said this, the game is not over: each of these attempts aroused strong opposition from mining companies, which have strong weapons to oppose government measures. Companies can threaten to suspend their operations, organise mass worker layoffs or go to international arbitration. Faced with such threats and their consequences, the Zambian government is currently in a more delicate position than the Congolese government for two main reasons. First, the contribution of the mining industry to employment and local and national development has always been an important political question in Zambia, where Copperbelt Province in particular has a reputation as a political bellwether. However, employment and foreign investment became a particularly sensitive issue after the Patriotic Front put it front and centre in their campaign in the mid-2000s and subsequently came to power in 2011. The leaders of the Patriotic Front, and Zambian politicians more widely, are thus in a more difficult position than Congolese leaders when mining companies threaten to suspend their operations and to retrench thousands of workers.

Second, when the Patriotic Front came to power in Zambia, it invested in numerous infrastructure projects and social programmes, considerably increasing the country's external debt (Siachiwena 2017; Hinfelaar and Sichone 2019). In November 2020, hard hit by the coronavirus crisis, the country was the first in Africa to default on sovereign debt. This debt makes the government particularly dependent on the mining industry, which in in the mid-2010s, directly accounted for 10 per cent of Gross Domestic Product (GDP) and provided just under 20 per cent of government revenue (EITI Zambia 2017; Dobler and Kesselring 2019). The contribution of the mining sector to state revenues is higher in Congo where the government has also increased public spending in the past decade: in 2017, the sector accounted for 17 per cent of GDP and 55 per cent of government revenues (Congo EITI 2017). But the country's external debt has remained comparatively low since it reached the completion point of the Heavily Indebted Poor Countries process in 2010 (Unceta 2020). Though still narrow, the Congolese government's margin for manoeuvre in its relationship with mining companies is therefore greater.

Despite differences in policy and politics on either side of the border, there are nonetheless overarching trends to the labour practices emerging amidst the diverse set of investors. Based on our research and review of available literature, it is possible to outline the principal dynamics of a new kind of labour regime. We identified five general trends in the post-privatisation labour practices of new mining companies in both copperbelts.

1. The new investors claim to break with the paternalism of the past, to focus on their core business, copper production. Those among them which bought mining and industrial assets from ZCCM and Gécamines sought to avoid any responsibility for their housing estates and social infrastructure. Their proclaimed aim is to put responsibility on the workers individually by paying their wages in cash. Benefits provided by law are generally converted into cash allowances or provided for by subcontractors. In large cities such as Kitwe or Lubumbashi, these allowances (e.g. the housing allowance) do not necessarily allow workers to access the corresponding goods or services (e.g. to find a family house). To compensate for low wages, several mining companies have signed agreements with banks to provide loans to workers. As in South Africa, this new credit market has led to the emergence of a culture of borrowing among workers, especially in Zambia (Musonda 2021; see James and Rajak 2014). Aspiring to a better life, a more sustainable economic base for their families, or a middle-class lifestyle, many take loans they are unable to repay and fall into the trap of over-indebtedness.

2. New investors outsource a larger range of activities to subcontractors than SOEs did in the past. Outsourcing has become widespread in the industry since the 1990s. Far from being limited to non-core activities such as catering, transport, cleaning, or security services, it is now extended to all the operations of a mine, including development, mining, maintenance and plant management. As this is one of the principal means through which companies cut costs and increase their flexibility to respond to market pressures, the fall of copper prices in 2008, and then again in 2011, gave subcontracting a new impetus. Today, between 40 and 60 per cent of the people working onsite at mines in Congo and Zambia are contract workers. Generally speaking, these workers have lower wages, fewer benefits and lower rates of unionisation than direct workers. This development of subcontracting contrasts with the strategy historically followed by mining companies in the copperbelts, which had progressively internalised activities necessary for their own development (Gécamines went as far as to produce maize for its workers). This trend had a long history: in the late colonial period, mining companies were already criticised for leaving little room for subcontracting to enable the development of small and midsized private firms.

3. If new mining projects produce more copper than ZCCM and Gécamines in the past, they also directly hire fewer workers. Apart from the abandonment of social infrastructure and the development of subcontracting, this reduction in workers' numbers is often attributed to mechanisation: mining is far more capital-inten-

sive today. This is however a long-term tendency, which does not correspond exactly to the liberalisation of the Congolese and Zambian mining sectors in the early 2000s; the mechanisation of production was already well underway in the 1960s. Another factor, however, has come into play. Like workers across many sectors, mineworkers, especially those in supervisory and administrative positions, have experienced the development of a do-it-yourself management culture and sharp reductions in administrative and support staff. Indeed, executives today must perform tasks – drive their car, send emails, or write reports – that would have been carried out by a driver, secretary, or an assistant in the time of ZCCM and Gécamines.

4. The direct jobs offered by new mining companies are more precarious than in the past. Following the financial crisis in 2008, and the decline of copper prices in 2011, several mining companies undertook mass layoffs. Retrenchments are more frequent and large-scale in Zambia than in Congo; production costs are also higher in Zambia, especially in the old underground mines of Copperbelt Province. As soon as copper prices go down, investors announce that their mines will be put under 'care and maintenance' and that their workforce will be reduced accordingly. Similarly, when Zambia's government intends to raise taxes on the mining industry, companies do not hesitate to exert pressure by threatening mass layoffs.

5. Finally, the establishment of new investors has been accompanied by the formation of an 'ethnotechnical hierarchy' (Hecht 2002: 699; see Rubbers 2019) made up of three distinct categories: expatriate senior managers and technicians; national skilled managers and employees from the country's major cities; and local unskilled workers recruited from nearby communities. The discrepancies in power, opportunity and privilege between these three categories generate frustrations that give rise to claims based on local, regional and national identity in both countries. This is particularly the case for mining projects in remote rural areas, where local communities feel marginalised by more skilled workers coming from large cities or established mining areas. On both sides of the border, feelings of marginalisation and exclusion have led local political leaders to demand employment quotas for local communities (Negi 2009; Rubbers 2019; Kapesa and McNamara 2020).

These trends point to the emergence of a new labour regime that might be termed 'neoliberal'. However, if used as a steamroller concept, flattening the irregularities observed on the ground, the concept of neoliberalism does not lead us very far. Following Brenner, Peck and Theodore (2010), neoliberalism is understood here as a variegated process, which takes different forms depending on the country and the domain of activity under study. What these scholars call 'neoliberalisation' – or, in an earlier version, 'actually existing neoliberalism' (Brenner and Theodore 2002) – exists in the form of historically situated restructuring projects shaped by pre-existing regulatory frameworks. From this perspective, neoliberalism is the starting point of the research process: it is an ideal-typical concept which invites further study of the different processes involved in the formation of a new labour regime.

To understand how a new labour regime comes into being and how it functions, it is necessary to delve into the micropolitics of work, the interactions between the wide range of players involved in the politics and practice of labour. The subsequent chapters thus explore the recent trends in labour practices of new mining investors in more depth, and the way they are experienced, negotiated and contested by a wide range of actors, most especially workers, trade unionists and managers.

Bibliography

Andrae, G. and Beckman, B. (1998). *Union Power in the Nigerian Textile Industry: Labour Regime and Adjustment.* Uppsala: Nordic Africa Institute

Bakajika, T. (1993). Capitalisme, rapport salarial et régulation de la main-d'oeuvre: la classe ouvrière dans les camps de l'Union minière du Haut-Katanga, 1925–1967. PhD thesis, University of Laval. Available at: https://corpus.ulaval.ca/jspui/handle/20.500.11794/17647 (accessed 19 February 2021)

Bancroft, J.A. (1961). *Mining in Northern Rhodesia: A Chronicle of Mineral Exploration and Mining Development.* London: British South Africa Company

Beckman, B. and Sachikonye, L.M. (2001). *Labour Regimes and Liberalization. The Restructuring of State–Society Relations in Africa.* Harare: University of Zimbabwe Press

Berger, E. (1974). *Labour, Race, and Colonial Rule: The Copperbelt from 1924 to Independence.* Oxford: Oxford University Press

Bezuidenhout, A. (2004). Post-Colonial Workplace Regimes in the Engineering Industry in South Africa, Swaziland and Zimbabwe. Crisis States Programme Working Paper 1. Available at: www.lse.ac.uk/international-development/Assets/Documents/PDFs/csrc-working-papers-phase-one/wp53-post-colonial-workplace-regimes-in-engineeering.pdf (accessed 19 February 2021)

Brenner, N. and Theodore, N. (2002). Cities and the Geographies of 'Actually Existing Neoliberalism'. *Antipode* 34(2): 349–79

Brenner, N., Peck, J. and Theodore, N. (2010). Variegated Neoliberalization: Geographies, Modalities, Pathways. *Global Networks* 10(2): 182–222

Brion, R. and Moreau, J.-L. (2006). *De la mine à mars. La genèse d'Umicore.* Tielt: Lannoo

Burawoy, M. (1985). *The Politics of Production: Factory Regimes under Capitalism and Socialism.* London: Verso Books

Carter Center (2017). A State Affair: Privatizing Congo's Copper Sector. Report for the Carter Center. Available at: www.cartercenter.org/resources/pdfs/news/peace_publications/democracy/congo-report-carter-center-nov-2017.pdf (accessed 19 February 2021)

Coderre, M. *et al.* (2020). La vision minière pour l'Afrique et les transformations des cadres règlementaires miniers: les experiences du Mali et du Sénégal. *Canadian Journal of Development Studies* 40(4): 464–81

Commission de revisitation des contrats miniers (2007). Rapport des travaux. Tome 2. Partenariats conclus par la Gécamines. Kinshasa: Ministère des mines. Available at: http://congomines.org/reports/182-rapport-revisitation-tome-2-contrats-gecamines (accessed 19 February 2021)

Corneille, A. (1945). *Le syndicalisme au Katanga*. Elisabethville: Les Editions congolaises

Craig, J. (2001). Putting Privatisation into Practice: The Case of Zambia Consolidated Copper Mines Limited. *Journal of Modern African Studies* 39(3): 389–410

Crehan, K. (1997). *The Fractured Community. Landscapes of Power and Gender in Rural Zambia*. Berkeley: University of California Press

Cunningham, S. (1981). *The Copper Industry in Zambia: Foreign Mining Companies in a Developing Country*. New York: Praeger

Cunningham, S. (1985). Nationalization and the Zambian Copper Mining Industry. PhD thesis, University of Edinburgh. Available at: https://era.ed.ac.uk/handle/1842/7503?show=full (accessed 19 February 2021)

Custers, R. (2019). Le Congo, exportations libérales des richesses. Blogpost for the Groupe de Recherche pour une Stratégie Economique Alternative. Avalaible at: https://gresea.be/Le-Congo-exportations-liberales-des-richesses (accessed 19 February 2021)

Cuvelier, J. (2011). Men, Mines and Masculinities: The Lives and Practices of Artisanal Miners in Lwambo (Katanga Province, DR Congo). PhD thesis, Katholiek Universiteit van Leuven. Available at: www.researchgate.net/publication/292334629_Men_mines_and_masculinities_the_lives_and_practices_of_artisanal_miners_in_Lwambo_Katanga_province_DR_Congo (accessed 19 February 2021)

Das, S. and Rose, M. (2014). Copper Colonialism. Vedanta KCM and the Copper Loot of Zambia. Report for Foil Vedanta. Available at: www.foilvedanta.org/wp-content/uploads/FV-Zambia-report1.pdf (accessed: 19 February 2021)

Dibwe dia Mwembu, D. (2001). *Bana Shaba abandonnés par leur père: structures de l'autorité et histoire sociale de la famille ouvrière au Katanga. 1910-1997*. Paris: L'Harmattan

Dobler, G. and Kesselring, R. (2019). Swiss Extractivism: Switzerland's Role in Zambia's Copper Sector. *Journal of Modern African Studies* 57(2): 223–45

EITI Zambia (2017). Eighth Report for the Fiscal Year Ended 31 December 2015 Extractive Industries Transparency Initiative. Available at: https://eiti.org/files/documents/zeiti-2015-reconcilation-final-report-220217.pdf (accessed 19 February 2021)

EITI Congo (2017). Rapport ITIE 2015. Available at: https://eiti.org/files/documents/finergies_-_itie_congo_-_rapport_2015.pdf (accessed 19 February 2021)

Epstein, A.L. (1958). *Politics in an Urban African Community*. Manchester: Manchester University Press

Ferguson, J. (1999). *Expectations of Modernity. Myths and Meanings of Urban Life on the Zambian Copperbelt*. Berkeley: University of California Press

Fraser, A. and Lungu, J. (2007). For Whom the Windfalls? Winners and Losers in the Privatisation of Zambia's Copper Mines. Report for the Civil Society Trade Network of Zambia (CSTNZ). Available at: https://sarpn.org/documents/d0002403/1-Zambia_copper-mines_Lungu_Fraser.pdf (accessed 19 February 2021)

Fraser A. and Larmer, M. (2010). *Zambia, Mining and Neoliberalism. Boom and Bust on the Globalized Copperbelt*. New York: Palgrave Macmillan

Frederiksen, T. (2010). Unearthing Rule. Mining, Power and the Political Ecology of Extraction in Colonial Zambia. PhD thesis, University of Manchester. Available at: www.escholar.manchester.ac.uk/uk-ac-man-scw:273400 (accessed 19 February 2021)

Gann, L.H. (1969). *A History of Northern Rhodesia: Early Days to 1953*. New York: Humanities Press

Gécamines (1969–1999). Rapports annuels. Lubumbashi: Générale des Carrières et des Mines

Gewald, J.B. and Soeters, S. (2010). African Miners and Shape-Shifting Capital Flight: The Case of Luanshya/Baluba. In Fraser, A. and Larmer, M., eds, *Zambia, Mining, and Neoliberalism*. New York: Palgrave Macmillan, pp. 155–83

Gluckman, M. (1960). Tribalism in Modern British Central Africa. *Cahiers d'études africaines* 1(1): 55–70

Greenberg, E. (1986). Review of *The Politics of Production: Factory Regimes Under Capitalism and Socialism* by Michael Burawoy. *American Political Science Review* 80(1): 309–10

Guene, E. (2017). *Copper, Borders and Nation-Building: The Katangese Factor in Zambian Political and Economic History*. Leiden: African Studies Centre

Haglund, D. (2010). Policy Evolution and Organisational Learning in Zambia's Mining Sector. PhD thesis, University of Bath. Available at: https://researchportal.bath.ac.uk/en/studentTheses/policy-evolution-and-organisational-learning-in-zambias-mining-se-2 (accessed 19 February 2021)

Hecht, G. (2002) Rupture–talk in the Nuclear Age: Conjugating Colonial Power in Africa. *Social Studies of Science* 32(5–6): 691–727

Henderson, I. (1972). Labour and Politics in Northern Rhodesia 1900–1953: A Study in the Limits of Colonial Power. PhD thesis, University of Edinburgh. Available at: https://era.ed.ac.uk/handle/1842/6830 (accessed 19 February 2021)

Henk, D.W. (1988). Kazi ya Shaba: Choice, Continuity and Social Change in an Industrial Community of Southern Zaire. PhD thesis, University of Florida. Available at: https://ufdc.ufl.edu/AA00037631/00001 (accessed 19 February 2021)

Higginson, J. (1989). *A Working Class in the Making. Belgian Colonial Labor Policy, Private Enterprise, and the African Mineworker, 1907–1951*. Madison: University of Wisconsin Press

Hinfelaar, M. and Sichone, J. (2019). The Challenge of Sustaining a Professional Civil Service Amidst Shifting Political Coalitions: The Case of the Ministry of Finance in Zambia, 1991–2018. Pockets of Effectiveness Working Paper 6. Available at: http://dx.doi.org/10.2139/ssrn.3467490 (accessed 19 February 2021)

Hughes, M. (2003). Fighting for White Rule in Africa: The Central African Federation, Katanga, and the Congo Crisis, 1958–1965. *International History Review* 25(3): 592–615

James, D. and Rajak, D. (2014). Credit Apartheid, Migrants, Mines and Money. *African Studies* 73(3): 455–76

Juif, D. and Frankema, E. (2018). From Coercion to Compensation: Institutional Responses to Labour Scarcity in the Central African Copperbelt. *Journal of Institutional Economics* 14(2): 313–43

Kalusa, W.T. (1993). Aspects of African Health in the Mining Industry in Colonial Zambia: A Case Study of Roan Antelope Mine, 1920–1964. MA thesis, University of Zambia

Kapesa, R. and McNamara, T. (2020). 'We Are not Just a Union, We Are a Family'. Class, Kinship and Tribe in Zambia's Mining Unions. *Dialectical Anthropology* 44: 153–72

Katz-Lavigne, S. (2020). 'Qui ne risque rien n'a rien': Conflict, Distributional Outcomes, and Property Rights in the Copper- and Cobalt-Mining Sector of the DRC. PhD thesis, University of Groningen and Carlton University. Available at: https://research.rug.nl/en/publications/qui-ne-risque-rien-na-rien-conflict-distributional-outcomes-and-p (accessed 19 February 2021)

Kayamba, B. (1986). Capitalisme et déstructuration des sociétés lignagères dans l'ancien territoire de Sakania au Zaïre (1870–1940). Unpublished PhD thesis, University of Lubumbashi

Kennes, E. and Larmer, M. (2017). *The Katangese Gendarmes and War in Central Africa: Fighting their Way Home*. Bloomington: Indiana University Press

Larmer, M. (2005). Unrealistic Expectations? Zambia's Mineworkers from Independence to the One-Party State, 1964–1972. *Journal of Historical Sociology* 18(4): 318–52

Larmer, M. (2006). 'The Hour Has Come at the Pit': The Mineworkers' Union of Zambia and the Movement for Multi-Party Democracy, 1982–1991. *Journal of Southern African Studies* 32(2): 293–312

Larmer, M. (2007). *Mineworkers in Zambia. Labour and Political Change in Post-Colonial Africa*. London: Tauris

Larmer, M. (2017). Permanent Precarity: Capital and Labour in the Central African Copperbelt. *Labor History* 58(2): 170–84

Lassourd, T. (2018). La fiscalité du nouveau code minier de la République Démocratique du Congo. Report for the Natural Resource Governance Institute. Available at: https://resourcegovernance.org/sites/default/files/documents/la-fiscalite-du-nouveau-code-minier-de-la-republique-democratique-du-congo.pdf (accessed 19 February 2021)

Lee, C.K. (2017). *The Spectre of Global China. Politics, Labor, and Foreign Investment in Africa*. Chicago, IL: University of Chicago Press

Lundstol, O. and Isaksen, J. (2018). Zambia's Mining Windfall Tax. World Institute for Development Economics Research Working Paper 51. Available at: www.wider.unu.edu/sites/default/files/Publications/Working-paper/PDF/wp2018-51.pdf (accessed 19 February 2021)

MacMillan, H. (2012). Mining, Housing and Welfare in South African and Zambia: An Historical Perspective. *Journal of Contemporary African Studies* 30(4): 539–50

Manley, D. (2013). Caught in a Trap: Zambia's Mineral Tax Reforms'. International Centre for Tax and Development Working Paper 5. Available at: www.ictd.ac/publication/2-working-papers/5-caught-in-a-trap-zambia-s-mineral-tax-reforms (accessed 19 February 2021)

Manley, D. (2015). A Guide to Mining Taxation in Zambia. Report for the Zambia Institute for Policy Analysis and Research. Available at: www.africaportal.org/publications/a-guide-to-mining-taxation-in-zambia/ (accessed 19 February 2021)

Marysse, S. and Tshimanga, C. (2012). La renaissance spectaculaire du secteur minier en RDC. Où va la rente minière? In Marysse, S. and Omasombo, J., eds, *Conjonctures congolaises 2012. Politique, secteur minier et gestion des resssources naturelles en RDCongo*. Paris: L'Harmattan, pp. 11–42

Mitchell, J.C. (1956). *The Kalela Dance. Aspects of Social Relations among Urban Africans in Northern Rhodesia*. Manchester: Manchester University Press

Money, D. (2016). 'No Matter How Much or How Little They've Got, They Can't Settle Down': A Social History of Europeans on the Zambian Copperbelt, 1926–1974. Unpublished PhD thesis, University of Oxford

Mottoulle, L. (1934). Contribution à l'étude du déterminisme fonctionnel de l'industrie dans l'éducation de l'indigène congolais. *Mémoires de l'Institut Royal Colonial Belge* 3(3)

Mottoulle, L. (1946). Politique sociale de l'Union Minière du Haut-Katanga pour la main-d'oeuvre indigène et ses résultats au cours de vingt années d'application. *Bulletin des séances de l'Institut Royal Colonial Belge* 17

Mulwanda, M. (1995). Structural Adjustment and Drought in Zambia. *Disasters* 19(2): 85–93

Musambachime, M.C. (1989). Escape from Tyranny: Flights Across the Rhodesia–Congo Boundary 1900–1930. *Transafrican Journal of History* 18: 147–59

Musambachime, M.C. (1990). Military Violence Against Civilians: The Case of the Congolese and Zairian Military in the Pedicle 1890–1988. *International Journal of African Historical Studies* 23(4): 643–64

Musonda, J. (2021). Modernity on Credit: The Experience of Underground Miners on the Zambian Copperbelt. *Journal of Southern African Studies* 47(3): 369–85

Mususa, P. (2014). There Used to Be Order: Life on the Copperbelt After the Privatisation of the Zambia Consolidated Copper Mines. PhD thesis, University of Cape Town. Available at: https://open.uct.ac.za/handle/11427/9291 (accessed 19 February 2021)

Negi, R. (2009). Copper Capitalism Today: Space, State and Development in North Western Zambia. PhD thesis, Ohio State University. Available at: https://etd.ohiolink.edu/apexprod/rws_olink/r/1501/10?p10_etd_subid=69258&clear=10#abstract-files (accessed 19 February 2021)

Noiriel, G. (1988). Du patronage au paternalisme: la restructuration des formes de domination de la main-d'œuvre ouvrière dans l'industrie métallurgique française. *Le Mouvement Social* 144: 17–35

Parpart, J. (1983). *Labor and Capital on the African Copperbelt*. Philadelphia, PA: Temple University Press

Perrings, C. (1979). *Black Mineworkers in Central Africa*. London: Heinemann

Poupart, R. (1960). *Première esquisse de l'évolution du syndicalisme au Congo*. Bruxelles: Editions de l'Institut de Sociologie Solvay

Powdermaker, H. (1962). *Copper Town: Changing Africa: The Human Situation on the Rhodesian Copperbelt*. New York: Harper & Row

Prain, R.L. (1956). The Stabilization of Labour in the Rhodesian Copper Belt. *African Affairs* 55(221): 305–12

Rakner, L. (1992). *Trade Unions in Processes of Democratisation. A Study of Party Labour Relations in Zambia*. Bergen: Michelsen Institute

Rakner, L. (2003). *Political and Economic Liberalisation in Zambia 1991–2001*. Uppsala: Nordic Africa Institute

Readhead, A. (2016). Transfer Pricing in the Mining Sector in Zambia. Report for the Natural Resource Governance Institute. Available at: https://resourcegovernance.org/sites/default/files/documents/nrgi_zambia_transfer-pricing-study.pdf (accessed 19 February 2021)

Reid, D. (1985). Industrial Paternalism: Discourse and Practice in Nineteenth-Century French Mining and Metallurgy. *Comparative Studies in Society and History* 27(4): 579–607

Roberts, A.D. (1982). Notes Towards a Financial History of Copper Mining in

Northern Rhodesia. *Canadian Journal of African Studies* 16(2): 347–59

Rubbers, B. (2010). Claiming Workers' Rights in the Democratic Republic of Congo: The Case of the 'Collectif Des Ex-Agents de La Gécamines.' *Review of African Political Economy* 37(125): 329–44

Rubbers, B. (2013). *Le paternalisme en question. Les anciens ouvriers de la Gécamines face à la libéralisation du secteur minier katangais (R.D.Congo).* Paris: L'Harmattan

Rubbers, B. (2019). Mining boom, Labour Market Segmentation and Social Inequality in the Congolese Copperbelt. *Development and Change* 51(6): 1555–78

Schumaker, L. (2001). *Africanizing Anthropology. Fieldwork, Networks and the Making of Cultural Knowledge in Central Africa.* Durham, NC: Duke University Press

Seibert, J. (2011). More Continuity than Change? New Forms of Unfree Labor in the Belgian Congo, 1908–1930. In Vanderlinden, M., ed., *Humanitarian Intervention and Changing Labor Relations.* Leiden: Brill, pp. 369–86

Seibert, J. (2013). 'Winds of Change': Worker's Unrest and the Transformation of Colonial Capitalism in Katanga – Belgian Congo. In Fall, B., Phaf-Rheinberger, I. and Eckert, A., eds, *Work and Culture in a Globalized World: From Africa to Latin America.* Paris: Karthala, pp. 253–71

Serageldin, I. (1992). Strategy for African Mining. World Bank Technical Paper 181. Available at: http://documents1.worldbank.org/curated/en/722101468204567891/pdf/multi-page.pdf (accessed 19 February 2021)

Siachiwena, H. (2017). Social policy reform in Zambia under President Lungu, 2015–2017. *Centre for Social Science Research* Working Paper 403. Available at: www.cssr.uct.ac.za/cssr/pub/wp/403 (accessed 19 February 2021)

Siegel, B. (1989) The Wild and Lazy Lamba. In Vail, L., ed. *The Creation of Tribalism in Southern Africa.* Berkeley, CA: James Currey and University of California Press, pp. 350–71

Stoever, W.A. (1981). *Renegotiations in International Business Transactions: The Process of Dispute-Resolution between Multinational Investors and Host Societies.* Lexington, MA: Lexington Books

Tone, A. (1997). *The Business of Benevolence. Industrial Paternalism in Progressive America.* New York: Cornell University Press

Toussaint, E. (1956). Le personnel congolais. In *Union Minière du Haut-Katanga. Evolution des techniques et des activités sociales. 1906–1956.* Bruxelles: Cuypers, pp. 213–76

UMHK (1956). *Union Minière du Haut-Katanga. 1906–1956.* Bruxelles: Cuypers

Unceta, R.A. (2020). République démocratique du Congo : Revenus miniers et dépenses publiques pour le développement. *Mondes en développement* 1(189): 55–80

Van Nitsen, R. (1933). *L'hygiène des travailleurs noirs dans les camps industriels du Haut-Katanga.* Brussels: Hayez

Vanthemsche, G. (1994). Genèse et Portée du Plan Décennal du Congo belge (1949–1959). *Mémoires de l'Académie Royale des Sciences d'Outre-mer* 51(4).

Vellut, J-L. (1981). Les bassins miniers de l'ancien Congo belge. Essai d'histoire économique et sociale (1900–1960). *Cahiers du CEDAF* 7: 1–70

Vellut, J-L. (1983). Articulations entre entreprises et Etat : pouvoirs hégémoniques dans le bloc colonial belge (1908–1960). In Coquery-Vidrovitch, C. and Forrest, A., eds, *Entreprises et entrepreneurs en Afrique (XIXième et XXième siècle)*, volume 2. Paris: L'Harmattan, pp. 49–79

Von Holdt, K. (2003). *Transition from Below. Forging Trade Unionism and*

Workplace Change in South Africa. Scottville: University of Natal Press

Von Holdt, K. and Webster, E., eds (2005). *Beyond the Apartheid Workplace: Studies in Transition*. Scotsville: University of KwaZulu-Natal Press

White, L. (2000). *Speaking with Vampires. Rumor and History in Colonial Africa*. Berkeley: University of California Press

Zahavi, G. (1988). *Workers, Managers, and Welfare Capitalism: The Shoeworkers and Tanners of Endicott Johnson, 1890–1950*. Urbana: University of Illinois Press

2

Safety: The Politics of Life in a Neoliberal Labour Regime

JAMES MUSONDA AND FRANCESCA PUGLIESE

One of the most noticeable changes brought by new mining investors in the Congolese and Zambian copperbelts since the early 2000s is the promotion of a new work culture, in particular, a safety culture. Any visitor to a mine can observe its significance in the workplace. After passing through electronic gates and breathing into the breathalyser, one undergoes a short safety training. Once this training is finished, one receives a full set of personal protective equipment (PPE), including a helmet, glasses, a mask, earplugs, boots and, sometimes, overalls that one is asked to wear during the duration of the visit. Once one is in the car and puts on the seatbelt, the driver honks before starting and scrupulously obeys speed limits for fear of being flashed by a speed camera. If he needs to refuel, one is asked to put on the helmet and leave the vehicle to wait in a shelter. When one gets out of the car and visits a place on foot, the guide shows the way with reminders of the rules in that area. At every step one sees, posted on walls, billboards or rocks, various safety messages: signs, rules, procedures, but also letters, graphs and posters bearing slogans and threats. These are the same posters – usually featuring a smiling worker in full PPE, with a slogan conveying the importance of safety to the company – as those found outside the mining concession, along the road leading to the entrance. Indeed, mining companies do not only post safety messages for workers in the workplace, but also along the main roads of the town, at the events they organise, in the reports they make public, and on their website. The discourse of safety literally saturates the space of the mine.

Of course, the significance of safety rules and procedures is not limited to mining companies in the Central African Copperbelt. The phenomenon has, in recent times, been noted by social scientists researching mining in other parts of the world, and can be viewed as a key characteristic of the labour regime currently emerging in the global mining industry. As such, the processes behind it as well as its effects, deserve attention. Yet, there is little analysis of these processes and effects in the literature on safety in the workplace, which is dominated by two approaches: a psychological approach, which seeks to identify risk factors in workers' behaviours (Heinrich 1959; Kemery, Mossholder and Bedeian 1987), and a sociological approach, which emphasises workers' practical knowledge and employers' responsibility (Leger 1992; Webster and Leger 1992; Baugher and Roberts 1999; Mayhew and Quinlan 1997; Nichols, Walters and Tasiran 2007; Phakathi 2017; Stewart and Nite 2017). These two approaches correspond to different political views of the trust to be granted to workers, the role that rules and procedures may play to avoid accidents, and the respective responsibilities of employer and employees when an accident occurs. As such, they show that safety provides a useful lens for studying the interplay between work practices, workplace power relations and production politics – in sum, the micropolitics of work. Yet they cannot account for the growing significance of safety in the mining industry, and the effects that it has on workers in the Central African Copperbelt.

To address this broader issue, this chapter proposes to analyse safety as a government technique aiming at placing responsibility and blame for safety lapses in the hands of workers. To better understand how safety policies are implemented, this chapter compares two mining projects that we will call Kopala mine (Zambia) and Kinke mine (Congo). James Musonda did a nine-month internship at Kopala, which involved three months of safety training and six months underground work with mineworkers. This experience gave him the opportunity to see first-hand how safety is learnt, perceived and put into practice by the workers in an underground mine. Francesca Pugliese did comparative research between different mining projects for a period of nine months and spent two one-month periods as an intern in the Human Resource (HR) department and the Social Department of two mining companies, one of which was Kinke mine. This stay allowed her to study safety from the point of view of office employees in an opencast and underground mines. Although we had different research experiences, their comparison turned out to offer interesting insights on how safety rules and procedures are implemented, the different factors that come into play, and how workers respond to them.

Although Kopala mine is in Zambia while Kinke mine is in Congo, the difference between the two countries is not analytically relevant as labour officers on both sides of the border are poorly equipped to enforce labour and safety regulations (on Zambia, see Haglund 2010; Ministry of Labour 2017; on Congo, Ministère de l'emploi 2011; Benjamin Rubbers, personal communication). As we will see, if Kopala and Kinke mines are interesting to compare, it is principally because they do not operate the same type of mine – Kopala operates an underground mine, Kinke an opencast mine – and do not follow the same investment strategies. They therefore allow for a better understanding of the variations in labour management techniques among mining investors (see Introduction).

In the first section of this chapter, we analyse the safety policies of Kopala and Kinke as disciplinary government techniques in Foucault's (2012 [1975]) sense of the word. In the second section, we discuss some new dimensions of these policies that have to be understood in the light of the dynamics of the mining industry in the twenty-first century. If the same power rationale can be found behind the safety policies of both mining projects, they also show some differences that we attempt to account for in the third section. Finally, on the basis of our interviews and conversations with them, we look at how mine employees critically make sense of the power of safety.

A Disciplinary Technique

Like most mining projects in the world, those found in the Zambian and Congolese copperbelts are keen to trumpet that their priority is the life and well-being of their employees.[1] On the website of the company that owns Kopala mine, one reads: 'Our priority in the workplace is to protect the health and well-being of all our workers. We take a proactive approach to health and safety; our goal is continuous improvement in preventing occupational disease and injuries.' Likewise, in its 2017 annual report, Kinke states: 'Safety is a crucial element of our culture. It is our first value and our highest operating priority.' Usually, some space is also devoted to explain the company's safety aims and methods. Kopala flags up its safety strategy, which is based on the identification of twelve common fatal hazards and of nine appropriate life-saving behaviours. In its sustainability report of 2017, Kinke describes its safety philosophy: 'We think safety first. We stop and think then act to prevent injury. [...] We are focused on building a safety mindset in all of our employees and contractors, while also ensuring that supporting behaviours, cultures and processes are in place across every area of our operations.'

As these quotes illustrate, safety is used as a public communication tool to demonstrate that the company cares for the well-being of its employees. At first sight, this message is principally for external audiences: the project's funding bodies, which may organise audits to ensure compliance with international safety standards; the project's stakeholders in the country where it is established, such as state representatives, trade unions, civil society organisations, or local communities; and of course, potential critics – journalists, advocacy organisations, or social science researchers. This message is intended to avoid scandal, external control, and the possible withdrawal of financial and political support. As with the discourse on Corporate Social Responsibility (Rajak 2011), the discourse on safety is aimed at promoting the image of a 'caring' corporation and, in doing so, at preventing the risks that emanate from the social environment of the mine.

When it comes to workers, the corporate discourse on safety provides a justification for the cumbersome rules and procedures workers must comply with in their everyday work routines and a response to critiques of the deprivation and precariousness in which new mining investors leave

1 A key role has been played in the promotion of occupational health and safety by the International Council on Mining and Metals (ICMM), an organisation created in 2001 with the aim to champion responsible mining globally.

them. However, safety is not merely a discourse here. From a Foucaultian perspective, it can also be studied as a disciplinary government technique, that is, a power strategy that seeks to improve workers' bodily dispositions through the control of space and the dispensation of both rewards and sanctions. As with the disciplinary techniques studied by Foucault, its underlying rationale is not only to increase workers' efficiency, but also to protect their lives and preserve the company's human capital.

First, the power of safety operates through the control of space and the dispensation of rewards and sanctions. As soon as workers enter the mine, whether at Kopala or Kinke, they are subject to this power strategy. They are greeted by a forest of symbols (notices, warnings, signs, etc.) posted on almost every surface, from the doors of company vehicles to the walls behind toilets in the changing rooms. Most of these messages remind the workers of the hazards specific to the place where they are displayed and the appropriate safety behaviour to be adopted. But they can also indicate no-go areas which cannot be entered without authorisation, or remind workers of the sanctions prescribed for safety offences. A poster at the entrance of Kopala mine, for example, says: 'Under the influence of alcohol? You will be dismissed!' To ensure that workers comply with safety rules and procedures, they are constantly monitored by their supervisors and surveillance cameras. They can also be subject to surprise controls by safety officers, who can impose sanctions ranging from simple verbal warning, severe reprimand to dismissal.

However, this political topography is far from homogeneous. Safety communication, control and surveillance tools are particularly concentrated in production sites and along the concession roads, and are less prevalent in offices, canteens or changing rooms. Outside the mining concession itself, the presence of safety is still more diluted and less threatening, taking the form of billboards with a slogan about the importance of safety for the company – here there are no stern declarations of rules or sanctions. Kopala also conducts safety campaigns (role plays, roadshows, etc.) in the communities where the workers live. In 2017, for instance, it organised an essay competition on family safety for miners' wives and children. The winners received cash prizes, household items and scholarships. As one Kopala mine official explained, 'We do not want workers to think about safety only when they are at work. We also want their children, the future miners, to understand safety before they come to the plant.' Thus, the mining company seeks to extend the power of safety beyond the workplace, and to use the workers' social environment to induce broader changes in their habits (drinking, driving and so forth). As mining companies are keen to point out, safety is not just a set of rules specific to the space of the mine, it is a 'culture', a new way of perceiving and being that workers have to embody.

Second, safety is used to impose time discipline on the workers. The presence of cameras in the workplace is officially justified by the need to monitor the production process and make sure that safety conditions are met. But they also serve to keep an eye on miners for non-compliant behaviour such as taking shortcuts, engaging in horseplay or sleeping whilst on duty. At Kopala mine, headlamps and oxygen boxes issued to workers also serve as a form of monitoring. They are allocated individually, instead of being taken from a pool, and each box is equipped with a chip. This chip allows the company to identify the location of every miner and to note the time spent at any given location whilst underground. If these measures are justified for safety reasons (they ensure that all miners come back to the surface alive after their day's work and if they do not, can trace their exact whereabouts), they also provide the opportunity to better control workers' movements underground for company officials to quickly detect delays and absenteeism. Since 2017, Kopala mine displayed a timetable for when different categories of miners can access the cage and be issued headlamps and oxygen boxes. Those who fail to meet this timetable must inform control services and ask for permission to access the mine.

Take for instance the experience of Patson, an underground miner. When he reported for work one day in 2018, he was thirty minutes late and the clock-in system did not allow him to enter the mine. To have his access card reconfigured by the IT team, he had to explain the reasons for his delay to his supervisors. After going through the automatic gates, he was again stopped at the mine entrance. The officers there did not let him use the cage because his helmet was not the right colour.[2] He had to wait another thirty minutes to get to his workstation. To be sure, Patson will do everything to avoid being in the same situation again. Faced with a highly developed control system, workers are quick to internalise time discipline.

Finally, safety is justified by the need not only to increase workers' efficiency, but also to preserve the company's human capital. There is a biopolitical rationale behind safety which leads companies to make a distinction between their direct employees, whose health is monitored and protected, and the people employed by subcontracted firms, whose health is not their direct responsibility. In both mines, these contract employees account for over 70 per cent of the workforce. While Kopala and Kinke provide PPE to all their permanent employees, it is up to the subcontracted firms to provide it for their own employees. Although they have to comply with the mining company's safety rules, in practice some do not fully provide it, or provide equipment of poor quality.

As a prerequisite to direct employment, both mining companies subject would-be workers to medical checks to determine their suitability. Such medical checks have a long history on both sides of the Central African Copperbelt. What is new is that they are justified by safety reasons, that they are performed regularly on workers, and that they are used to exclude those who are 'not fit' from employment. As one Congolese safety officer explained, 'if a miner cannot see or hear properly, he is very vulnerable to mobile equipment and the dangers of mining'. Far from being limited to

2 Miners are assigned helmets of different colours according to their rank and the section of the mine where they work. Specific times during which they can use the cage have been established for these different categories of workers.

eyes and ears, medical checks involve a full examination of the body, and, in Kopala, include tests for sexually transmitted diseases. In both mines, the workers who fail medical checks are liable to receive termination of employment on medical grounds. Their presence in the workplace is viewed as a possible danger to their own safety and to that of others.

Making Workers Responsible

Although safety can be viewed as a disciplinary government technique, it is not merely a renewed form of industrial discipline. When discussing discipline in the workplace, Foucault (2012 [1975]) gives central place to the factory regime of the late nineteenth and early twentieth centuries. The most accomplished expression of industrial discipline can be found in applications resulting from the psychophysiology of factory work in that period: a science – whose most famous representative was F.W. Taylor – which aimed at dissecting workers' tasks into simple physical acts in order to optimise and redistribute them along a production line. This is obviously not the aim of safety under a neoliberal labour regime, which calls upon workers' reflection as they perform complex tasks. Indeed, safety does not only push workers to internalise practical automatisms, but also reflexive automatisms, to 'stop, look and think' before acting. Instead of making workers' movements faster, this reflexive dimension leads to sequencing and slowing them down. Incidentally these cumbersome procedures are the subject of recurrent criticism among Congolese and Zambian workers. They complain of the complexity of the rules and procedures, the frequent meetings devoted to them, and the lengthy training necessary to obtain the authorisation to perform simple tasks.

Thus, safety should not be understood as the simple continuation of the industrial discipline characteristic of paternalistic labour regimes. The rationale behind its rules, procedures and messages must be sought elsewhere than in the pursuit for ever-increasing efficiency and productivity of workers' bodies.

Our research suggests two complementary lines of interpretation. On the one hand, the new importance given to safety must be understood in the light of the increasingly capital-intensive nature of the mining industry. Most mines now depend more on machines than on workers. In this context, safety appears as a government technique which must ensure the continuity of production.[3] If it does not increase workers' individual productivity, it increases the productivity of the mine as a whole. From a management point of view, an accident can stop production for several

[3] Although the mechanisation of production is a long-standing trend in the Central African Copperbelt, it has not been accompanied by a corresponding development of safety policies. Indeed, these remained almost unchanged since the 1950s. Safety as a key government technique to ensure the continuity of production was introduced by new mining investors in the 2000s.

hours, and this lost time represents a greater cost to the company than the money invested in safety equipment and personnel or the time dedicated to safety training and meetings. This link between safety and production – the crude economic rationale behind safety – is made explicit in the precise accounting that contemporary mining companies, including Kopala and Kinke, hold of lost-time injuries and deaths. These figures are displayed everywhere – at the mine's entrance, in the company's annual reports, during safety meetings and so forth – to encourage workers to share the company's concern for production and the creation of value. The value that the company gives to workers' health, life and well-being is here fused with its own shareholder value.

On the other hand, safety allows the employer to transfer responsibility for accidents onto workers. Regular training, the provision of PPE, the wide range of rules and procedures, the display of safety messages, the establishment of systems of control, collectively remind workers that the company has taken all precautions to guarantee their safety and that it cannot be held responsible for accidents. If an accident occurs, it is generally attributed to workers' negligence. This is a lesson that Larry, a miner at Kopala, learnt at his own expense. He had repeatedly reported to his superiors that the shovel of the loader he operated was defective. Nothing was done, however, until it injured and killed another miner. The company charged Larry for gross negligence and dismissed him from employment. 'I don't know if you have noticed,' one of his colleagues observed, 'whenever there is a mine accident, it is always the worker who is at fault.' Larry's case is not exceptional. As long as production proceeded it was common for safety officers to turn a blind eye to unsafe practices or to neglect repairs but to punish mineworkers when accidents occurred.

It is in the light of this transfer of responsibility onto the workers that the obligation to refuse to work when safety conditions are not fulfilled must be understood. As we will see in the next section, this obligation is difficult to follow in practice for some workers, especially miners employed by subcontractors. Nevertheless, workers are constantly reminded of it in documentation, during pre-shift safety assessments, or in post-accident reports reviews. This transfer of responsibility for accidents also sheds some light on the obligation to get 100 per cent on safety exams. For example, in 2014, Musonda, participated in a three-month safety training course organised by Kopala mine. It was mandatory for participants to obtain a 100 per cent score before being employed. Those who failed received their certificates only after passing repeat examinations. One of the participants stressed the novelty of this requirement in comparison to the prevailing practice at the time of Zambian Consolidated Copper Mines (ZCCM): 'in ZCCM, we just went to sit in classes and listen to the lesson. Today you have to pass an examination.' The words of an HR employee at Kinke helps to understand the reasoning: 'The strength of the company is in training workers so that they internalise the safety culture and make it part of their values. We aim to make everyone responsible for their safety and that of others.'

From this, safety may thus be understood as the expression of a neoliberal mode of government. The confusion of market values with moral values, as well as the transfer of responsibility to individuals, have been identified by various scholars as key characteristics of neoliberalism (see, e.g., Rose 1999; Shamir 2008; Trnka and Trundle 2017; Rubbers and Jedlowski 2019). As suggested in Chapter 1, however, it is important to go beyond this concept to develop a more grounded analysis of the labour policies put in place by different mining companies. Two main differences emerge from the comparison between the safety policies of Kopala and Kinke.

First, although both companies operate a zero-tolerance policy to alcohol consumption, Kopala enforce sanctions more strictly and reported more disciplinary cases than Kinke. Between 2013 and 2017, Kopala reported 528 alcohol-related offences. Of these, the company dismissed from employment 219 offenders for exceeding the alcohol limit and issued final warnings to the remainder, whose alcohol levels remained within acceptable limits. Kopala also prohibits the dismissed workers from seeking re-employment there for the next three years. Kopala conducts alcohol tests on accident victims, including those who have died, to rule out the possibility of alcohol consumption.

In contrast, Kinke records very few alcohol-related offences, and dismissals for disciplinary reasons in general are between three and five per year. In addition, while Kopala punished all workers, including contract workers, in case of non-compliance, at Kinke safety officials referred non-compliant workers to their employers. As subcontractors usually have a looser approach to safety, this meant workers received less punitive sanctions, or even no sanction at all.

Second, although the percentage of contract workers is more or less the same in both companies, they do not enjoy the same conditions of employment. Kinke works with a limited number of large and midsized subcontracting firms, which make substantial profits. Such firms offer employment conditions (wages, benefits, etc.) that are slightly lower than those provided by the mining company. By contrast, Kopala puts a large number of small and midsized subcontracting firms in competition with one another to operate its underground mines. To win contracts during tenders, these firms are pressured to make offers with a low price. As they make small profits, many tend to not provide for their workers adequately. This competitive tendering is coupled with a bonus system which ties the profits made by subcontracting firms and the wages of contract workers to their level of production.

As most contract workers receive a very low base salary, this bonus is critical for them to make ends meet at the end of the month. As Collinson's (1999) and Phakathi's (2017) work on South Africa show, this type of system pushes miners to take liberties with safety rules and procedures. They are more likely to ignore safety rules to increase production. Worse, if they do not take such risks, they may lose their job.

This is what happened to George, an underground miner at Kopala mine. One day, he refused to work in an unsupported area of the underground mine. The following day, his supervisor reassigned him to the surface where there was nothing to do. His colleagues mocked him labelling him 'Mr Safety'. A week later, he was informed that his contract had expired. He reported this matter to the company safety officers but they could not help. When a contract expires the employer is not under any obligation to renew it. As this example illustrates, although in theory, all workers have a right to refuse dangerous work, in practice contract workers do not enjoy this right.

It is tempting to make sense of the contrasting safety practices at Kopala and Kinke on the basis of the parent company's investment strategy. Confidentiality clauses do not allow us to say much about those companies here. Suffice it to say that Kopala's parent company is a private global company that seeks to make short-term profits to increase its shareholder value, while Kinke's is a Chinese State-Owned Enterprise (SOE) that works with a longer-term perspective (on this contrast, see Lee 2017). In view of Kopala's capital ownership and investment strategy, it is unsurprising that it puts subcontractors in competition to both raise production and reduce costs without taking responsibility for the consequences of this policy on the safety of contract workers.

But this contrast, we believe, is of lesser significance than the types of mines that Kopala and Kinke operate. While Kinke operates opencast mines, Kopala operates old and deep underground mines that are famous for being particularly wet. As is well known, the risks in underground mines are much higher than in surface mines. This may explain Kopala's greater insistence on respect of safety rules and procedures by its own employees – its human capital. However, the operating costs of underground mines, including labour costs, are much higher. To make a profit, Kopala tends to focus on the reduction of labour costs, which is the only variable cost category. This pushes the company to outsource its activities to subcontractors on a competitive basis, and to conveniently turn a blind eye to their safety practices.

Critiques from Below

Generally speaking, employees at both Kopala and Kinke mines are ambivalent about safety. On the one hand, they believe that safety measures are an effective way to avoid accidents and protect their lives. The safety measures that mining companies put in place are used by workers and their families to compare their employment conditions, the care they show towards employees. PPE is itself a status symbol in the community. On the other hand, when it comes to their everyday experience in the workplace, our informants complain about the ubiquity of safety, its intrusive and threatening presence.

Indeed, the first thing workers in both countries highlighted is the ubiquity of safety in their everyday lives. Take for instance the underground miners of Kopala. In the company bus, on their way to work, safety is already one of their main subjects of conversation. At the entrance to the mine, they are greeted by safety posters and a self-administered breathalyser before proceeding to the mandatory alcohol test conducted by security officers. After putting on their work clothes, they clock in and collect their headlamps and oxygen boxes. Once they reach the underground office, the pre-shift safety meeting begins. At the stope, each miner has to individually conduct an assessment of the work area for any hazards to be reported or rectified before commencing work. As work proceeds, the supervisor performs targeted observations on every mineworker on safety compliance, skills and technique, posture and PPE. Safety officers also conduct their inspections and supervisions routinely and randomly.

As this example suggests, safety is experienced as both a series of monotonous routines and a pervasive form of control in time and space. It is present when workers work individually, during meetings and informal conversations, as well as when they move from one place to another on the mine site. As some workers told us, this extensive surveillance apparatus expresses the employer's profound distrust toward workers: 'When we report for work,' a miner of Kopala said, 'they test us for alcohol when at work, they observe everything we do. Maybe they have even put cameras in the toilet. They do not trust us. To them, we are not just workers but drunkards and criminals.'

This impression was reinforced in both mines since employers have implemented double-check mechanisms. At Kopala mine, before the new safety policy, miners recorded all safety incidences in one report book. Since 2017, there has been a book for recording pre-shift meetings which is separate from the one in which assessments are recorded. Safety interventions are recorded in yet another document. Further, when conducting individual assessments, supervisors record their observations on separate forms, while spot checks are also recorded on a separate document. At Kinke, the new safety policy increased the number of required authorisations before specific tasks can be performed. In the past, there was only one office issuing work authorisations. With the new system, each work team has two supervisors, one for the work area and the other for supervising the tasks performed by workers. This double-check mechanism is meant to stop shortcuts and unsafe acts. For many workers, however, this is just more bureaucracy, consuming time and energy at the expense of their work.

Workers in both mines also criticised the employer's intransigence when it comes to safety, noting that the slightest offence becomes the subject of reprimand and punishment. This is especially the case at Kopala, where the company has the reputation of being unforgiving. As a miner at Kopala put it, 'when one is found guilty of having alcohol in his breath, he feels stupid. Many are remorseful, but the company does not care.' At Kinke, the number of dismissals, temporary layoffs, or reprimands for safety reasons is lower. However, the company also has a reputation of inflexibility. Stories about workers dismissed for minor safety offences circulate among workers. Valérie, a female employee, said:

> At the entrance, everybody has to do it (the alcohol test) compulsorily. Some people got fired after the test. Alcohol can make you lose the job. Indeed, in case of an accident, the family of the worker can ask compensation from the company. However, this is on condition that the victim of injury or accident was not drunk at the time of accident. [...] Also, the company observed strict enforcement of speed limits on the site. Cars cannot exceed 40 km/hour and the sanctions can consist of a dismissal. Also, in case one of the passengers is not wearing the safety belt, they were sanctioned together with the driver.

For the workers in Kopala, one of the main means by which their employer controls their behaviour is through video surveillance. Even though the cameras primarily serve to monitor the production process, they also capture any 'deviant' behaviour by workers, such as sleeping, horseplay or non-compliance with the regulations. The simple fact that they can be used for this purpose arouses – like Bentham's panopticon in Foucault (2012 [1975]) – a feeling of being constantly watched. Having said this, surveillance is not understood by workers as an anonymous form of power; it is concretely embodied in the figure of safety officers. At Kopala, they are seen as 'fault finders' working in the hands of management: 'Safety officers,' a miner said, 'always side with the bosses to make sure that they find fault in a worker when there is an accident.' Such 'traitors', another miner added, tend to show no empathy towards other workers: 'They know that sometimes things are difficult in the mine and a person can take a shortcut, but they report you to the bosses. They do not mind that by reporting you to the bosses, you will lose the job and your children will suffer.' Similar critiques could also be heard on the Congolese side of the border, with some variations across mining projects. At Kinke Pugliese heard a few conversations in which safety officers were presented as being on the side of the employer. At Kishi, another Congolese mine where she did research, the question was less whether safety officers are on the side of the employer than if they treated workers differently, depending on their personal connections with them: 'we know of someone who reported for work drunk', a worker of this company told Pugliese, 'however, being the sole breadwinner in his family and the security officers knowing him, they did not report him. Instead, they sent him home'.

Discourses about safety inevitably led to comments about the unequal treatment of workers by mining companies. At Kinke, workers denounced the impunity of some 'bosses' who are seen to be above safety rules and sanctions. They do not wear full PPE, they breach the driving rules, but they are never reprimanded by the safety officers. There are thus double standards in the implementation of safety for executive managers and the bulk of the workforce. At Kopala, comments were more geared towards the inequalities between permanent workers and contract workers. As we have seen above, these two categories of employees do not receive the same PPE. Consequently, most contract workers experience the safety policy with a deep sense of exclusion. As Charles, an underground miner complained, 'We do the most difficult job, but we feel that we are not needed here. We work with torn gloves, boots and overalls. Look at our friends; they have everything. It is not fair.' In practice, only the permanent workers enjoy the right to refuse dangerous work. In addition, they can call upon their unions for protection in safety offences. By contrast, as George's story shows, contract workers cannot refuse dangerous tasks without risking losing their jobs and, since 80 per cent are not unionised, they have no recourse against sanctions by safety officers. Worse still, the production bonus system pushes them to take risks – to operate in unsupported areas, take shortcuts, work without the appropriate equipment, etc. – and to conceal accidents in order to maximise production and increase their insufficient wages.

Mineworkers who experienced the ZCCM or Générale des Carrières et des Mines (Gécamines) era were keen to compare the safety policy of new mining companies with the one that prevailed in the SOEs of the past. Some Congolese workers, for instance, remembered that, at Gécamines, safety training was given to specific categories of workers on the basis of the tasks that they had to perform, and that compliance with safety rules and procedures was the responsibility of supervisors. In new mining companies, by contrast, all the employees must participate in regular safety training, and compliance with safety rules and procedures is regarded as the responsibility of the workers themselves. As their behaviour is subject to different forms of control, it is more difficult for workers who commit offences to seek leniency from their supervisor and to escape sanctions. Similarly, former ZCCM workers referenced the tolerance attached to safety non-compliance: 'when you failed to obey the rules, they put you under the disciplinary regime but they rarely dismissed you from employment'.

Generally speaking, our respondents contrasted the insistence on safety by new companies with the paternalistic policy of ZCCM and Gécamines in the past. In the discourse of the new mining companies, safety is presented as a generous gift showing that they care for the lives of their employees and the well-being of their families. The workers, on the other hand, oppose these new safety policies, which focus primarily on workers' biological lives and physical safety, to earlier social policies which covered every aspect of the lives and well-being of workers and their families.

From this perspective, safety campaigns serve as bitter reminders of the difficulties caused by the withdrawal of social welfare, the mass layoffs, the rise of subcontracting and the low wages paid to mineworkers. In the Zambian mining community where Kopala mine conducted its safety campaigns, many residents perceive safety to be meaningless when people have no access to jobs or social welfare. As one argued:

> It is annoying to see safety campaigns in the communities where the mining companies do nothing to help the people who live there. During ZCCM, the mines provided schools, healthcare, sports and entertainment and public sanitation. However, today, all this has been removed, and people have lost jobs. Bringing safety to where workers live does not make sense. How does the community benefit from these safety campaigns?

One can find in this critique of safety the expression of a paternalistic moral economy, that is, a set of expectations towards employers that have to do with the subsistence of workers and which takes as a standard the social policies of previous mining companies (Rubbers 2010; see Thompson 1971; Scott 1977). The new investors are criticised for breaking with the concern of their predecessors, ZCCM and Gécamines, for workers' social life and reducing it to a concern for their biological life. To use Agamben's conceptual distinction (1998), while paternalism allowed them to aspire to a certain conception of the good life (*bios*, or the life worth living), safety reduces their prospects to mere physical existence (*zoë*, or bare life).

Conclusion

This chapter, through its discussion of the safety policies of new mining companies in the Central African Copperbelt, suggests that they have not completely broken with the industrial paternalism of the past. Like the social policies of colonial companies, and then of postcolonial SOEs, safety in the neoliberal labour regime appears as a discourse stressing the care that companies show for the lives and well-being of their workers, a government technique to control and discipline them, and a modern form of production management. Like paternalism in the twentieth century, safety in the twenty-first conflates all these aspects – care, life, well-being, control, discipline, production and modernity – all together.

Safety in the twenty-first century is however grounded in a different power rationality than the paternalistic policies that preceded it. It reflects the increasingly capital-intensive nature of the mining industry, which is based less on the productivity of workers individually than on the productivity of the mine as a whole. In these circumstances, workers' primary responsibility is not to increase their own efficiency but to ensure that the production process is not halted. Safety also reflects a new corporate strategy that aims to transfer responsibility for work accidents to the workers themselves. What the safety discourse does is to make the mining project's various stakeholders understand that accidents are the responsibility of the workers, not of the company.

If the same neoliberal power rationality underlies the safety policies of contemporary mining companies, it is important to account for the different ways in which such policies are implemented. Our comparison between Kopala in Zambia and Kinke in Congo shows significant variations in their safety policies, and suggests that these variations can be understood in the light of their labour management practices, the type of mine being operated, and the type of investor behind them. If a general conclusion can be drawn from this comparison, it is that safety policies are likely to be more flexible and less discriminatory in opencast mines operated by mining companies investing with a longer-term perspective.

In a sense, workers' comments allow light to be shed on the dynamics behind the safety policies which emerged in the Central African Copperbelt as foreign mining investors succeeded the large SOEs of the past. From their perspective, the importance given to procedures, surveillance and sanctions reveals the distrust of management towards workers while the discrimination mining companies practice between different categories of employees suggests that they do not value the latters' lives equally. The ways in which safety measures are implemented contribute to the emergence of new types of inequalities in the workplace that were absent under state paternalism. Above all, in comparison to the social policies that were developed by mining companies in both copperbelts (from the 1920s to the 1980s), the safety policies of new mining investors are grounded in a narrow conception of care and protection, which reduces workers' lives to mere physical existence, as if their own conception of the good life has no importance.

Bibliography

Agamben, G. (1998). *Homo Sacer: Sovereign Power and Bare Life*. Stanford, CA: Stanford University Press

Baugher, J.E. and Roberts, T.M. (1999). Perceptions and Worry about Hazards at Work: Unions, Contract Maintenance and Job Control in the US Petrochemical Industry. *Industrial Relations* 38: 522–41

Collinson, D.L. (1999). 'Surviving the Rigs': Safety and Surveillance on North Sea Oil Installations. *Organization Studies* 20(4): 579–600

Foucault, M. (2012 [1975]). *Discipline and Punish: The Birth of the Prison*. New York: Knopf/Doubleday Publishing Group

Haglund, D. (2010). Policy Evolution and Organisational Learning in Zambia's Mining Sector. PhD thesis, University of Bath. Available at: https://researchportal.bath.ac.uk/en/studentTheses/policy-evolution-and-organisational-learning-in-zambias-mining-se-2 (accessed 19 February 2021)

Heinrich, H.W. (1959). *Industrial Accident Prevention: A Scientific Approach*. New York: McGraw-Hill

Kemery, E.R., Mossholder, K.W. and Bedeian, A.G. (1987). Role Stress, Physical Symptomatology, and Turnover Intentions: A Causal Analysis of Three Alternative Specifications. *Journal of Organizational Behavior* 8(1): 11–23

Lee, C.K. (2017). *The Spectre of Global China. Politics, Labor, and Foreign Investment in Africa*. Chicago, IL: University of Chicago Press

Leger, J.P. (1992). 'Talking Rocks': An Investigation of the Pit Sense of Rockfall Accidents amongst Underground Gold Miners. Unpublished PhD thesis, University of the Witwatersrand

Mayhew, C. and Quinlan, M. (1997). Subcontracting and Occupational Health and Safety in the Residential Building Industry. *Industrial Relations Journal* 28(3): 192–205

Ministère de l'emploi, du travail et de la prévoyance sociale (2011). Programme d'actions prioritaires et cadre de dépenses à moyen terme (2012–2016). Democratic Republic of Congo, unpublished document

Ministry of Labour and Social Security (2017). Annual report. Available at: www.mlss.gov.zm/?wpfb_dl=54 (accessed 19 February 2021)

Nichols, T., Walters, D. and Tasiran, C. (2007). Trade Unions, Institutional Mediation and Industrial Safety: Evidence from the UK. *Journal of Industrial Relations* 49(2): 211–25

Phakathi, S. (2018). *Production, Safety and Teamwork in a Deep-Level Mining Workplace. Perspectives from the Rock-Face.* Bingley: Emerald Insight

Rajak, D. (2011). *In Good Company. An Anatomy of Corporate Social Responsibility.* Stanford, CA: Stanford University Press

Rose, N. (1999). *Powers of Freedom: Reframing Political Thought.* Cambridge: Cambridge University Press

Rubbers, B. (2010). Claiming Workers' Rights in the Democratic Republic of Congo: The Case of the 'Collectif Des Ex-Agents de La Gécamines'. *Review of African Political Economy* 37(125): 329–44

Rubbers, B. and Jedlowski, A. (2019). Introduction. Regimes of Responsibility in Africa: Towards a New Theoretical Approach. In Rubbers, B. and Jedlowski, A., eds, *Regimes of Responsibility in Africa. Genealogies, Rationalities and Conflicts.* Oxford: Berghahn, pp. 1–20

Scott, J.C. (1977). *The Moral Economy of the Peasant: Rebellion and Subsistence in Southeast Asia.* New Haven, CT: Yale University Press

Shamir, R. (2008). The Age of Responsibilization: On Market-embedded Morality. *Economy and Society* 37(1): 1–19

Stewart, P.F. and Nite, D.K. (2017). From Fatalism to Mass Action to Incorporation to Neoliberal Individualism: Worker Safety on South African Mines, c.1955–2016. *Review of African Political Economy* 44(152): 252–71

Thompson, E.P. (1971). The Moral Economy of the English Crowd in the Eighteenth Century. *Past & Present* 50: 76–136

Trnka, S. and Trundle, C. (2017). Introduction. Competing Responsibilities: Reckoning Personal Responsibility, Care for the Other, and the Social Contract in Contemporary Life. In Trnka, S. and Trundle, C., eds, *Competing Responsibilities: The Politics and Ethics of Contemporary Life.* Durham, NC: Duke University Press, pp. 1–26

Webster, E. and Leger, J.P. (1992). Reconceptualising Skill Formation in South Africa. *Perspectives in Education* 13(2): 53–68

3

Gender: Navigating a Male-Dominated Space

FRANCESCA PUGLIESE AND JAMES MUSONDA

This chapter analyses the challenges, motivations and strategies of women working for new mining projects in the Central African Copperbelt. Although they remain few, their employment is an increasingly debated and polarising topic within families and broader society on both sides of the border. By examining the different ways women navigate the male-dominated environment of mining, we seek to assess the extent to which, in an area that has been strongly marked by the legacy of industrial paternalism, the development of a neoliberal labour regime was accompanied by a change in gender roles. Through a micropolitical lens, we explore the continuities, changes and disruptions in gender dynamics and highlight the new forms of gender inequality generated by the boom in mining investments.

Female employees in the mining industry have been largely overlooked in the literature on the Central African Copperbelt.[1] Yet gender is key to study changes in power relations in the workplace and the social space within which it is located. As Lindsay and Miescher (2003: 21–22) argue, gender norms are strongly related to the operation of power: 'Gender relations are produced, reproduced and transformed through discourses, practices and subjectivities in interaction with local and broader structures and processes.' Drawing inspiration from the growing corpus of research on female mineworkers in other parts of the world (Gier and Mercier 2006; Lahiri-Dutt 2006; Rolston 2014; Benya 2016), we focus on the specific features that people use to depict the proper behaviour of men and women. Such features contribute to assign people in certain positions, and influence the way they think about their own experience at work, at home, and in broader society.

This chapter is based on ethnographic fieldwork conducted by the authors between 2016 and 2019 in the Central African Copperbelt. Francesca Pugliese completed a one-month internship in two mining companies in Congo, during which she stayed in the companies' camps

[1] In Central Africa, studies dealing with gender dynamics are exclusively about artisanal mining (Mususa 2010; Cuvelier 2011; Hayes and Perks 2012; Bashwira *et al.* 2013). Exceptions are Musonda (2020) and Pugliese (2020) dealing with female employees in mining companies in Zambia and in Congo, respectively.

with mine employees. She also lived for a total of seven months with different mineworkers' families in town. James Musonda spent nine months as a helper at two underground mining companies in Zambia. During this period, we had informal interactions with various categories of mine employees in the workplace, at home and during leisure activities. We also conducted over two hundred interviews, of which approximately a third were with women. The difference in the authors' gender, age, nationality, background and familiarity with the field certainly influenced our approach to gender issues. While Pugliese tried to establish a confidential relationship with women on the basis of her own experience as a (white) woman, Musonda – a Zambian man who grew up in Kitwe – drew on his own personal knowledge and his large social network in the miners' community.

Below, after providing a brief historical background, we analyse the motivations that have pushed women to look for employment in new mining projects. We then turn to the ways in which they navigate the male-dominated environment of the mines. Finally, we discuss the implications that jobs in the mining sector have on their marital and family life. In each section, we provide a comparative perspective to better make sense of the similarities and differences between the two sides of the Central African Copperbelt, and of the gender dynamics in this region of Central Africa since the twentieth century.

Women in Mining

As Benjamin Rubbers and Emma Lochery show in Chapter 1, from the 1920s onwards mining companies in the Central African Copperbelt progressively put in place a paternalistic labour regime. The aim of this regime was to generate a new category of workers, who would be more stabilised, skilled, disciplined and educated than the migrant workers who preceded them. Women, who were banned from working in the mines, had a crucial role to play in this project (Chauncey 1981: 139; Rubbers 2015: 216). Provided that they learned to behave as 'modern' housewives, women could make life in the mines more comfortable for male miners, encourage them to become more responsible, and raise the next generation of workers under the supervision of the employer. Their place was at home to take care of their husband and children, not in the workplace. Until the 1940s, these gender policies were more effectively enforced on the Congolese side of the Copperbelt, as Union Minière du Haut-Katanga (UMHK) received more support from the colonial administration and the Catholic missions (Vellut, 1983; Dibwe 2001; Rubbers 2013) than Rhodesian Selection Trust (RST) and Rhodesian Anglo American (RAA) (Parpart, 1986: 38–39). After the Second World War, mining companies on both the sides of the Central African Copperbelt adopted similar policies and sponsored educational programmes that taught married women 'to be better wives and mothers' (Hunt 1990: 456; Parpart 1986: 42). For girls, therefore, educational opportunities were limited and tailored to domestic roles rather than wage work. Generally speaking, women's wage work was seen as superfluous, if not harmful for the husband, who risked being seen as unable to provide for his family (Epstein 1981; Dibwe, 2001, pp. 64–65). The only activity that was tolerated, and even encouraged, among workers' wives was urban agriculture as it could supplement the food ration received from the employer (Peša 2020: 537).

From the 1970s onwards, however, mineworkers in the Central African Copperbelt were confronted with declining wages and social welfare services. Although Générale des Carrières et des Mines (Gécamines) and Zambian Consolidated Copper Mines (ZCCM) largely endorsed the gender ideology promoted by colonial mining companies and Christian mission, the conditions they offered to mineworkers no longer allowed them to develop a 'modern' family lifestyle (Ferguson 1999; Dibwe 2001; Mususa 2010; Rubbers 2015). A growing number of women began to engage in income-generating activities such as gardening, trade, or beer brewing to contribute to family budgets. With the deterioration of their living conditions in the 1980s and 1990s, households came to increasingly depend on these activities for their daily needs, and model of the modern family was gradually put into question (Henk 1988; Ferguson 1999; Rubbers 2015).

Besides those who developed income-generating activities in agriculture or trade, a minority of women – who have largely remained unnoticed by previous scholars writing on gender in the Central African Copperbelt – worked in the mining industry. In 1976, the percentage of women employed by Gécamines and ZCCM was 4.5 and 4 per cent respectively (Rapports annuels de la Gécamines, 1969–99; ZCCM labour reports, 1964–97; see Lando 1978; Munene 2018; Dibwe 2019). Most worked in subaltern positions such as secretaries, nurses, cleaners, or cooks. Only a few, generally with a middle-class background, were in executive or middle management positions. Most were employed in administration or in the companies' social institutions such as schools or hospitals. As Dibwe (2019: 4; our translation) notes about Gécamines, 'the exploitation and production sector remains until now the prerogative of men'. Although this is certainly not specific to the Central African Copperbelt (see Gier and Mercier 2006), this division of labour reflected widely held assumptions about the characteristic features of men and women in the area.

Over the course of the last two decades, with the growth of the urban population, the decline of state-owned mining enterprises and the establishment of new foreign mining companies, the proportion of women on the labour market seems to have increased. Although most women remain active in the informal economy – including artisanal mining, where their share is estimated at 30–50 per cent (World Bank 2017) – a growing number have sought formal employment. The increasingly visible presence of women in wage employment more generally has not gone unnoticed. On social media, it has become commonplace to see memes ridiculing the declining power of the man in a couple circulating among friends.

The mining sector has not escaped this broader trend. Although new foreign mining investors do not hesitate to dismiss workers and offer fewer social benefits than their predecessors, the jobs they advertise are still seen as stable and well-paid compared to those offered by most national firms. As a result, a growing number of women, especially those with higher education degrees, try their luck with these companies. This is all the more so since a growing number of mining companies claim to be committed to gender diversity and to give preference to female candidates: for instance, some companies in Congo mentions in their job advertisements that 'Women's applications are given high priority' (our translation). Indeed, gender equality campaigns have progressively found their way into the mining sector and new foreign investors feel increasingly under pressure to conform with Western corporate ethical standards. In the Central African Copperbelt, this is especially true of companies that are part of the International Council on Mining and Metals (ICMM), an international organisation that champions the Corporate Social Responsibility movement in the global mining industry.

To date, however, women represent less than 10 per cent of the workforce of most mining companies in both countries (World Bank 2017).[2] There are several reasons for this. Most girls are discouraged to take scientific and technical subjects at school and university. Thus, although it has increased, the number of women applying for jobs in the mining sector remains limited. Secondly, recruitment committees are usually composed only of men. In a region marked by a high unemployment rate, where a man's honour is defined by his ability to provide for his family, to hire a woman in a mining company is considered by many as a waste, as it deprives men of job opportunities. While some households have two salaries, others have no stable source of income. Consequently, women not only have a lower likelihood of being hired at all, they are also the first to be dismissed. Finally, executive managers themselves may prioritise male workers to avoid interruptions in the production process caused by pregnancy and women's family obligations. This explanation was provided – among others – by Regina, one of the few female managers to run a subcontracting firm in the Zambian copperbelt: 'Women are not as productive as men. They have a lot of responsibility. A lot of days off, looking after the husband who is sick today, tomorrow the child, the other day funeral. Mining does not work like that.'

[2] In contrast to South Africa (Benya 2016: 7), Congo and Zambia have not adopted affirmative action policies compelling mining companies to speed up the inclusion of women. Thus the number of female employees in a mining company largely depends on its own commitment to gender equality and the pressure exerted by local civil society organisations.

A small but significant change associated with the development of new mining projects is that some women now work as mechanics, loader drivers or dump truck operators in core functions such as processing, maintenance or mining. Their number is small, however. As in the past, most of the women who find employment in these projects work in auxiliary departments and services (human resources, finance, administration, social, hospital, canteen, cleaning, etc.). In both countries, their presence underground remains strictly regulated: in Congo it is prohibited for women to work in this environment; in Zambia, they are only authorised to perform non-manual work and must be accompanied by a man while underground.[3] While it is still generally accepted that, as in many mining countries, women's bodies must be protected from the dangers of underground work, this excludes women from wage increases and bonuses offered to workers in the production departments based on the company's performance. All mineworkers know that such bonuses make a significant difference in what they get at the end of the month.[4]

All this indicates that various initiatives have been formally taken to facilitate women's inclusion in the mining sector. While states introduced legal changes to allow women to work at night (in Congo) or underground (in Zambia), some mining companies advertised female-friendly jobs, set up shorter shifts for breastfeeding mothers, or simply put up posters showing women in company uniforms. Nevertheless, the situation for female workers has only changed slightly. Women working on these projects remain few and far between, and most are assigned to positions that are not essential to the functioning of the mines. Worse still, in Congo, the emergence of subcontracting in the industry has strongly impacted on women. Many who once worked for mining companies now work for subcontracting companies, which offer them fewer stable jobs and lower wages. In cleaning and catering firms, their number can reach half of the workforce. In the Zambian copperbelt, the situation is different because the bulk of the workforce is employed in underground mining operations. The development of subcontracting in this country has thus affected men more than women.

This reproduction of women's position in the workplace must be understood in the light of the gender ideology that was promoted by mining companies in the twentieth century, which professed that women had to be obedient to men, that their place was at home, and that their role was to take care of children. As Acker (1990: 152) argues, 'the ranking of women's jobs is often justified on the basis of women's identification with childbearing and domestic life'. Even in the masculine domain of

3 Following the legislative changes to allow women to work underground, three women were recruited to work underground at Kopala mine, where Musonda did fieldwork.

4 In Congo, although women cannot benefit from this underground bonus, a law promulgated in July 2016 allows them to work at night, and hence to receive the bonus for night work.

the mines, women are generally expected to perform a woman's job. As this quote from Sandra, a Congolese executive secretary, suggests, female mineworkers internalise and reproduce these normative expectations while being keenly aware that: 'Bosses prefer people who do not contradict and women usually do not. [...] Men like to control, and women are used to being controlled. That is why women are well employed in administrative positions or as secretaries taking care of the boss' practical stuff.'

Motivations

Women are found at all levels of the employment hierarchy and may be grouped into three categories based on their position and their level of education. In the first category, we find women with an upper or middle-class background and a local or foreign university degree. Most work as executive or middle managers in administration, the Human Resource (HR) department, or the social development department. Added to this category are the few female geologists, chemists, or engineers in departments involved in the production process. The second category comprises women of various social origins with a degree from a technical school or, in few cases, a local university. They are employed as office workers (secretaries, translators, accountants, etc.) or skilled manual workers (electricians, truck drivers, mechanics, etc.). The final category is composed of women who work as cleaners, cooks or logistics personnel. Although some of them may have a university degree, they perform unskilled work.

These differences in terms of job position and education level are connected to the ways in which our informants talked about their decision to work. Those at the top of the hierarchy (the first category) tend to downplay the importance of money and to highlight their personal aspirations, while the women in the second and third categories mostly emphasise the need for work and responsibility towards their family. For Maria, a young Zambian technician working underground, it is the passion for the job, the competition with men and the desire for climbing the social ladder that has prompted her to embark on this career. This thirst for success and recognition, she said, must be understood in the light of her childhood. She is one of two children brought up by a single mother. The difficulties she faced as a child pushed her to develop masculine behaviours: 'During my childhood, I did literally everything boys did. I herded cattle, sold fruits at the market, and worked in the fields to help my mother to raise money for my young brother and me'. Upon completing secondary school, she got interested in rock mechanics and decided to pursue it as a career. Her passion bore fruit when, in her final year at university, she won a competition sponsored by a mining company and was offered a job.

For Rose, a 35-year-old woman who works as a geologist in an underground mine in Zambia, the salary is important as she has to provide for a household comprising her mother, her daughter and herself.

But money is not everything. As with some other women from mining families, she developed an early interest in the world of mining thanks to her father, a ZCCM geologist: 'I always admired my father's boots and overalls every time he came back from work. He told me a lot about the underground, and it is like I knew what the underground looked like even before I started work.' As for Maria, competition with men also played a role when she started studying geology at university: 'When a guy performed well,' she explained, 'I also wanted to do better, that is how I managed to finish with excellent grades.'

Responsibility towards the children and the family is an aspect that was more frequently brought up by the women in the second and third categories. For Gisèle, a Congolese technician who holds a degree from a local university, working for a mining company was less a choice than a family necessity: 'If I had a good husband that takes care of my children and me', she said, 'I would not work. [...] I work because I need it, but I would like to rest and take care of my children.' Gisèle is married with two children but her husband, who is never at home, does not earn enough to fully provide for the family. This is why she started to work for a mining company, a choice that brings her some satisfaction: she is proud of having been selected among many candidates and she feels respected by her peers. Finally, she now has the means to provide for her family and to occasionally assist a relative or neighbour. However, as the quote above makes explicit, being a miner is not her ambition. She would prefer to stay at home and take care of her children. As she confided to Pugliese, to satisfy this ambition, she would like to find a new husband who can perform the role of breadwinner properly.

The same goes for Huguette, a 40-year-old Congolese woman, who had a difficult career before finding a job in a mining company. She struggled to obtain a secondary school diploma, and she could not afford to continue her studies due to economic problems and early pregnancies. During her life, she has had several jobs. In the mining sector, she first worked in different subcontracting catering companies and then obtained a contract working in logistics at a mining company. 'Everything I did,' she says, 'was for my family, and if I think about where I come from and the difficulties and humiliation I experienced as a single mother, I think I took the right decision. Now my children can study and have the life that I would have always wanted.' For her, however, the job that she currently holds is not the end of the story. It is a means to achieve her dream, opening a private kindergarten. But to save up enough money she has to work for a few more years.

As we can see from these stories, women describe different motivations to account for their decision to work for a mining company. It has to do, to varying extents, with their passion for the job itself, their aspirations for economic independence and social mobility, and their responsibilities as mothers. In all cases, the ways in which they present their motivations shows the centrality of gender norms, which unfold in different directions depending on the job position and level of education. Gender norms strongly influence their aspirations, the forms of dependence in which they find themselves and the responsibilities that they consider theirs. Such discourses, however, are not sufficient to account for their experience of the mine as a gendered workplace. In the next section, we study the challenges they face in this masculine environment and the strategies they put in place to deal with them.

A Gendered Workplace

Women working in the mining sector face different sorts of challenges. First, they must work in a material environment that has been designed for men's bodies. The most obvious example relates to the standard Personal Protective Equipment (PPE) provided to workers, which is often not suitable or comfortable for women (see Benya 2009: 96). In Zambia, the one-piece workwear presents special difficulties to women working underground as, when they must go to the toilet, they have to take off all of their equipment and clothes: the headlamp, the hard hat, the battery belt tied to the waist and then the whole work-suit. The company was unable even to find the right size of shoe for Rose because no manufacturer makes small sizes. As a result, she has to work wearing oversized shoes, which make walking underground very difficult: 'Wearing an oversized shoe feels like carrying a heavy burden and leads to tiring very quickly. It is like punishment,' she complained. The masculine nature of the mine is inscribed in the very materiality of its facilities and equipment, and this makes it easy for management to invoke practical reasons (e.g. the cost of equipment or of building toilets specifically for women) to normalise the exclusion of women.

Second, women are subject to strict restrictions about certain types of jobs such as those involving manual tasks underground. In the Zambian mine, despite the legal changes to allow women to work underground, restrictions persist. As already noted only three women, Rose, Maria and Beatrice are authorised to work underground. To obtain this authorisation required their employer to make a request to the government's mine safety department. According to the law, this request must stipulate that all the necessary measures to accommodate women in this environment have been taken, such as toilets for women, separate changing rooms, and a male escort while underground, etc. As explained above, the decision to open mine access to women is connected to transnational initiatives for equal rights and to the companies' own concern with their corporate image. But this opening is strongly constrained by legal provisions which continue to be justified by the imperative to protect women. This justification is generally well-accepted by male mineworkers. As a company manager explained, 'women's bodies cannot withstand the environment underground for a long time. So we need to specify where they work and for how long.'

Third, if women want children, they know that pregnancies can impose on them difficult choices and have a strong impact on their career. While this affects working women generally, it is, once again, especially the case for women working in the mines, whether underground or on the surface. Under both Congolese and Zambian law, due to the intrinsic hazards of the mines, pregnant women cannot be employed in this environment irrespective of the nature of the job. One of our respondents in Zambia, who was trained as a heavy-duty mechanic, explained that she lost a job opportunity in the mines because she became pregnant (the pregnancy test she took as part of the recruitment process was positive). After she gave birth, she failed to find another opportunity in the mines and she was therefore forced to retrain as a nurse: 'It was easier to get a job as a nurse than to get a manly job.'

As previously noted, when mining companies restructure their operations and/or organise mass layoffs, women are usually the first to lose their jobs. When Grace, a loader truck operator, came back from maternity leave in 2015, the downturn in copper prices led her employer to restructure its operations, and Grace and her fellow female colleagues were excluded from the mine site. Six were retrenched while she and three other women were assigned to the information desk. Her job now involved monitoring the production process underground via cameras. While management justified this action as a cost-cutting measure affecting all workers, the women saw it as a discriminatory practice based on gender. This opinion is shared by Cynthia, a Congolese mine employee who lost her job in 2016. As she put it, 'they prefer to keep men or people who have a family and just one salary. As if, when you do not have one, you were less responsible, and you do not need a job. People ask you: "What are you going to do with the money if you do not have a family?"'

Finally, women working in mining may experience derogatory comments made by colleagues. Like many other women interviewed in Congo, Rachelle, a HR officer, feels that men do not always consider women in the workplace as colleagues, but as sexual partners or housewives: 'At work,' she said, 'men always desire women or think that women are there for cooking and not for work in mining [...] They are curious, they harass you, they ask you to marry them just to have fun. In the bus, if you are not well dressed, they judge you.' Rumours about women workers may be spread as much by their female as by their male colleagues. In Congolese mines, where women are already 'out of place', rumours are rife about women workers who are alleged to have obtained their positions by flirting or having sexual intercourse with male supervisors.

To cope with these challenges, women express their agency by developing various strategies. Like many in high and mid-level positions, Rachelle insists on the importance for women of obtaining men's respect. To do so, women have to work hard – harder than men – and put some limits on the jokes and comments that male colleagues can make: 'Some colleagues need to be guided to understand when joking goes too far. You can laugh twice; the third time you say that you need respect.' In her view, it also involves putting aside gossiping and vanity, which she sees as their 'feminine part', to focus on the job.

This view is part of a broader strategy among women which consists of adopting so-called masculine traits (e.g. hard work, assertiveness, courage, indifference to dirt, propensity to joke with colleagues) in order to prove their ability to work on an equal footing with men. Our informants frequently stressed that they were recruited on the basis of their skills, not because of their physical attractiveness or sexual availability. Among them, only Huguette confided to us that she had had a love affair with a male supervisor at the beginning of her career: 'We have to fight with what we have,' she said. 'If we do not, we will not have any promotions, and we will just experience marginalisation.' Since women adopting masculine behaviour can be regarded with suspicion, it is important for them to not push it too far. This is a limit that Jessica, a female heavy truck driver, learned to delineate from experience: 'Sometimes I forgot the way I was working, and I behaved like a man [...] Men have a complex if women work, especially if they are better qualified than they are. To avoid harassment, I try to become friends and never make men feel less important.' To gain their male colleagues' respect and avoid troubles, women have to be careful not to humiliate them, and show that they comply with expected feminine behaviours by being faithful and dedicated wives at home.

In Zambia, the experience of the three female underground workers suggests that women can also draw upon their position of hierarchical superiority and mutual dependency with their male team members to cope with negative stereotypes. On the one hand, the three women relied on their crews to get the work done, achieve targets and hence get favourable performance assessments. On the other, the male miners depended on them for work assignments, rewards, breaks, recommendations for promotions and wage increases, technical knowledge and skills, and for possible protection during retrenchment. Interactions at work revolved mainly around production, safety and job security, and the importance of these concerns tended to obscure gender difference in significant ways. The successful integration of these women underground was thus based neither on the adoption of male behaviour nor on open resistance to male domination. Rather, these women attempted to neutralise gender differences by emphasising the demands of work or to reconfigure them differently by redefining work interactions in the language of the family (for a similar observation, see Rolston 2014: 8–10). In the latter case they came to assume a feminine role, that of a 'mother' or 'sister', but one that gives them authority over their co-workers.

A Miner and a Housewife

During an interview, the HR manager of a mining company in Congo explained that recruiting female workers contributes to improving the situation of families. In his view, women are more responsible than men, who tend to waste their wages on alcohol and girlfriends. This view can be found in other mining projects elsewhere. A senior expatriate manager interviewed by Lahiri-Dutt (2006: 363) in Indonesia, for example, believed that 'women are more careful in their jobs and as a result not one of them have had any accidents. They can also cope better with repetitive and tedious jobs, are easier to deal with, and tend to have a steadying impact on men.' In Congo, however, this opinion is not shared by the majority of workers, who tend to criticise new management practices aiming to increase the number of women as they consider that a woman's place is at home.

In this view, which endorses the gendered division of labour promoted by mining companies in the past, a woman's role is primarily that of wife and mother, not of breadwinner. If the family is in need, a married woman may engage in informal economic activities to supplement her husband's income but in this case the main concern is that her activities remain under the husband's sole supervision: men prefer their wives not have other 'bosses' in their lives, to prevent potential harassment or cheating. When women work alongside male colleagues under the supervision of other men, as is the case for female mineworkers, they are often the object of suspicion from their husband and in-laws. Female wage workers are frequently blamed by their in-laws of hiding their salary from the husband and playing the role of the boss at home. Many women are reluctant to work in this suspicious environment. Gisèle, who has to work night shifts with men, finds it shameful, as it may place her respectability into question and cause problems at home: 'A married woman returns home from work at eight in the evening, and has to decide between the house and the job, this is not good. I do not like to work at night; I would rather leave before six.'

In view of such suspicions, it is unsurprising that women are careful to show that they are faithful and dedicated wives. Bernadette, a Congolese technician, told us that it was crucial for her to be recognised not just as a competent worker but as a subservient wife, who takes care of the needs of her husband. To show her love and affection, every day when she comes back from work, she is keen to enact a sort of marital ritual in which her husband waits for her, sitting on the couch, and asks her to take off his shoes:

> It is my role. Luckily for my husband that I am Christian and I know how to respect him. Otherwise, he should have done a lot of work with me. [...] He knows how much I love my job and the efforts I made to get it [...] At work, I follow the orders just from the bosses and the colleagues

> above me and not from whoever thinks that the women are inferior. On the couple's level, I accept the submission. I cannot ask my husband to make the bed, clean the kitchen or to cook. He is the boss. If he wants to do it, it is because of the love he wants to show me. It is not me that I can order. It is in the Bible.

Like Bernadette, the majority of the female mineworkers interviewed by Pugliese stressed that they are not arrogant (*orgueilleuses*) at home, and that they accept the authority of their husbands. As Rubbers (2015: 227–28) explains in an article on spousal relationships among Gécamines workers, couples continue to refer to the colonial family model – namely to the ideals of monogamy, domesticity and male authority – to remind one another of their respective duties as docile housewives and responsible husbands, and to obtain respect as virtuous Christian families in the local community. To do so, it is particularly important for women to be transparent about their pay with their husbands. However, they do not have to hand it over to their husbands. According to Kahola (2014: 161–62), among Congolese couples, the husband has the responsibility to assume the main financial burden in the family, even when the wife earns more than him. Consequently, the wife does not have to spend money for the household; she can, if she chooses, keep it for herself and her relatives. That said, even though women are free to dispose of their own income freely, in practice most of our informants use it to meet family needs along with their husbands. This practice is becoming increasingly common among Congolese couples where both the spouses work (Muswamba 2006: 75). This indicates that women's work both inside or outside the mines follows similar patterns and challenges the prevailing gender values in society.

Our research tends to suggest that women's wage employment is more widely accepted in Zambia than in Congo. As Musonda (2020: 38) finds elsewhere, men are not as ashamed of having working wives as they were in the period from the 1950s to the 1970s. For these families, economic security is a more important determinant of a man's or a woman's position than gender difference. As such, men generally prefer to marry women who are in a position to work, or to develop a business, and to generate some income. As one of his friends told Musonda, 'it is suicidal to marry a woman who just sits at home and wait for your salary. A woman should bring something to the table.' If they do not marry a woman who is already working, many mineworkers are ready to pay to have their wives trained as teachers, nurses or safety officers. This increased recognition of women's economic role accords with recent findings on the Zambian Copperbelt which show women as breadwinners (Mususa 2010; Evans 2016). This is uncommon in Congo, where most men prefer that their wives stay at home or engage only in informal economic activities. If they pay for training it is for themselves, to improve their own employability, not for their wives to get jobs.

Problems can sometimes arise when women earn higher salaries then their husbands, as we saw in the story of Rita, a female mineworker whose wage is twice or thrice that of her husband. Like many other women, the fact that she works full time does not relieve her of household chores. She wakes up at four in the morning to prepare food and bathwater for her husband, and to get children ready for school. By five-thirty, she is at the bus station to go to the mine site and work until six in the evening. Given her difficult job in the mines, she usually returns home exhausted. Soon after she got her job, she hired a maid to help her at home, but this did not please her husband. A crisis broke out one day when she was so tired she could not cook for the husband. 'I cannot eat bread,' he said. 'What type of woman are you if you cannot cook for your husband?' He reminded her of her duties and called a meeting with her parents. During this meeting, he expressed what he saw as a lack of respect, and associated it with her new employment: 'it is a woman's responsibility to cook fresh meals for her husband regardless of her employment status. A man's pride is in the dish his wife cooks.'[5]

As Silberschmidt (1999: 7) argues, the failure of men to fulfil sociocultural expectations to provide, which in large part constitute their 'social value, identity, and sense of self-esteem', threatens their authority and in some cases reduces their role in the household to that of 'figureheads'. In the case of Rita's husband, his feeling of losing control finds expression in accusations of disrespect and infidelity: 'Sometimes', Rita told Musonda, 'when there is no food at home and I ask my friends to give me some money, he would not eat the food protesting that it may have come from my boyfriends.' Issues of jealousy and infidelity are well documented in the anthropological literature on the Central African Copperbelt (Powdermarker 1962; Epstein 1981; Ferguson 1999). Unsurprisingly, such issues are resurfacing in the context of the mining boom, with the increase in women's employment and the development of social media. Thus Linda, a warehouse worker, reported:

> The moment I reach home, I cannot answer my phone, especially if the call is coming from a man. My husband will ask who the man was and why he was calling a married woman after work. Switching off the phone was another problem because it meant avoiding calls. I cannot accept car lifts from male colleagues. I have to use the company or public bus. Being on social media such as Facebook and WhatsApp simply meant flirting with men. Having a password on my phone was not about security but about hiding a sexual relationship. If I knock off late from work, it means I was with my boss or another man. He was not like that before I started work.

5 Similar statements on food as a key medium of marriage and kinship are found in Congo. As noted by Mottiaux and Petit (2004: 189; our translation), a common expression in Congo is: 'a wife must know how to "treat" [cook for] her husband if she wants to keep him'.

Conclusion

Following a movement that has emerged in the global mining industry over the past thirty years, some among the new foreign mining companies operating in the Central African Copperbelt claim to support gender equality primarily by recruiting more women and, to a lesser extent, by creating a suitable work environment for them. However, although the presence of women in the mining sector is more visible than in the past, things seem to have changed little in terms of gender equality. The proportion of women in mining companies remains low and most work in subordinate positions to men in auxiliary departments. They are consequently more affected than men by the neoliberal labour regime introduced by new investors, especially the abandonment of social support, the repeated mass layoffs and low real wages. For various reasons, which derive from investors' pressures to cut labour costs, national employment laws and the family model prevailing in the Central African Copperbelt, the mines remain a gendered space that is numerically, socially and symbolically dominated by men.

The legacy of industrial paternalism, which contributed to promoting a family model based on a clear division of roles between men and women, is still very strong in the Central African Copperbelt. This does not mean, however, that this gendered model has had the same implications on both sides of the Copperbelt. Our research suggests that the legacy of this gender ideology is stronger in Congo than in Zambia because paternalism in Congo was adopted earlier, and became more total. The family policy was also more central to UMHK and Gécamines' social policy than in RST, RAA, or ZCCM. The current economic situation in the two countries is another reason for the variations in gender roles within the Central African Copperbelt: the cost of living and housing is higher in Zambian cities and Zambian families face a greater struggle to live on a single wage compared to Congolese families. In Zambia, women's desire to work receives more and more support from husbands; some men are even ready to participate in domestic chores to enable their wives to work and earn money.

Nevertheless, in both countries, a growing number of women obtain higher education degrees and look for work, including in the mining sector. This is due to a combination of factors. The challenges for the male breadwinners to provide for their families amidst high unemployment, widespread job losses and declining wages, have driven more women into the labour market to ensure the survival of their families. To some extent, this trend has been supported by gender equality policies and campaigns. In both countries, some of the legal restrictions on women's employment have been lifted, and although concrete and binding policy measures have not been implemented to support women's work (e.g. in recruitment processes or work–life balance), the rhetoric of economic gender equality has become increasingly present in institutional discourse and the media. In the mining sector, the active involvement of some mining companies in promoting gender equality has also had an impact: a greater female presence and better working conditions are generally more guaranteed in the large mining projects committed to ICMM mining principles. Finally, women themselves have helped to actively drive the feminisation of mining by taking advantage of emerging opportunities. Given the economic prominence of mining in the Central African Copperbelt, this sector was and continues to be an obvious choice, both for educated women looking for work matching their qualifications, and less educated women seeking financial security. Today, women occupy job positions that were once exclusively occupied by men and some supervise entire teams, services and departments composed of men. Proud to play such a role in society, the female mineworkers we met were, at the same time, increasingly aware of the discriminations they face in everyday life.

Few of our informants are ready to openly oppose these discriminations or join a struggle for women's rights. Instead, they express their agency by adopting various tactics in order to work and earn a living without compromising male authority in public (Scott 1990; see Hodgson and McCurdy 2001; Rolston 2014; Rubbers 2015). At work, they can adopt – within certain limits – so-called masculine behavioural traits to gain respect from their male colleagues or assume a feminine role, that of a 'mother' or 'sister', giving them authority over their co-workers. At home, their room for manoeuvre is more limited: they must play, and sometimes overplay, their role of housewives if they do not want to stir up their husband's jealousy, and possibly end up divorced from him. Indeed, being a miner and a housewife are roles that can be difficult to reconcile. At the same time, their interaction leads to something new. As Lindsay and Miescher (2003: 7) suggest, gender identities that are experienced and performed differently depending on the context contribute to the reproduction or transformation of gender systems. More specifically, in the Central African Copperbelt, having female employees in mining companies means that women participate to a greater extent both in the countries' economies and in contributing to household finances; sometimes they even become the main breadwinners. This enables them to have more decision-making authority and room for manoeuvre in accommodating new gender dynamics within the family and society at large. Moreover, in terms of changing societal values, having female employees in the mining sector and especially in production-related departments, has the added value of disrupting the idea of women's work as occurring only within female-coded sectors. Indeed, traditional gender roles are challenged when women hold a high position in the male-dominated mining sector and perform tasks considered primarily masculine because of the harsh, dangerous, dirty labour they entail. Depending on the job, women renegotiate prevailing gender norms: the higher the position at work and the greater the economic security, the more women emphasise their independence, even at home. Likewise, men are usually more inclined to share authority in the household when women are economically successful. These gender dynamics do not completely break down past norms and values, but reinvent them in line with men's and women's new aspirations and forms of interaction.

Bibliography

Acker, J. (1990). Hierarchies, Jobs, Bodies: A Theory of Gendered Organizations. *Gender and Society* 4(2): 139–58

Bashwira, M.-R. *et al.* (2013). Not Only a Man's World: Women's Involvement in Artisanal Mining in Eastern DRC. *Resources Policy* 40: 109–16

Benya, A. (2009). *Women in Mining: A Challenge to Occupational Culture in Mines.* MA Thesis, University of the Witwatersrand

Benya, A. (2016). Women in Mining: Occupational Culture and Gendered Identities in the Making. PhD thesis, University of the Witwatersrand. Available at: http://wiredspace.wits.ac.za/handle/10539/22425 (accessed 19 February 2021)

Chauncey, G. (1981). The Locus of Reproduction: Women's Labour in the Zambian Copperbelt, 1927–1953. *Journal of Southern African Studies* 7(2): 135–64

Cuvelier, J. (2011). Men, Mines and Masculinities: The Lives and Practices of Artisanal Miners in Lwambo (Katanga Province, DR Congo). PhD thesis, Katholiek Universiteit van Leuven. Available at: www.researchgate.net/publication/292334629_Men_mines_and_masculinities_the_lives_and_practices_of_artisanal_miners_in_Lwambo_Katanga_province_DR_Congo (accessed 19 February 2021)

Dibwe dia Mwembu, D. (2001). *Bana Shaba abandonnés par leur père: structures de l'autorité et histoire sociale de la famille ouvrière au Katanga. 1910–1997.* Paris: L'Harmattan

Dibwe dia Mwembu, D. (2019). Histoire du travail. Cours d'histoire du travail, Université de Lubumbashi.

Epstein, A.L. (1981). *Urbanization and Kinship: The Domestic Domain on the Copperbelt of Zambia, 1950–1956.* New York: Academic Press

Evans, A. (2016). The Decline of the Male Breadwinner and Persistence of the Female Carer: Exposure, Interests, and Micro-Macro Interactions. *Annals of the American Association of Geographers* 106(5): 1135–51

Ferguson, J. (1999). *Expectations of Modernity. Myths and Meanings of Urban Life on the Zambian Copperbelt.* Berkeley: University of California Press

Gécamines (1969–1999). Rapports annuels. Lubumbashi: Générale des Carrières et des Mines

Gier, J. and Mercier, L., eds (2006). *Mining Women: Gender in the Development of a Global Industry, 1670 to 2005.* New York: Palgrave Macmillan

Hayes, K. and Perks, R. (2012). Women in the Artisanal and Small-Scale Mining Sector of the Democratic Republic of the Congo. In Lujala, P. and Rustad, S.A., eds, *High-Value Natural Resources and Post-Conflict Peace Building.* London: Earthscan, pp. 529–44

Henk, D.W. (1988). Kazi ya Shaba: Choice, Continuity and Social Change in an Industrial Community of Southern Zaire. PhD thesis, University of Florida. Available at: https://ufdc.ufl.edu/AA00037631/00001 (accessed 19 February 2021)

Hodgson, D. and McCurdy, S. (2001). Introduction: 'Wicked' Women and the Reconfiguration of Gender in Africa. In Hodgson, D. and McCurdy, S., eds, *'Wicked' Women and the Reconfiguration of Gender in Africa*. Portsmouth, NH: Heinemann, pp. 1–26

Hunt, N.R. (1990). Domesticity and Colonialism in Belgian Africa: Usumbura's Foyer Social, 1946–1960. *Signs: Journal of Women in Culture and Society* 15(3): 447–74

Kahola, O. (2014). Dons cachés, normes matrimoniales et règles d'héritage dans les échanges au sein des ménages à Lubumbashi. *Nouvelles perspectives en sciences sociales* 9(2): 159–85

Lahiri-Dutt, K. (2006). Globalization and Women's Work in the Mine Pits in East Kalimantan, Indonesia. In Lahiri-Dutt, K. and Macintyre, M., eds, *Women Miners in Developing Countries: Pit Women and Others*. Farnham: Ashgate, pp. 349–69

Lando, L. (1978). Les cadres sociaux de la motivation féminine au travail. *Maadini, Bulletin d'information de la Gécamines 18–19–20*

Lindsay, L. and Miescher, S. (2003). Introduction: Men and Masculinities in Modern African history. In Lindsay, L. and Miescher, S., eds, *Men and Masculinities in Modern Africa*. Portsmouth, NH: Heinemann, pp. 1–29

Mottiaux, A. and Petit, P. (2004). Histoire et mémoire alimentaires. In Petit, P., ed., *Byakula. Approche socio-anthropologique de l'alimentation à Lubumbashi*. Bruxelles: Académie Royale des Sciences d'Outre-Mer, pp. 180–96

Munene, H. (2018). A History of Rhokana/Rokana Corporation and Its Nkana Mine Division, 1928–1991. PhD thesis, University of Free State. Available at: https://scholar.ufs.ac.za/handle/11660/10341 (accessed 19 February 2021)

Musonda, J. (2020). Undermining Gender: Women Mineworkers at the Rock Face in a Zambian Underground Mine. *Anthropology Southern Africa* 43(1): 32–42

Mususa, P. (2010). Contesting Illegality: Women in the Informal Copper Business. In Fraser, A. and Larmer, M., eds, *Zambia, Mining and Neoliberalism. Boom and Bust on the Globalized Copperbelt*. New York: Palgrave Macmillan, pp. 185–208

Muswamba R. (2006). *Le Travail des Femmes en République Démocratique du Congo : Exploitation ou Promesse d'Autonomie ?* Paris: UNESCO.

Parpart, J.L. (1986). The Household and the Mine Shaft. Gender and Class Struggles on the Zambian Copperbelt, 1926–1964. *Journal of Southern African Studies* 13(1): 36–56

Peša, I. (2020). Crops and Copper: Agriculture and Urbanism on the Central African Copperbelt, 1950-2000. *Journal of Southern African Studies* 46(3): 527–45

Powdermaker, H. (1962). *Copper Town: Changing Africa: The Human Situation on the Rhodesian Copperbelt*. New York: Harper & Row

Pugliese, F. (2020). Mining Companies and Gender(ed) Policies: The Women of the Congolese Copperbelt, Past and Present. *Extractive Industries and Society* 8(3). Available at: https://doi.org/10.1016/j.exis.2020.08.006 (accessed 19 February 2021)

Rolston, J.S. (2014). *Mining Coal and Undermining Gender: Rhythms of Work and Family in the American West*. New Brunswick, NJ: Rutgers University Press

Rubbers, B. (2013). *Le paternalisme en question. Les anciens ouvriers de la Gécamines face à la libéralisation du secteur minier katangais (R.D.Congo)*. Paris: L'Harmattan

Rubbers, B. (2015). When Women Support the Patriarchal Family. The Dynamics of Marriage in a Gécamines Mining Camp (Katanga Province, DR Congo). *Journal of Historical Sociology* 28(2): 213–34

Scott, J.C. (1990). *Domination and the Arts of Resistance. Hidden Transcripts.* New Haven, CT: Yale University Press

Silberschmidt, M. (1999) *"Women Forget that Men are the Masters": Gender Antagonism and Socio-economic Change in Kisii District, Kenya.* Uppsala: Nordic Africa Institute

Vellut, J-L. (1983). Articulations entre entreprises et Etat : pouvoirs hégémoniques dans le bloc colonial belge (1908–1960). In Coquery-Vidrovitch, C. and Forrest, A., eds, *Entreprises et entrepreneurs en Afrique (XIXième et XXième siècle),* volume 2. Paris: L'Harmattan, pp. 49–79

World Bank (2017). Advocacy for Women's Rights in DRC's Mines Gains Momentum. Online article. Available at: www.worldbank.org/en/news/feature/2017/12/13/advocacy-for-womens-rights-in-drcs-mines-gains-momentum (accessed 19 February 2021)

ZCCM (1964–1997). *Labour Reports.* Kitwe: Zambia Consolidated Copper Mines

4

Union Elections: Marketing 'Modern' Unionism

KRISTIEN GEENEN AND THOMAS McNAMARA

This chapter explores the relationship between trade unionists and employers in mining companies in the Central African Copperbelt, and analyses the way workers perceive this relationship. To do so, it focuses on union elections, as it is during this period of heightened competition that trade unionists' track records are discussed, assessed and finally valued or rejected. Our argument is that, although differences in union organisation on both sides of the border trigger a distinct electoral dynamism, they manifest similar power games, the same form of micropolitics of work. While on both sides trade unionists utilise repurposed discourses of union strength in their interactions with members, they are pragmatic in their dealings with management and justify this behaviour by claiming that this is the best way to deal with the Western and Asian managers that have been appointed since the mining boom in the 2000s. In their view, 'modern' unionism is primarily based on dialogue and conciliation, rather than on confrontation.

Far from being specific to the mining sector of the Central African Copperbelt, such a claim of modernity can be found in many places around the world (see Durrenberger 2017; McNamara and Spyridakis 2020). Botiveau (2013, 2017), for instance, has shown how the National Union of Mineworkers (NUM) in South Africa gradually adopted the workings and procedures of the companies it tried to fight, at the expense of a more militant stance. This copying of the bureaucratic system since 1994, as well as the adoption of soft rather than conflictual communication, was supposed to 'modernise' NUM as an organisation. This bureaucratic strategy proved effective in several respects for the union, in the face of the challenges it confronted, but also seriously deterred its members. This new unionism, it could be argued, is characteristic of our neoliberal area. As such, we may consider it an additional feature of the neoliberal labour regime described by Benjamin Rubbers and Emma Lochery in the first chapter.

The close cooperation between management and unions, however, is not as 'modern' as some may think. This conciliatory strategy – as well as the claim of modernity associated to it – has been favoured by state administrations, mining companies and some union leaders in Congo and Zambia since the beginning of African trade unionism in the 1950s, and it has been immediately met by workers' own demands for a more confrontational stand. This observation calls for a more detailed analysis of the processes that shape contemporary union dynamics on both sides of the border. To do so, this chapter draws on intensive ethnographic fieldwork carried out in Kolwezi (Congo), Kitwe and Ndola (both Zambia) between 2017 and 2019. During this period, we followed union elections and electoral campaigns, attended union meetings, collected electoral materials and observed the ballot procedures. We also conducted interviews with trade unionists, managers and employees. Most informants were approached several times, and we spent a considerable time with them, including in their family environments.

Below we will first highlight the differences in the way union representation is organised in Congo and Zambia and point to the implications for the micropolitics of everyday trade unionism in the workplace. In the second section we show that, despite these differences, the moral discourses about trade unionists during elections are similar on both sides of the border. This is a parallel we seek to elucidate further in the third and last section, by focusing on the diverse means the management of mining companies use to control the unions.

Two Union Systems

At first sight, the dynamics of trade unionism in the mining sector in Congo and Zambia stand in stark contrast. In Congo, African unions have always been toothless (Poupart 1960; Banza, n.d.; Mangwaya-Bukulu 1970; Mbili Kwa Mbili 1970; Martens 1999; Butedi 2013). Although the existence of trade unions was legally authorised in the aftermath of the Second World War, their effective creation proved to be a long and complicated process. The reason for this slowness was that, in the view of colonial authorities, Congolese workers were not yet ready for the modernity of trade union politics (Poupart 1960: 59). Following a paternalistic approach to the issue, large colonial companies such as the Union Minière du Haut-Katanga (UMHK) preferred to install *conseils indigènes d'entreprise*, in which workers' representatives were carefully selected by the employer, instead of autonomous trade unions (Dibwe 2001). While workers' representatives in these councils could make suggestions to improve living conditions in the camps, they were not allowed to organise the workers or to criticise the employer in public.

When, just after independence, trade unions were finally introduced, miners were slow to take part to the movement. A couple of years later, all the existing unions were brought together in a single union – the Union Nationale des Travailleurs du Zaïre (UNTZ) – under the control of the Mobutu regime, and all wage workers were considered as members. A check-off system was established to deduct their dues from their monthly salaries. Although the single union was occasionally used as a channel to voice workers' demands, it was primarily a government technique to educate the workers, not a protest organisation (Banza n.d.: 133–34).[1]

The political liberalisation of the 1990s saw the creation of myriad new trade unions. Today, according to the International Labour Organization (Cunniah 2010), there are more than four hundred unions in Congo. At least fifty of them – including about a dozen well-established unions – compete to represent the workers in mining companies and to collect their dues, which are still deducted from salaries by employers. As workers have no qualms in hopping from one union to another according to the prospects they offer, this competition is close to a free market. It has little to do with politics or ideology.

Across the border in Zambia, the union landscape offers a completely different picture (Parpart 1983; Cooper 1996; Larmer 2007). Like the Belgian authorities, British colonial authorities authorised trade unions just after the Second World War with the aim to channel workers' claims. Unlike what happened in Congo, however, the situation completely escaped their control. In a context marked by the presence of a strong white workers' union and the rise of settler politics, African workers seized this opportunity to create a union and defend their own interests. With its ability to organise mass strikes, the African Mineworkers Union, re-baptised the Mineworkers Union of Zambia (MUZ), played a key role in the struggle for the independence of Zambia in 1964.

The dependence of the postcolonial state on copper revenues, however, encouraged assaults on trade union autonomy. During the Kaunda era (1964–91), MUZ was the only union in the mining sector, and its leaders were close to the ruling party. In contrast to their Congolese counterparts, however, they exercised only limited control over the union base. In the 1970s and 1980s, with the support of shop floor-based junior union representatives, mineworkers organised a growing number of wildcat strikes to protest against declines in their living conditions. They also joined, in massive numbers, the opposition movement which eventually brought Frederick Chiluba to power in 1991.

Similar to what happened on the other side of the border, the political liberalisation of the 1990s profoundly reshaped the union landscape in the Zambian mining sector. Neoliberal reforms removed the 'one-union one-industry' rule and shifted from industry-level to company-level collective bargaining. While MUZ had been the only mining union for decades, it was joined by the National Union of Mine and Allied Workers (NUMAW) and the United Mineworkers Union of Zambia (UMUZ) in 2003 and 2010 respectively. These unions, which have vague ideological identities, use gifts and financial services to recruit members from each other. In the course of the past two decades, they have increasingly attempted to use business generation as a way to mitigate the decline of miners' real wages: they set

1 Articles about trade unionism in the Gécamines newsletter Mwana Shaba provide a clear illustration of this power rationale. See, for instance, Gécamines (1975, 1978a, 1978b, 1981, 1983).

up stores that sell essential commodities to miners on credit, or provide payday loans through a financial partner. They do so not only to support members and maintain their own financial viability, but also to support their own candidates during national government elections. Former executives of both MUZ and NUMAW have been elected into the governments of the Movement for Multiparty Democracy (MMD, 1992–2010) and Patriotic Front (2011 to present). When these officeholders headed the ministries of labour or of mines, they have focused on organising payouts for miners and mine communities when worksites were closed, employees subcontracted or salaries reduced.

The composition of the union delegations in mining companies reflects these differences between the countries. In Zambia, the three major unions have a union branch in each company; it consists of six delegates (the chair, the treasurer, the secretary and their deputies) elected by union members. Each company thus has three separate union delegations. During elections, unionised workers choose the candidates who will represent them on behalf of their union. When they need assistance, they will likewise address 'their' union. In Congo, on the other hand, twelve or more unions can be represented in a single company, and they are all grouped into one single union delegation (*délégation syndicale*). A union delegation is composed of a certain number of *délégués* (and their deputies) who represent different unions in the company in which they are employees.[2] They are selected from among the workers by a *permanent*, a union employee who supervises their union duties and participates in their meetings with management.[3] During elections, workers can vote for a candidate belonging to any union. A remarkable consequence of this system is that, after having fiercely competed during the elections, the delegates from different unions are asked to work together in the interests of all the workers, no matter the union whose candidate they voted or to which their fees go. Similarly, when workers face a problem with their employer, they can request assistance from any *délégué*, even if they did not vote for his/her union during elections.

2 The number of delegates (*délégués effectifs*) and their deputies (*délégués suppléants*) is proportionate to the number of workers at the company. At companies with 20–100 employees, workers are entitled to three delegates and three vice-delegates; at companies with 101–500 employees, they can have five delegates and five vice-delegates, and so forth. Thus, in a company of 3,000 employees, it is possible to find twelve different unions if each seat in the delegation is taken by a different union.

3 The *permanents* can be considered the equivalents of branch leaders in Zambia. In Kolwezi, however, *permanent* is only a part-time job: the salary paid by the union is insufficient and they must have other sources of income. During elections, the *permanent* in charge of the company decides the order in which the candidates will figure on the list. Only the first candidate is certain to get a seat if his or her union is elected. But sometimes unions proceed with the 'harmonisation of the list' after the election, that is, the rearrangement of the order of candidates on the list.

Both Zambian and Congolese delegates receive sitting fees for the union duties they fulfil. But the source and the amount of these fees differ. In Zambia, the fees are paid by the union, and the amounts are small. For a meeting between branch executives and shop stewards, for instance, the trade unionists receive US$ 5, while for major events like national union elections, they are compensated US$ 50 a day. In Congo, the sitting fees are paid by the company and their amount is usually more substantial. For the quarterly meetings, which can last several days, both delegates and *permanents* receive between US$ 50 and 100 a day. For extraordinary meetings, which are organised by management to negotiate on important unexpected issues, the sitting fees can be even higher.

The way the union fees are collected is yet another major difference, one that affects the financial core of a union. In Zambia, where unionisation is a free choice, about 80 per cent of permanent pensionable miners are unionised. In Congo, although the law stipulates that a worker has the right – but not the obligation – to unionise and to adhere to his/her union of preference, in practice, many companies continue to apply the system of *adhésion générale* or general membership inherited from the past: workers are automatically unionised unless they inform management in writing of their wish not to join. However, only a very small number of workers bother to navigate the red tape and undo unionisation. The management of mining companies automatically withdraws the monthly union fee from the salaries of all unionised workers and divides the total among the unions depending on the number of seats in the union delegation they obtained in the elections. Unions that did not win any seats lose all contributions, regardless of the number of workers who voted for them. The only exceptions to this system are two Glencore subsidiaries, where workers are free to unionise or not. Interestingly, less than half of the workforce in these mining projects chose to unionise.

As a result, there is far more at stake during the elections for the Congolese unions than for the Zambian unions. In Zambia, income through membership is independent of the elections, which only affect the inner order: the election results decide whom gets which position inside the union's hierarchal structure. There is no financial loss, as the members pay their fees anyway. The only possible loss comes from workers who swap unions or stop being unionised altogether. In Congo, by contrast, it is the number of votes that decides whether a seat in the delegation is granted and, thus, a share in the totality of the union fees. The very survival of unions depends upon the number of *délégués* they have in different companies.

Unsurprisingly, the two systems trigger completely different electoral dynamics on the two sides of the border. Whereas in Zambia members of the same union compete to obtain a seat in the union delegation, in Congo members from different unions compete. In Zambia, the whole delegation is usually replaced after the elections but since the head office takes care of the defeated delegates, this does not mean the end of their union careers. In Congo, if a union fails to obtain a seat in the union delegation, it loses everything, including its access to the company.

Electoral Discourses

Despite these differences between the two union systems, discourses during electoral campaigns are surprisingly similar; they are not that distinct from electoral discourse everywhere in the world either, for that matter. In Congo, electoral meetings take place either inside company buildings, following a schedule planned by the Human Resource (HR) department in advance, or outside, in bars and other venues. In the former case, trade unionists are impeded not only by strict time limits – with more than twenty unions competing, they are limited to thirty minutes per union – but also by the presence of HR officials which hinders the presenters from speaking frankly and obliges them to refrain from criticising other unions. For this reason, although these inside meetings are virtually cost-free, campaigning trade unionists usually prefer to gather workers outside company buildings. At these outside meetings, between twenty and two hundred people can show up. When the meeting is held in a bar, this involves spending money on drinks, but also on 'transport', an amount of money that always exceeds the actual cost of travel. As they are well known to most workers, the eligible *delegués* do most of the talking but the *permanents* also take the floor.

In Zambia, fellow trade unionists compete to obtain a seat in the branch of their union at the company. Zambian workers occasionally take the initiative to hear out the candidates, and call the candidates for chairmanship to campaign in their section well before the legislated campaign time. During the elections, members often vote on the basis of these preliminary and informal meetings. But other meetings are also held in bars for many weeks before the elections. Candidates speak to their co-workers, tapping into dissatisfaction with current union leaders and promising to raise wages and 'be tough' with management. They also stress their own leadership experience, often highlighting the time they have spent as scout leaders, church elders or volunteers.

The presenters' aim in these meetings is, obviously, to convince the workers to vote for their union. In both countries, being an accomplished public speaker is a major asset. The scholarly literature has indicated the importance of the public performance of the trade unionists who present their programme to a crowd: clear and straightforward language is most effective in getting a message through, empty rhetoric and glib talk are pointless. The Railway Workers Union in Ghana, for instance, organised culturally inspired mass-meetings 'with speakers trying to outdo each other in bravado' (Jeffries 1974: 50; see also Jeffries 1975, 1978) to gather support from the workers, verbal skills and inspirational performances being crucial.

The discourse during the meetings touches upon different issues, some of which are double-edged. Take a union's track record, for instance. Some candidates put forward the long-standing existence of their union, which guarantees a professionalism that others cannot offer: 'just google our union's name' a Congolese *permanent* said to the crowd during a meeting to underline its seriousness. This seems to be the core cleavage in Zambia too. During a mass meeting in Kitwe, the more experienced candidates circulated posters that read 'We need Maturity and Experience' and 'Vote for Credible Leaders'. Echoing these messages, the Head Office representative preached: 'better the devil you know than the angel you don't'.

In Congo, it is not hard for well-established unions to bring down newer unions which are numerous and unorganised. During one meeting, Jacky, a *permanent* with an impressive track record, used vivid metaphors to illustrate how hard it is to cooperate with all the green trade unionists in a delegation:

> They often just make a lot of noise, and although everyone listens to them, they do not achieve a thing in the end. Take two barrels, a full one and an empty one, and roll them down the streets. The empty one will make a lot of noise while rolling, and everyone will look at it, but it will have no direction, and zigzag its way down. The filled barrel on the other hand, will gently roll without making the slightest noise, no one will notice it, but it goes in a straight line right to its goal. So if you want to achieve something, you need very experienced unionists in the delegation, if not, you will not obtain any results.

Workers are receptive to such messages, and state that potential bargaining power is an important rationale in their electoral choice. At a post-electoral meeting in a Zambian company, one attendee explained why he had refused to vote for a younger man: 'I spoke to him and said, "you are a small boy, you are not a big man, the title you are looking for is fatter than you are, how will you fulfil your union duties?"' However, lengthy experience can also be tricky if the accomplishments of experienced candidates are poor. One Congolese worker stated that he would never vote a union that was present at Générale des Carrières et des Mines (Gécamines), 'just look at what happened to that company!' he exclaimed, in reference to the deep water in which it landed (see Rubbers 2013). To counter attacks from the experienced unions, the candidates of newly founded unions stress their clean and uncorrupted status and present themselves as 'a breath of fresh air' or deserving 'the benefit of doubt', to use the words of some Congolese *permanents.*

So the incumbent and the challenging delegates usually have conflicting discourses. Being a member of a delegation that has not achieved considerable improvements in labour conditions is definitely a drawback. In Congo, incumbent candidates who worked together during their previous tenure become divided while campaigning as they now compete among themselves. In these circumstances, some trade unionists do not hesitate to pass the buck for the unchanged labour conditions to the fellow *délégués* of another union. In the words of one *permanent*, 'we failed because the other unions obstructed us'. The challenging candidates, on the other hand, get a free run at these meetings. They can afford to attack the delegation and cultivate an image as change agents. In Zambia, however, as the competitors are members of the same union, the head office attempts to discourage them from attacking their opponents. Rather, they prefer the campaigners to say nice things. A MUZ head office representative said: 'When you campaign, don't do politics, don't say bad things about the current executive, say what you will do. And tell the truth, don't say you will get a 100 per cent increment when we have never got that at Chambishi.'

The main topic during speeches and the Q&A that follows is the proximity of the candidates to management. While attending a meeting of an incumbent union, one worker asked out loud 'are you the union of Glencore, or the union of us, workers?' Challenging candidates about this perceived closeness to management acts as a strategy to undermine the candidates of the incumbent delegation. In Zambia, despite head office's instructions, those running against the incumbents can tap into a genuine stream of anger. Former executives claim that the current branch executives are unpopular because they do not communicate with members during the negotiations, instead 'they become very big when they get elected, they become like management'.

In both countries, this familiarity with the employer raises questions among the workers. Several candidates put forward their belief that the incumbent executives are corrupt and receive help from the company, either by being promoted past their station or by being offered cash. During a gathering in Zambia, a challenger mockingly proclaimed that 'As soon as we become executives, we will take that car', in reference to the car granted to the president of the union delegation. Indeed, being part of the union delegation or branch comes with benefits. These include not only attendance fees, but also a phone, call credit and a car. Whereas in Zambia, it is generally the union's head office that puts a car at the disposal of the branch chairman, free fuel included, in Congo, it is the company management that does so for the president of the delegation. On both sides of the border, the car regularly showed up in the discourses we captured during union campaigns. To the workers, it illustrates the proximity of the delegates to the management of the company, regardless of who granted the car. That a vehicle illustrates workers' remoteness from the union leadership reflects continuity from the time of industrial paternalism. Already in the early 1970s, one Zambian miner defined a trade unionist as someone he 'just sees move in a car' (Burawoy 1972: 79).

In Congo, where the mining company offers the car to the union delegation, this gift, or benefit in kind, could be viewed as what Blundo and Olivier de Sardan (2001: 17) call an *investissement corruptif*, a favour that will bring a return in the future. A car enhances the grip the employer has upon the delegation as it can be (temporarily) withdrawn as punishment whenever the delegates turn uncompliant. This is why Bernard, a Congolese *permanent*, is not in favour of this bonus. Ideally, he said, the union itself should offer its branch chairmen the car, as occurs in Zambia. Alas, it lacks the money to do so. Fully aware of the predicament it would put him in, the Congolese president of one delegation even refused to accept the gift. This was perceived by management as an act of insubordination and he was dismissed soon after. Most union representatives, however, show less aversion. When one union won the presidency of the delegation in a transnational mining company, the first thing its *permanent* did was to claim a car for his delegate, a benefit that had not previously been granted by that company.

In Zambia, the car serves as a way to discuss dissatisfaction with unions. It was frequently mentioned during informal conversations with union members. The chairman was constantly either using it or lending it to the head office and the members saw this as evidence that he was too close to the head office and to the company, rather than to them. Similarly, the *permanent* of a Congolese union explained why the incumbent delegation president failed to be re-elected thus: 'the car had aroused much jealousy, the workers saw it as a sign that the president was as thick as thieves with management'. When the election results were made known, the outgoing president had to hand in the car keys on the spot.

A 'Modern' Pact

In both countries, there is a long tradition of representing employer and employee as hand in glove. Unions under the Mobutu and Kaunda regimes in Zaire and Zambia respectively were already conceived as transmission belts whose aim was to educate the workers on industrial discipline and national development and, in return, to express workers' grievances to management. At that time, unions were already presented in official discourses as the 'partners' of the company and the government, which had the duty to act 'responsibly' – that is, to moderate workers' demands.[4] Workers were frequently reminded during union meetings that their interests were not different to the interests of the company and the nation. This message was also conveyed to workers through company newsletters. A 1978 issue of *Mwana Shaba*, the Gécamines newsletter, stated: 'union representation involves the delicate mission of defending the interests both of the employees and the employer' (Gécamines 1978b: 10).

[4] This alignment of unions with the interests of the employer and the state is characteristic of many authoritarian regimes, but not all (see, for instance, Nash 1993 [1979] on Bolivia and Von Holdt (2003) on South Africa). In liberal democracies, unions tend to defend workers more actively, even though their action is everywhere based on conciliation with management. By definition, unions are not revolutionary organisations.

Many actors in the union field seem to ignore, or to have forgotten, this past when they claim that the 'modern' trade unionist does not oppose management anymore, but collaborates with it to increase production, profits and wages. Both Western and Asian employers present management and unions as collaborators, not as opponents. This discourse enables them to posture as benevolent figures towards the workers. The manager from a subcontracting company went as far as to identify himself as a trade unionist: 'the prime union is the employer himself', he said without a trace of irony. It also serves to obtain the cooperation of union delegates and to keep them under management's thumb.

This discourse is not only used by the management of mining companies, however. In Congo, many *permanents* feel that delegates should lift themselves above workers and avoid causing any turmoil. As one of them put it, 'a modern union does not think with its muscles'. In his view, management should even have a say in the appointment of the president of the union delegation because 'it is a very collaborative job, so the candidate must suit the employer'. By urging moderation and negotiation, the main concern of the *permanents* is to highlight the modern professional character of the union and to maintain the union's access to mining companies. Indeed, many employers do not hesitate to tell *permanents* that they do not want unions with the reputation of being troublemakers.

Finally, union representatives can be called to order by state labour officials, who do not hesitate to remind them of their responsibilities. Immediately after the union elections, a Zambian labour officer advised the incoming executives thus:

> Union negotiations today are about needs-based bargaining. We are not going to go to the management making demands, rather, we will present our needs. This is a modern system and we are now in partnership with management. So we must only go to the bargaining table after having increased productivity and we will see that the management will have to give us an improvement. We want a dialogue, a sensible one, not one based on unreasonable demands.

Of course, this discourse about management and unions collaborating on an equal footing does not deceive anyone. The president of the union delegation at a Chinese company in Congo explained that he was asked to address the Congolese HR manager as *partenaire* [partner], but that he was incapable of doing so: 'after all, this man is my superior, and I cannot shake that image off. So I just call him 'boss' even if he consistently calls me "*partenaire*".' Unsurprisingly, talking on equal terms with the expatriate managers is even harder for him. From a strategic perspective, our informants had contrasting opinions about the opportunity to call executive managers *partenaire*. To most, being subservient to management is probably the best strategy to obtain improvements in labour conditions. Building on a well-established cultural repertoire in Central Africa, they do not hesitate to declare their dependence on the 'boss' in the hope of putting him in a benevolent mood (see Bayart 1993, 2000; Ferguson 2013). The workers see right through his flattering discourse. Trade unionists and workers alike make jokes about it, and it certainly does not influence their behaviour during electoral campaigns. One informant, however, suggested that it is better to address the employer as 'partner':

> I do it on purpose, this means that you will talk as equals, you do not put yourself in a subordinate position right from the start, and negotiating will become hard. You have to formulate your arguments very carefully, but beginning with 'partenaire' is a good start to get things done when you really need something; then you start the discussion at the same level. Even in communications by mail, it is better to use 'partenaire', for instance if you want to obtain some obsolete material (a vehicle, some batteries, an old fridge…) that the company is about to throw out. If you write 'madame, est-ce que je pourrais avoir…' you put yourself in a begging position, but if you say 'partenaire, ce vieux frigo me sera très utile…' you give him the impression that he is doing a favour to a friend by giving it to you, and this is what you want to reach. On top of this, the language use remains soft, not hard.

Not all trade unionists agree about the necessity of working in close collaboration with management. In the eyes of a Congolese *permanent*, such practices lead to unions that have 'lost all value, and even all sense'. He would prefer his *délégués* to keep their distance with the employer, but he acknowledges that this is hard to do, even physically. In some cases, the office of the union delegation is next door to the office of the HR manager, lowering the threshold and facilitating regular contact. The location of the union delegation's office at Gécamines is illustrative of this point. Previously situated next to the shop floor, a couple of years ago it was moved closer to the management's main building because trade unionists wanted to avoid what they called 'harassment' by workers. Some *permanents* do not like this physical proximity and advise their delegates to email their managers before popping into their offices; this is a matter of maintaining distance.

Some delegates would like to defend workers' rights more assertively. Being a vocal trade unionist is not without risks, however. It is not unusual for a union delegate to miss out on a promotion as a form of punishment, because he or she refuses to do the management's bidding. This is why, one Zambian head office representative explained, women with the requisite skills usually prefer to avoid union positions from the start, knowing it might hamper their career. In certain cases, a critical stance can become a pitfall: management sometimes offers trade unionists who fulfil their union duties with extreme dedication and expertise a promotion in order to neutralise them. To accept the offer, they must quit the union to focus exclusively on their new position, as the latter is incompatible with union duties.

Besides promotion, the money and the benefits trade unionists get from management also matter. Corruption is latently present on either side of the border. In both Congo and Zambia, the trade unionists receive sitting fees and travel allowances to attend negotiations in which they have very little bargaining power. After returning from a wage negotiation with almost no salary raise, they are often accused of corruption regardless of the truth of the accusation. This being said, the trade unionists themselves do not deny these accusations. In her book on the Zambian mining industry, Lee (2017: 140) notes that 'some managers and unionists told me about giving and receiving bribes, even though both sides claimed that the money did not change their positions at the bargaining table'. In Congo, trade unionists openly talked about a corrupt practice, *le package*, when a fat envelope slides over the table at the fancy restaurant to which the employer has invited the trade unionists, one by one. In the eyes of the management, accepting this envelope inevitably means that the delegate will not make any claims and do all he can to keep the workers from striking. To the unionist, however, it is mere strategy. Some are expert at the game of *package*; they threaten management that, due to the harsh labour conditions, it is extremely hard to keep peace and that not only are minor improvements needed, but an extra envelope as well. Being a good trade unionist and a bribable one is not mutually exclusive.

To point out which goals are achievable, workers and trade unionists alike compare conditions at the different mining companies (Rubbers 2019: 14). Workers pay attention to the wage increases or bonuses obtained in other companies to push their union representatives to make new claims. It is often when these claims are not met that wildcat strikes break out (see Chapter 5). As far as trade unionists are concerned, it is first and foremost when they negotiate the company collective agreement that they refer to the agreements of other companies in an attempt to obtain similar labour conditions. Some trade unionists suggest that a collective agreement for the entire mining sector – with similar conditions in all mining companies – might be a solution, but the idea has not been taken up by the political authorities or the companies.

Nevertheless, today the primary goal of trade unionists is not to obtain salary increases for mineworkers. Confronted with repeated mass layoffs, it tends to be increasingly limited to saving jobs. As we show in the next chapter, trade unionists feel morally responsible for workers' ongoing employment. Moreover, to the unionists, having saved jobs might guarantee a successful election outcome. This is at least what the experience of Didier, the president of the union delegation at a major company in Congo, suggests. Mass layoffs were threatened when production was put on hold for two years, but Didier convinced the employer to limit dismissals to one-fifth of the workforce and have the remainder work one month and take (paid) leave the next. In the following elections, Didier had no problem being re-elected and reinstalled as president of the union delegation.

Conclusion

Although the way union elections are organised is completely different on both sides of the border, the discourses of trade unionists and workers are strikingly similar. The workers perceive their union representatives as being close to management. Yet, this close cooperation is largely seen as business as usual, not as an anomaly against which workers should fight, and it does not really influence their voting behaviour. Rather, their voting rationale is based on the positive achievements of the incumbent delegates or on the popularity of their challengers. From trade unionists' point of view, working in close cooperation with management is the best way not only to take advantage of their function, but also to obtain better employment conditions for workers. Moreover, executive managers, union leaders and labour officials alike push them to adopt this subservient behaviour by presenting it as the right way for a 'modern' trade unionist to behave, especially when negotiating with foreign mining investors. In the name of the development of both the mining companies and the nation, union representatives are expected to refrain from asking too much during negotiations and do what is in their power to prevent strikes.

Not every trade unionist is pleased with this subservient behaviour and the control exercised by management on union elections. A Congolese *permanent* framed union elections as 'bogus elections', and one of his Zambian peers concurred, saying 'we have guided elections'. Some scholars argue that the privatisation of Zambian mining companies has diminished the power of the unions, leaving room for alternative civil organisations to fill in the void (Fraser 2010; Negi 2011). To be sure, repeated mass layoffs and the rise of subcontracting have weakened the unions. These new labour practices are not, however, sufficient to account for the power games characteristic of the union arena, which remains marked by logics of action that have a relatively long history in the two copperbelts.

Since the late colonial period, trade unionists in both countries have been pressured to act 'responsibly', that is, to not infringe on the interests of mining companies and governments by defending workers' interests. To maintain this cooperative behaviour, or to dismiss recalcitrant trade unionists if necessary, mining companies have since had various means, or government tools, at their disposal, such as sitting fees and other benefits in kind, promotion opportunities, or dismissing troublesome trade unionists for professional misconduct. Congolese and Zambian trade unionists have learned to deal with these constraints and to instrumentalise their dependent position to obtain personal advantages, to rule out competitors, and to win victories for the workforce. This is a pragmatic form of agency that is fostered by competition within the union field and that new foreign investors have to deal with. Of course, it facilitates their dialogue with union partners. It is not certain, however, that this is a very effective approach. After all, workers who are suspicious of senior union leaders can, on occasion, organise wildcat strikes behind their backs, as will be discussed in the next chapter.

Bibliography

Banza, M.N. (n.d.). *L'unification du mouvement syndical en République démocratique du Congo.* Bruxelles: De Clercq Monique

Bayart, J.-F. (1993). *The State in Africa. The Politics of the Belly.* London: Longman

Bayart, J.-F. (2000). Africa in the World: A History of Extraversion. *African Affairs* 99(395): 217–67

Blundo, G. and Olivier de Sardan, J.-P. (2001). La corruption quotidienne en Afrique de l'Ouest. *Politique africaine* 83: 8–37

Botiveau, R. (2013). Forces et faiblesse de l'organisation syndicale: le cas du National Union of Mineworkers sud-africain. *Politique Africaine* 3(131): 75–99

Botiveau, R. (2017). *Organise or Die? Democracy and Leadership in South Africa's National Union of Mineworkers.* Johannesburg: Wits University Press

Burawoy, M. (1972). *The Colour of Class on the Copper Mines: From African Advancement to Zambianization.* Manchester: Manchester University Press

Butedi, F. (2013). *Cartographie des syndicats en RDC: vers une compréhension du monde syndical congolais.* Yaounde: Presses universitaires d'Afrique

Cooper, F. (1996). *Decolonization and African Society. The Labor Question in French and British Africa.* Cambridge: Cambridge University Press

Cunniah, D. (2010). Pluralisme syndical et prolifération des syndicats en Afrique francophone. Report for the International Labour Organization. Available at: www.ilo.org/wcmsp5/groups/public/---ed_dialogue/---actrav/documents/publication/wcms_143550.pdf (accessed 19 February 2021)

Dibwe dia Mwembu, D. (2001). *Bana Shaba abandonnés par leur père: structures de l'autorité et histoire sociale de la famille ouvrière au Katanga. 1910–1997.* Paris: L'Harmattan

Durrenberger, P. (2017). *Uncertain Times: Anthropological Approaches to Labor in a Neoliberal World.* Boulder, CO: University Press of Colorado

Ferguson, J. (2013). Declarations of Dependence: Labour, Personhood, and Welfare in Southern Africa. *Journal of the Royal Anthropological Institute* 19: 223–42

Fraser, A. (2010). Introduction: Boom and Bust on the Zambian Copperbelt. In Fraser, A. and Larmer, M., eds, *Zambia, Mining, and Neoliberalism: Boom and Bust on the Globalized Copperbelt.* New York: Palgrave Macmillan, pp. 1–30

Gécamines (1975). Installation du comité de la JMPR ouvrière Gécamines. *Mwana Shaba* 241 (September): 3

Gécamines (1978a). Les qualités d'un bon délégué syndical. *Mwana Shaba* 278 (October): 11

Gécamines (1978b). Elections syndicales à la Gécamines. *Mwana Shaba* 273 (May): 10

Gécamines (1981). Les élections syndicales édition 1981. *Mwana Shaba* 307 (May): 1–4

Gécamines (1983). Installation des comités de base MPR à la Gécamines. *Mwana Shaba* 337 (November): 6

Jeffries, R. (1974). The Politics of Trade Unionism in Ghana: a Case-Study of the Railway Workers Union. PhD thesis, University of London. Available at: https://eprints.soas.ac.uk/28806/ (accessed 19 February 2021)

Jeffries, R. (1975). Populist Tendencies in the Ghanaian Trade Union Movement. In Sandbrook, R. and Cohen, eds, *The Development of an African Working Class. Studies in Class Formation and Action.* Londres: Longman, pp. 261–80

Jeffries, R. (1978). *Class, Power and Ideology in Ghana: The Railwaymen of Sekondi.* Cambridge: Cambridge University Press

Larmer, M. (2007). *Mineworkers in Zambia. Labour and Political Change in Post-Colonial Africa*. London: Tauris

Lee, C.K. (2017). *The Spectre of Global China. Politics, Labor, and Foreign Investment in Africa*. Chicago, IL: University of Chicago Press

Mangwaya-Bukulu, C. (1970). Réflexions sur les pouvoirs des délégués syndicaux dans les entreprises congolaises. *Congo-Afrique* 10(47): 387–97

Martens, G. (1999). Congolese Trade Unionism: The Colonial Heritage. *Brood en Rozen* 2: 129–49

Mbili Kwa Mbili. (1986). Esquisse du syndicalisme au Zaïre: d'hier à aujourd'hui. *Africa* 41(2): 271–80

McNamara, T. and Syridakis, M. (2020). Introduction. Trade Unions in Times of Austerity and Development. *Dialectical Anthropology* 44: 109–19

Nash, J. (1993 [1979]). *We Eat the Mines and the Mines Eat Us. Dependency and Exploitation in Bolivian Tin Mines*. New York: Columbia University Press

Negi, R. (2011). The Micropolitics of Mining and Development in Zambia: Insights from the Northwestern Province. *African Studies Quarterly* 12(2): 27–43

Parpart, J. (1983). *Labor and Capital on the African Copperbelt*. Philadelphia, PA: Temple University Press

Poupart, R. (1960). *Première esquisse de l'évolution du syndicalisme au Congo*. Bruxelles: Editions de l'Institut de Sociologie Solvay

Rubbers, B. (2013). *Le paternalisme en question. Les anciens ouvriers de la Gécamines face à la libéralisation du secteur minier katangais (R.D.Congo)*. Paris: L'Harmattan

Rubbers, B. (2019). Mining boom, Labour Market Segmentation and Social Inequality in the Congolese Copperbelt. *Development and Change* 51(6): 1555–78

Von Holdt, K. (2003). *Transition from Below. Forging Trade Unionism and Workplace Change in South Africa*. Scottville: University of Natal Press

5

Strikes: Claiming Union Power in Chinese Companies

THOMAS McNAMARA AND KRISTIEN GEENEN

In April 2017, a strike occurred at a subsidiary of the Chinese Non-ferrous Metals Mining Group (CNMC), which we refer to as ChinMin, in Chambishi, Zambia.[1] The strike started when the union branch chairmen of Mineworkers' Union of Zambia (MUZ) and National Union of Mine and Allied Workers (NUMAW) gathered their members to inform them that, for the third year in a row, they would receive no increase in their basic monthly salary of a little under ZMK 1,100 (US$ 110).[2] During these three years, Zambia's inflation had totalled 24 per cent, the kwacha had devalued by almost 50 per cent against the US dollar and the cost of living had risen by a similar amount (JCTR 2019). The union chairmen moved between the departments of the mine processing plant, delivering the bad news to angry cries about the hardship of Zambian life and accusations of bribery and betrayal. A disgruntled former trade unionist ran ahead, spreading rumours that the union branch leaders had been corrupted by 'the Chinese' and informing workers that a strike was the only way they would receive a fair pay rise. By the time the union executives had reached the heart of plant, employees had downed tools and locked the gates. They had left sophisticated machinery running, causing hundreds of thousands of dollars of damage. This strike was quickly resolved through the intervention of the Member of Parliament (MP) for Kalulushi Constituency, where Chambishi is located. She demanded that workers receive a significant pay rise and that no one be fired for striking. The MP was cheered on by the union chairmen, who claimed to have assisted her. However, these chairmen later worried that the strikes would damage the relationships between the union, the company and the workers.

Striking miners were mobilised through, utilised and responded to, narratives about 'the Chinese'. While wages and conditions at ChinMin were not drastically different to those at other Zambian mine sites, the workers described the Chinese managers as corrupt, greedy and

1 This pseudonym is necessary to protect anonymity in McNamara (2021), where the wage negotiations leading up to this strike are explored.

2 The exchange rate oscillated between ZMK 8 and 15 to the US dollar during the time Thomas was in Zambia. For simplicity's sake, this article pegs US$ 1 to ZMK 10.

inhumane. After the strike had been resolved, Kalulushi's MP assured workers and the media that the Chinese did not understand 'human rights' – i.e. the responsibilities of an employer to a Zambian wage earner – but that they could be educated without a strike. MUZ's national leaders disagreed, asserting their continued utility to workers by stating that 'the Chinese need to learn that this is our country… that we will not be colonised'. They warned that Chinese businesses would become the targets of deserved future militancy.

Meanwhile, in November 2017, on the premises of Sino-Congolaise des Mines (Sicomines)[3] near Kolwezi, in Congo, a union-negotiated collective agreement was similarly rejected through industrial action. Low pay and the thwarted ambitions of university-educated Congolese inspired graffiti on the walls of toilets, conspiratorial conversations over walkie-talkies and whispers on company buses. The workers of the maintenance department were the first to stop work. The employees of the commercial section soon followed, and they were joined by colleagues from other departments. When the strike occurred, trade unionists declined to be identified as the workers' leaders, and the workers did not want their representation. Instead, employees sang the praises of an opposition political leader and demanded, among other things, that their salaries be tripled. While the striking workers received some of the benefits they desired, the union and politicians eventually persuaded them to return to work. Despite discouraging the strike and then refusing to lead it, Congolese union leaders later claimed that militancy had helped their cause, they explained that: 'During such a strike, management is forced to approach the trade unionists to find a solution, they will finally listen to us.'

Mirroring the situation in Chambishi, industrial action was shaped by intra-workplace and national discourses about 'the Chinese'. For example, workers claimed that Chinese management had difficulties understanding and meeting their demands. In the words of a union leader who participated in the negotiations: 'The Chinese had problems to grasp that such an agreement [a collective agreement] should contain an improvement of the conditions as stipulated in the labour law… they just wanted to stick to the legally mandated minimum.' Indicting the relationship between the national government and Chinese companies, striking workers sang songs praising regional opposition leaders to enhance their political position.

This chapter contributes to the book's examination of the emergence of a neoliberal labour regime in the Copperbelt by exploring its momentary fracturing and rapid reconstitution. Strikes offer a unique opportunity to explore the micropolitics of work when the usual governance techniques involved in wage negotiations have failed: industrial action renders visible workers' expectations, unionists' tactical strengths and weaknesses,

[3] The main shareholders of Sicomines are the SOEs China Railway Group (CREG) and Sinohydro Corporation – and Gécamines and the Société Immobilière du Congo.

and the political costs and rewards of industrial harmony. This chapter uses two Copperbelt strikes to illustrate how unions' relationships with workers, employers and the government are reconfigured, while workers' lives grow ever more difficult (see Chapters 2 and 3). In both Chambishi and Kolwezi, strikes expressed workers' rejection of collective agreements and, through this, the legitimacy of the relationship between themselves, their union, their employer and their government, creating a space of potential renegotiation. However, evidencing a core claim of this book, both the processes that led to the strikes and the strikes' resolution were driven more by the needs of capital than the goals of the state. In Chambishi, a temporary increase in political interest led to a one-off wage increase; in Kolwezi, opposition political involvement led to local authorities withdrawing their support for striking workers, yet a small wage increase was also provided. Key to these micropolitics were challenges to – and the partial reassertion of – the brokerage role of junior workplace-based unionists, and their control over the disjuncture between workers and Human Resource (HR) managers. As this chapter shows, this was a fragile role. In Zambia, unionists and management undertook significant discursive labour to maintain the status of the unions as the workers' supposed voice. In contrast, in the DRC, it was the government, more than the company or even the unions themselves, that reasserted the legitimacy of collective bargaining.

In comparing the involvement of Zambian and Congolese unions' involvement in workers' strikes, this chapter investigates how new foreign investments are grafted onto the historic trajectories of the Copperbelt (see Chapter 1). Under state paternalism in Congo, the union body Union Nationale des Travailleurs Zaïrois (UNTZ) was overtly an appendage of the regime and workers' militancy was violently supressed. In Zambia, while senior MUZ leaders worked with Kaunda to minimise industrial action, miners regularly utilised militancy to demand improved working conditions and, by linking their militancy to decolonisation and democratisation, created narratives of powerful, militant mining unions. A key distinction between our case studies in the neoliberal era is not the strength of these unions – almost all have been neutered by ongoing layoffs – but the way their histories lead to differing expectations of those who adopt union roles. Linking the book's insights to the limited ethnography on strikes, this chapter considers how the union power field shapes workers' expectations, solidarity and bargaining power (Britwum 2018; Fredricks 2019; McQuinn 2018; Werbner 2014).

An important characteristic of the most recent mining boom is the increased role of Chinese State-Owned Enterprises (SOEs) in the Central African Copperbelt. Lee (2017) argues that these SOEs prioritise long-term production over short-term profits and are more likely than private capital to respond to political pressure with concessions to workers. We build upon Lee's (2017) insights by exploring why Chinese SOEs are more likely than other mines to experience political pressure. To do so, we introduce the concept of the 'emic Chinese'; monolithic constructions of 'the Chinese' that emerge through media reports, local gossip and national political campaigns. Where other works demonstrate the need to challenge simplistic and often sinophobic narratives of 'Chinese colonisation' and 'China in Africa', we show that the 'emic Chinese' constructed has genuine political and economic affects (cf. Alden 2007; Mawdsley 2014). In both operations, anti-Chinese resentment accelerated militancy, in Chambishi it encouraged national political support for strikers, in Katanga it motivated rapid repression.

Strikes and the Micropolitics of Work

Anthropology and labour studies often romanticise strikes as sites of instability, renegotiation and resistance (Lazar 2017; Werbner 2014). These works see industrial action as evidencing and generating workers' power to demand improved wages and conditions, and interpret any response to militancy other than unionists' unconditional support as evidence of cowardice or corruption (Kieran 2010; Zlolniski 2019). Several studies of workers' experiences of militancy state that employees strike in response to a failure by unions to effectively represent their members or to guide their demands; the unions discourage the strike but lack the legitimacy to either prevent or end it; and local political leaders use the disturbance as an opportunity to enhance their status, siding with the workers or employers as is politically expedient (Uzar 2017; Zlolniski 2019). This chapter attempts to add nuance to the micropolitics of militancy, comparing the acts of junior unionists in two strikes to explore how their tactical agency shaped and responded to differing political and ideological histories and economies on the central African Copperbelt.

Workers' ability to improve wages through militancy reflects their bargaining power and their solidarity, interacting with legal structures and cultural norms. Key determinants of the threat of militancy (and through it the ability to use bargaining to raise wages) are the availability of skilled replacements for striking workers and the effectiveness of militancy in impeding production (Mwanika and Spooner 2017). Linked to these economic factors is employees' sense of unity with their co-workers (von Holdt and Webster 2005). A strike is an overt demonstration of employees' economic significance and, by uniting against management, striking workers affirm and create their workplace identity. Further, the relationship between workers and management is mediated by various moral expectations (Kasmir 2014). Strikes often arouse when employers or workers attempt to alter this moral economy (Fredricks 2018).

The limited anthropology of unions explores the times when unions lead, rather than respond to, strikes (Fredricks 2018; Kasmir 2014). These studies focus on how unionists decode members' claims, strengthen their resolve, and articulate to management the ways in which it has failed its moral obligations. Unions are therefore presented as the employees' voices within a larger society, and strikes as opportunities that empower unions through entwining them with workers' identity. Durrenberger and Erem (2005: 92, 99), for instance, explain that: 'Unions are able to provide the infrastructure to use spontaneous actions creatively for longer-term goals for the individual, for the bargaining unit and for the union.' Further, 'By various means... and negotiating from the base of strength... [trade unionists] tried to bring the frames of reference of members into alignment with those of the union by involving them in successful action.'

Building upon this understanding of industrial action, Keskula and Sanchez (2019) and Lazar (2017) describe grand narratives of strikes and militancy as motivating union leaders and members. Keskula and Sanchez (2019) then explore slippage between union discourses, which emphasise strikes and militancy, and the mundane tasks of trade unionism, which are unromantic, bureaucratic and centred on compromise rather than struggle, a disjuncture that they claim is core to workers' disillusionment with unions.

Where Keskula and Sanchez (2019) and Lazar (2017) attempt to understand how unionists are motivated, other works try to analyse their ability to meet their own and their unions' goals. These studies often draw on actor-network approaches and classic brokerage literature (Darlington 2014). They conceptualise unionists as a double-sided screen, controlling the miscommunications between employees and management (Cohen 2014). Under the right circumstances, this enables unions to make demands on HR, who are worried about disharmony and ignorant about workers; at other times, it allows them to facilitate concessions to employees while maintaining the associational identity of the workforce (Britwum 2018). Unionists are also often understood to profit from this disjuncture, by either receiving promotions or siphoning off resources for themselves (Zlolniski 2019). These studies share some of the key flaws of much brokerage literature: the unionist in question is presumed to embody all the powers of the union, without considering these actors' (often junior) intra-institutional status, and there is little attention paid to how unionists' motivations and moral projects guide and are shaped by their brokerage capacity (James 2011; McNamara 2019). We focus on the moral discourses and emotional labour of relatively junior, shop floor-based, union officials. These workers discourage strikes, yet for them a career in politics, or a substantive bribe, is unlikely, and they would benefit from the same pay rises as other unionised workers. This chapter shows how Zambian trade unionists attempt to reconcile the disconnect between a belief in the union's strength and their experience of disempowerment. In contrast, in Congo, which does not have a culture of 'strong' unions, junior union officials put less effort into reconciling their structural position with their union's historical project and their own experience of development.

Often underexplored in analysis of strikes is the role of political history, real and imagined, in shaping the likelihood and potential of militancy. When comparing the micro-politics of work across the Copperbelt a key distinction is the role of unions under paternalism, and how this role influences workers and unionists in the neoliberal labour regime.

The Congo has little history of union-led social change and, as the previous chapter shows, Congolese mineworkers are relatively ambivalent towards their union. In Zambia, miners' strikes were crucial to both the decolonisation and the democratisation movements (Larmer 2007). While this has generated significant nostalgia for the powerful unions of the pre-privatisation era, workers are aware that their militancy was not always supported by union leaders. They therefore invoke their proud trade unionist history even when appealing past unions to political figures (Uzar 2017). This nostalgia shapes union members' and junior representatives' belief in the power of the union, and in the potential efficacy of strikes and industrial action. In Congo there is no such nostalgia; unions have never held significant power and were subordinated through a corporatist structure under Mobutu (see Chapter 4). Unions in both nations therefore have similarly limited legal powers, but junior union officials in the two countries draw from and respond to differing obligations and moral economies.

Across the Central African Copperbelt, workers and unionists have been challenged by neoliberal legal and political changes. In the Congolese copperbelt today, workers are more precariously hired than under state or industrial paternalism. They are subject to mass layoffs and are more likely to be subcontracted than ever before (see Chapter 1). In these circumstances, the unions defend workers in disciplinary disputes and participate in wage negotiations, sometimes successfully improving salaries and working conditions. In Zambia, workers have found their wages and working conditions diminished as investor primacy has been combined with discourses that link national development to low salaries and labour flexibility. Over the ten-year period that followed mine privatisation, sympathy strikes were outlawed, multi-unionism was introduced, and collective bargaining shifted from an industry to enterprise level (Lee 2014). In responding to miners' worsening wages and conditions, Frederick Chiluba, Zambia's first democratically elected president and a former union leader, famously asked mine workers to 'die a little' to revitalise the economy (Fraser 2010: 11). Uzar (2017: 292) claims that Zambian mining unions have 'surrendered to the dominant ideology of "industrial peace", yielding the strike weapon to corporate hegemony'.

This creates a strange situation on the Zambian side of the Copperbelt. When strikes occur they are often reasonably effective, with companies incentivised to increase workers' miniscule salaries in exchange for not paying the shutdown and upkeep costs of their enterprises (Lee 2017). The Copperbelt is crucial to Zambia's politics and is deeply unionised. Workers' strikes therefore encouraged rapid involvement by senior unionists and politicians (Fraser 2017). In most cases these unionists and politicians urged miners to return to work, publicly condemning their irresponsibility, even as they covertly brokered salary increases (Uzar 2017). Workers therefore have the potential to demonstrate their bargaining power and build unity through militancy, but this process often encourages them to be sceptical of their union.

Workers' disempowerment in the Copperbelt is complicated by the prominence of Chinese state and private capital. Chinese companies have a growing presence on both sides of the Copperbelt, generating anxiety among workers, who believe that they pay less than other employers, and among local businesspeople, with whom they compete for customers (Fraser and Larmer 2010; Rubbers 2019). As Lee (2017) observed, the way these enterprises are structured and their links to the Chinese state make them susceptible to political pressure and more flexible in responding to workers' demands. We show how this pressure is created and deployed, with miners' invocations of 'the Chinese' requiring a response, and with political figures unwilling to be associated with Chinese companies.

In describing the effects of this 'emic Chinese' we contribute to the near sub-discipline of 'China in Africa' (Alden 2007). Much of these literature problematically conflates Chinese migrants, investment capital, diaspora and the state. An emerging topic in studies of Chinese workplace regimes and China in Africa more generally, is differentiating among actors labelled 'Chinese' and unpacking the often sloppy conflation of Sinophobic rumours, exuberant media reports and actual data (McNamara 2017). CNMC, the Chinese SOE behind ChinMin, has appeared frequently in this literature. In 2011, a Human Rights Watch report claimed that NFCA underpays, prohibits unionisation and is uniquely dangerous to work for. Rebutting this report, Hairong and Sautman (2013) presented data that showed that wages and working conditions actually meet industry standards. Human Rights Watch, in their view, was merely reporting Sinophobic rumours. In 2017, Lee (2017) reconciled these claims, stating that NFCA – another CNMC's subsidiary in Zambia – offered a compact whereby lower wages were a trade-off for security of tenure, which is increasingly unavailable to other workers. While we discuss the precise level of CNMC wages below, what is undeniable is Zambians' perception that CNMC, and an amalgamation of 'Chinese' hawkers, construction companies, and the diaspora, are brutal employers and a potential threat to Zambia's political independence and development (Fraser and Larmer 2007). Similar ideas are expressed by workers, and spread by various media and civil society organisations in Congo (Rubbers 2019). What interests us here is not the veracity of these beliefs, but how they came into play in the context of the strikes under study. As we will see, they influenced the jostling for moral position between the union, state and company, and the political imperative not to be seen as weak in front of the Chinese enhanced workers' ability to make demands on political figures.

Unionisation in Chinese SOEs

Chinese SOEs in the Copperbelt are judged against Zambian Consolidated Copper Mines (ZCCM), Générale des Carrières et des Mines (Gécamines) and other current investors. These investors often, but not always, have links to former colonial powers, and many of their operations were crucial in shaping the transition from state paternalism to early neoliberalism. Chinese SOEs' deviation from the norms set by these organisations guides and creates additional opportunities for brokerage and political action.

After international investors pulled out of the Chambishi mine in 2004, CNMC, China's 29th largest SOE, bought this mine for US$ 50 million, with a commitment to invest another US$ 150 million in the region (Lee 2017). Chambishi was designated a Special Economic Zone, where CNMC would invest in other businesses, including a construction company and a copper smelter, in exchange for tax concessions (Lee 2010). Initially, mineworkers were not unionised, and in 2017, they were paid a monthly salary of ZMK 1,228 (US$ 123). By comparison, at Mopani Copper Mines, a permanent miner received ZMK 2,239 (US$ 224).

Workers at CNMC subsidiaries obtained permanent employment and unionisation through a series of strikes. Wages for permanent workers at CNMC subsidiaries had consistently hovered around two-thirds of what permanent miners at other enterprises made. However, at ChinMin's worksite, over 70 per cent of employees are on permanent contracts, while at other mines only 30 per cent of workers were salaried, with the rest employed as subcontractors, earning as little as ZMK 650 (US$ 65) (see Kumwenda 2015). Despite this, the absence of any permanent high-paying mining jobs appeared to many Zambians as a form of betrayal (see Lee 2014). Rather than ChinMin's workers being ascribed the high social status of *shimaini* (miner), they are referred to derogatorily as '*awomba ama Chinese*' (worker for the Chinese).

Zambian discourses about 'the Chinese' combine their disappointment in the differences between *shimaini* and *awomba ama Chinese* with their interactions with Chinese storekeepers and construction workers, both of whom are alleged to brutalise workers, as well as with regular announcements by opposition politicians that 'the Chinese' control Zambia's government (Fraser and Larmer 2010). While this emic construction is imprecise, it is clear that politicians and union leaders fear any perception that they are allied with the Chinese and this gives striking workers additional leverage.

In 2011, following a series of strikes, ChinMin workers achieved unionisation, with NUMAW, but not MUZ, allowed to represent them. While preventing workers from choosing their union is illegal, NUMAW is considered to be less confrontational than MUZ (see Kapesa and McNamara 2020). When allowed on site, NUMAW head office staff promised the miners it would take a 'tough' stance with the Chinese. NUMAW's first branch chairman led a work stoppage that turned violent, with Chinese security guards firing into the crowd. He was dismissed shortly afterwards with the blessing of NUMAW's national leadership. The next branch chairman was widely perceived to be corrupt and incompetent. Workers claimed he was unable to defend them in disciplinary disputes and wage growth during his tenure was nearly non-existent. When their branch chairman lost his bid for re-election in 2013, he used his connections with management and local political leaders to establish a MUZ branch. A combination of his personal patronage and widespread dissatisfaction with NUMAW meant that he quickly obtained almost half the plant's workers as members. This experience disillusioned workers, but almost all still asserted the importance of unionism, linking union presence to the successful strike, their positive experience of other union activities, and Zambia's political history (see Larmer 2007).

Even with both unions negotiating, wage growth remained negligible and in 2017, four months before the strike, workers learnt that the chairmen of both MUZ and NUMAW had recently received an all-expenses-paid study tour to China. This entwined their cynicism about 'the Chinese' with their experience of union corruption. Yet they also saw the need to corrupt unionists as evidence of union strength. This tension was crucial to understanding workers' and junior unionists' belief in the union's potential power and in seeing its failures as evidence of corruption rather than of weakness.

At Sicomines in Kolwezi, unionisation was similarly discouraged and traits that the workforce associated with the Chinese were key to a shutdown. Sicomines mine was part of a notorious deal signed in Congo in 2007 for Chinese-built infrastructure in exchange for access to mineral resources. The infrastructure works were carried out by Chinese SOEs, including CREG and Sinohydro, and financed through loans from the China Exim Bank. In exchange, the Congolese government granted access to mineral deposits near Kolwezi. Sicomines was created as a result of this deal, to ensure China's guaranteed access to minerals.[4] Initially, the deal was perceived by academics and the media to be detrimental for the Congolese state (for a review, see Jansson 2013; Landry 2018). However, it fitted nicely into President Kabila's widely advertised *cinq chantiers* programme, which promised structural improvements in five domains: healthcare, employment, education, water and electricity supply, and urban infrastructure. Sicomines was therefore heavily associated with Kabila, and its success or failure reflected upon the president.

Working and unionising at Sicomines combined frustrations common to many Congolese mineworkers with specific complaints about Chinese management. Importantly, Sicomines did not begin the unionisation process when it had ten employees, as required by Congolese law. According to one *permanent*, this was because of the close ties between

[4] Except Zhejiang Huayou Cobalt, which has only a very small share, Sicomines' Chinese parent companies are all SOEs. The project currently exploits two copper and cobalt mines: Dikuluwe and Mashamba West.

President Kabila and the Chinese managers. Sicomines' lowest paid workers earned just US$ 104 a month. This was less than the industry's average salary and much less than the estimated US$ 400 needed to support a family in Kolwezi. Among the 1,200 Congolese employees at Sicomines, only eleven occupied a position requiring a tertiary degree. In an environment of high underemployment, Sicomines did not consider tertiary education in hiring. This led to the presence of a large number of *universitaires cachés* at the company: employees who, eager to get any job rather than remain unemployed, had hidden their actual degree while applying. This topsy-turvy hierarchical structure created frustration, as Congolese employees resented being bossed over by someone who was less educated than themselves. Employees imagined that Chinese managers were rude people originating from 'rural and backward provinces' and often framed complaints as explicit rebukes of the Chinese; as one put it, for example: 'The Chinese boss treats you as if you were an idiot; you really need a lot of endurance to cope with this.'

More generally, miscommunication between the local staff and the Chinese migrants was endemic. Many Chinese employees were unable to express themselves in Swahili, French or English. All employees had rudimentary dictionaries in their phones, which they would pull out when necessary, leading to mongrelised expressions. Many directives were lost in translation, if they were translated at all. For instance, to the surprise of security guard John, he received a map of the plant labelled exclusively in Chinese, which was totally unreadable and unusable for him and the security staff.

In 2016 several *permanents* reminded management of its legal duties and introduced an application to unionise. The installation of this union delegation proved an arduous task. Whereas the law dictates that workers elect the union delegates by ballot, and consequently that the unions would be represented at the company, an HR manager went through the applications of about fifteen *permanents*, and invited those unions that seemed reliable for an interview. 'Reliability' depended on criteria such as owning an office, having long-standing experience and being rooted nationwide. As one of the *permanents* who was invited put it, 'the managers stated they did not want any "*syndicat troubadour*"' – a union which makes unrealistic promises to workers. According to a high-level HR manager, an equally important requirement was that the union had a presence in another Chinese company and consequently had experience in negotiating with Chinese managers. After these interviews, the HR manager chose three unions.

Management asked the heads of each department to appoint a suitable union delegate who was articulate, well-educated and polite. The eighteen selected employees had no choice but to accept union duties. André, who was amongst the chosen ones, was worried because he was not allowed to choose which union he would represent. He explained: 'But the branch leaders said that this does not matter, as the only important thing is to establish a collective agreement, so all delegates should work together.'

Management fabricated a vote to decide which union was entitled to the presidency of the union delegation. These proceedings are similar to those found in China, where it is the employer who appoints the delegate (often his own relative), and not the votes of the workers (Chen 2003: 1025). However, they also reminded older Congolese trade unionists of the workings of union elections under the Mobutu regime.

The union delegation at Sicomines lacked legitimacy in the eyes of the workers. Both employees and the community more generally associated it with the belief that the company was protected by the national government, which enabled this government to be evaluated through the actions of Sicomines. As in Chambishi, this has led members to be disappointed with their unions. However, the trade unionists themselves were less embedded in a history of struggle and do not have the same loyalty to their unions as their Zambian counterparts. This had consequences on the way they negotiate wages and working conditions with their employer.

Wage Negotiations

The negotiations explored in this chapter occurred at times when worker dissatisfaction with their unions and employer was very high. In Chambishi, the unions and their newly elected branch leaders saw negotiations as a way to repair their relationship with workers. Without the ability to strike, or a rapid and equitable arbitration process, wage negotiators' core tactic was to draw upon the moral relationships between workers and their employers and to link these to technical discourses. The failure of these negotiations is crucial to understanding dissatisfaction with unions in Zambia and the limits of one of unionists' key brokerage roles. Unions presented their supposed ability to improve workers' wages as legitimising their presence. Their inevitable failure led to them being seen as corrupt or 'on the side of management', reducing their ability to help workers during a strike, and yet encouraging them to consider themselves the leaders of that strike, and to then discourage future strikes.

After learning of their chairmen's study trips to China, MUZ and NUMAW both organised elections to select new branch executives shortly before their 2017 wage negotiations. These elections were harshly fought. As members and candidates attributed their low wages to the previous chairman's corruption, outlandish pay rises and daily wage negotiation updates were promised by the candidates. Those elected decided to ask ChinMin for a 'needs based' increment of ZMK 2,500 (US$ 250). To support this claim they produced a document explaining that even salaries of ZMK 3,700 (US$ 370) would fall below the industry average for permanent workers and the basic-needs basket calculated by Zambia's Jesuit Centre for Theological Research (JCTR 2019). They also compiled data implying that the company was healthy. However, when they brought their arguments to NUMAW's deputy general secretary, he questioned their technical expertise and linked this to the brutal legal structures, exclaiming:

> We are supposed to be leaders, lets not be like those normal Zambians, who whenever they see a truck say 'the company is rich'... if we ask for too much the company will just say 'we are in dispute' and then they will show our demands and say we were being unreasonable, we need demonstrate that we know about the company and that our claims make sense.

He suggested instead asking for ZMK 1,000 (US$ 100) and stressed the need to manage miners' expectations. Further contradicting the promises made during the branch elections, the MUZ General Secretary called his chairman to remind him that the negotiations were confidential and suggested that he avoid members until they concluded.

During Chambishi's negotiations, it was clear that legal structures were more important than argument in determining wages. ChinMin's Zambian HR manager and its Chinese director presented the company as poor and explained that, despite any moral obligation they felt to workers' families, ChinMin simply could not increase salaries. The Zambia HR manager, did most of the talking, she said that the diminishing value of the kwacha was reducing profits, that the government had removed their energy subsidy, and that they could not find a market for sulphur, a by-product of copper production. In response, the MUZ chairman found an earlier ChinMin annual report which stated that the only impact of the devaluing kwacha was an 11 per cent reduction in ChinMin's wage bill and the branch executives obtained the prices on essentials from various markets, demonstrating the increased cost of living.

Over the course of negotiations, the HR manager acknowledged many of the union's arguments. However, she argued that they were irrelevant if the company could not find a buyer for their sulphur, meaning that any pay rise would endanger its health.[5] After three weeks, the HR manager gave the union two options: the company could increase the transport allowance by ZMK 30 (US$ 3 a month) or it could give a pay-rise of ZMK 1,000 (US$ 100), but would balance operational costs by laying off nearly half of its employees. The unionists made a counter offer the next day, they would accept 10 per cent (about US $10) and the company would not lay off any workers. The HR manager declined their offer. She said that if the union did not accept 0 per cent, the company would declare a dispute. She adjourned the meeting until the following morning.

That evening, the MUZ general secretary told the branch chairman that he must accept the increment offered. MUZ would not pay for a legal challenge, and if the negotiations stalled, the company might fire him. As the night progressed, members desperately called the chairman,

5 Several months later we learned that sulphuric acid accounted for less than 4% of ChinMin's revenue.

seeking information about their diminishing wages. He protested that he was not allowed to inform them. A co-worker reminded him that he had committed to update members on negotiations, unlike his predecessor. Linking his own disempowerment to the nation's perceived prostration before the Chinese, he told a caller:

> The things people say when they are in opposition is different to what they do in office. When [former Zambian president] Michael Sata was in opposition he was always saying, the Chinese are parasites, the Chinese are parasites. Then he was elected and he came to parliament and he said, my Chinese are not the Chinese of [the president before Sata] Rupiah Banda. What had happened was the powerful people had told him that he must keep quiet and that keeping quiet is good for the country, it is the same for us [the unionists].

Workers saw his silence as evidence of his incompetence or corruption. The next day it was agreed that the company would increase the transport allowance by 30KW and retrench no workers. The branch chairmen were sent to explain this to members. They read a factsheet detailing the company's struggles to sell sulphur, without mentioning the threat of retrenchment. They began this task in one section of the company at 9 a.m., but found that by their 11 a.m. appointment in the heart of the plant, all miners knew the results of the negotiation and believed that union executives had been bribed by the Chinese. A strike began and the trade unionists switched from advocating for the workers to attempting to cajole them back to work.

Negotiations at Sicomines were similarly laborious, yet without the burden of promises of success by union leaders or a history of labour activism. Executives needed to continuously delay proceedings to consult their head office in China. The poor software translations of the drafts led to misunderstanding and renegotiations. Cultural differences also caused disagreements. Management understood the legal minimum as indicative of what workers should be entitled to. In the eyes of the Chinese negotiators, wages and social advantages that are not enshrined in the labour law are 'priceless gifts', not to be embedded in workplace agreements. Further, exemplifying these cultural differences, the president of the union delegation attempted to explain to his Chinese interlocutors the importance of a decent burial and an extended (and costly) period of mourning in the eyes of Congolese workers. But the only answer he received was: 'Dying is a natural thing... so why spend so much money on something that is so natural?... Death is a family affair, not a company affair.'

The legitimacy of the union was also challenged during the negotiations. Weeks were spent on one clause which stated that 'not the least kind of pressure' is to be put upon the members of the union delegation. The Chinese side vigorously opposed this expression. Instead, the agreement was changed to read that both parties shall refrain from putting 'pressure that might hinder or compromise the execution of the union delegations' duties'. Eventually a single-digit increment was agreed upon, increasing the lowest wage by US$ 6 to about US$ 110.

As was the case in Zambia, communication between trade unionists and members was prohibited during the negotiations, encouraging sentiments of mistrust and dissatisfaction to be aimed at the unions. After many months of difficult negotiations, the collective agreement came into force at the end of October 2017. In Congo, the unions are typically the key advocates of the agreement. However, on this occasion each department received just one copy, and the members of the union delegation relied upon HR staff to explain the agreement, who in turn passed this task on to the foremen. The negotiation process had left the workers predisposed to question the legitimacy of the document and malicious rumours spread about the agreement's supposed failures. Workers started to whisper that it was a very disadvantageous agreement and his sparked a general feeling of unease on the work floor. The disgruntlement particularly concerned the meagre single-digit salary increase. A member of the union delegation gauged this unease and warned the Chinese HR staff that a strike was percolating. The HR manager retorted that it was precisely the union delegation's job to prevent workers from striking. When Chinese officers were directly confronted by disgruntled employees, they replied that they should channel their anger towards the union delegates, as they were the ones who had signed the agreement.

Common to these negotiations was how little power the trade unionists held vis-a-vis employers. Despite their disempowerment, however, it was they, not management, who had to persuade the workers that the negotiation outcomes were fair. In both Chambishi and Kolwezi, they failed, and the disgruntled workers went on strike. Paradoxically, these strikes strengthened the negotiating of the trade unionists who had worked to prevent them. This observation is important for distinguishing between unions and unionists as brokers. These junior unionists had little capacity to change their wage agreement's outcome without militancy, yet they were crucial to maintaining the disjuncture between workers and management. As we will see, this enabled multiple actors to claim responsibility for the success of negotiations, while abrogating themselves from their failure.

Strike Resolution

The specifics of Zambia and Congo's political economies, combined with internal concerns about the Chinese, encouraged workers in both nations to use strikes to obtain political patronage rather than union leadership. In Zambia, the success of this patronage further divorced workers' associational identities from their unions. In Congo, trade unionists claimed after the event to have advocated for the strike, in stark contrast to their actions at the time. In both cases, by firing workers but not union leaders, the company could reduce the union's moral credibility without damaging a negotiating process that was advantageous to the employer, or inhibiting the daily running of their operations.

While the strikes were caused by similar dissatisfactions, how they were resolved demonstrates the contrasting political significance of miners across the Copperbelt. Chambishi is in Kalulushi, one of Zambia's most significant electorates. It has never been held by the same MP for more than one electoral cycle and is politically and economically crucial to the nation. It is also among the largest electorates by population, which is significant because several analysts of Zambian politics argue that miners' votes have a multiplier effect: rural family members follow the voting patterns of the urban miners who assist them financially (Fraser 2017). The area's MP and the Patriotic Front government feared the perception that they were cowering before the Chinese, a perception that was toxic not just in their electorate but all urban electorates where Chinese retailers were outcompeting Zambians (Fraser and Larmer 2007).

When the Chambishi strike began, the branch chairmen addressed strikers, imploring them to return to work. The NUMAW chairman explained that his appeal reflected his genuinely held belief that they had obtained the best wage increase that was economically viable. The MUZ chairman did not disagree, but noted also that management had threatened to fire him if the strike continued. Workers hurled rocks at their supposed comrades and accused them of corruption.

Management was in the process of sending the trade unionists home when Kalulushi's MP flew into Chambishi on the president's private jet. She berated the Zambian HR manager and claimed that the Chinese did not know what an appropriate salary was but that the HR manager 'was greedy with her fellow Zambians'. She explained 'it is as easy as drinking water, you must take this allowance and add it to the basic' (essentially a 35 per cent pay increase) and she demanded that no one be disciplined for the strike. The ChinMin CEO agreed, and the MP addressed the striking workers. The MP then returned to Lusaka, where she gave a press conference explaining that she had educated the Chinese about their responsibilities to Zambia.

Over the next few months, the MP loudly and publicly blamed the union's head offices for trouble in the Chambishi Zone and in Chinese operations more generally, deflecting criticism from the company while asserting her own significance to the strike's outcome. She explained that 'the Chinese must be taught that this is Zambia' but that 'we Zambians are being betrayed by our own people [i.e. bribe-taking trade unionists]'. While CNMC could not publicly challenge the MP, company HR could punish junior unionists. While no one was fired for striking, many MUZ members were dismissed and union branch staff were charged on unrelated matters.

To remain effective, the MUZ chairman had to draw ever closer to management. HR overtly blamed the junior unionists and explained: 'If the union had been honourable, they would have said "this is a matter for the union and the company, the politicians have no mandate to be part of it."' She noted that the politicians' involvement reflected badly on both the union and herself, even as it had strengthened workers' identity and raised their wages. Despite being proud of the wages they had achieved after the strike, most unionists were committed to preventing another strike from occurring.

The Sicomines strike's resolution reflected Katanga's weaker political position, but still invoked 'the Chinese'. The ability to call upon national political concerns was a key tactic for the disgruntled workers who, right from the start, politicised the strike to support their demands. The particular political context also assisted, with elections that seemed continuously pending and a vulnerable president, which in turn triggered a tense climate throughout the country, with regular rallies and marches. Lacking a union-based industrial relations structure and having no close relationship with an influential local political figure, Sicomines lacked a clear resolution strategy and therefore attempted to break the strike through divide-and-rule. Supervisors put pressure on individual workers and handed out cash to those who were willing to work or to guard company property. Within one day, management had succeeded in halving the number of strikers.

Without a long-established union role, the Congolese delegates faded into the strikes. The provincial ministers of mines, labour and home affairs, as well as the labour inspector and the deputy mayor, came to the plant to try and soothe the workers. When the authorities asked the strikers to put together a group of representatives with whom they could negotiate, the strikers all pointed to each other, and no one dared to step forward. Instead, hostile songs rang out about the corrupt union delegation. The strikers praised Moise Katumbi and Dieudonné Mwenze Kongolo, two prominent opponents of President Kabila. As the governor of Lualaba Province, where Kolwezi is located, is known to be a protégé of Kabila, these acclamations represented a challenge to the provincial authorities who visited the workers.

Nevertheless, even without union leadership, the strikers managed to put their grievances on paper and handed it to the provincial minister of labour, who was determined to assert the union's role as workers' representatives. Among their demands was a minimum wage of US$ 300, two bags of cassava meal a month, a new system of shifts, higher funeral allowances, increased severance payments, more suitable positions for educated Congolese with appropriate transport provided for them, and finally an end to the contempt and insults the Chinese colleagues inflict on them. The minister called upon two union delegates to sign this document, to make it 'official'. She then handed this to management, and ordered them to give their reply to the union delegation, who would pass the response on to the workforce. As in Zambia, a local political figure thus restored the duties of the union delegation after determining wages and conditions on their behalf. A trade unionist claimed: 'A wildcat strike [like this one] gives us power. Because during such a strike, management is forced to approach the unionists to find a solution, they will finally listen to us.'

The following day, Monday, 20 November 2017, one of the workers' claims was met on the spot: all workers received two bags of cassava meal. Management promised to take the strikers' demands into account and assess the possibility of meeting them. An increase in salary was a possibility as well, but the union delegates convinced the strikers one way or another that tripling the lowest wage (from US$ 100 to US$ 300) would be impossible and would undermine the company's viability and, consequently, job security for all. One by one, the employees got back to work. As spontaneously as the strike had begun, it ended.

The strike had dramatic repercussions on the workforce. As many as seventy-two strikers who were identified by surveillance cameras in the plant lost their jobs. To find out who the instigators had been, however, proved hard. The HR staff believed it was the *universitaires cachés*, those who had hidden degrees, the intellectuals among the blue-collar workers. This was rejected by the workers, as one explained: 'we all wanted respect for our educated people'. Seeing a Chinese boss being rude or disrespectful to someone who is their own superior is hard to bear. There was enormous solidarity among the workers, and they all refused to identify the strikers from the pictures that the HR staff showed, let alone to name the instigators. Annual leave went from twelve to fourteen days, there was a slight salary increase and workers received two monthly bags of cassava meal. In addition, management made some efforts to create a more pleasant atmosphere and suppress the insults. Posters appeared throughout the plant exhorting the Chinese staff to 'put the worker at ease'. Management dismissed a Chinese supervisor who was known for being particularly harsh and rude towards Congolese workers, who had nicknamed him 'Mobutu'.

Despite the limited role of unions in both strikes, they contributed to consolidating their structural power and give meaning to the role of junior trade unionists. In Zambia, junior trade unionists came to reposition themselves as having led the strike, and to see themselves, rather than workers, to have made moral claims to management and the community. In doing so, they could draw upon and emboldened a well-established myth of union strength (see Kesküla and Sanchez 2019). In Congo, trade unionists pointed out that strikes such as these show management the importance of having strong unions to represent the workers and to listen to their demands. In both cases, these claims were considerably facilitated by the fact that the strikes broke out in Chinese mining companies, and that the labour practices of such companies have emerged as a public issue which can be leveraged for the support of a political patron. Problematically for the unions, miners used militancy to obtain improved working conditions, strengthening their own identities as workers even as this identity was divorced from their union.

Conclusion

This chapter has used strikes in Chambishi and Kolwezi to explain the extent to which trade unionists, and workers in general, are able to influence new investors' labour practices. As has been a key claim of the book, we have shown that the requirements of capital take precedence over the aspirations of the state in shaping labour regimes. However, we have also shown that as the neoliberal regime emerges, state authorities can on occasion play a crucial role in supporting workers' militancy, a role they rarely played under state paternalism, when they were necessarily entwined with management. We also explored how and why politicians are particularly incentivised to intervene when militancy occurs at Chinese SOEs.

The similarities and differences between these strikes demonstrate how labour regimes are contested, negotiated and reshaped. In both Zambia and Congo, the fragmentation of the union power field, threats of mass layoffs, and the development of subcontracting has encouraged conservative union projects, oriented towards surviving as an organisation and saving workers' jobs. Unions, and the unionists within them, attempt to broker the relationship between workers (whom they represent), companies (on whom they depend) and the state (whose legislation constricts their actions). Where Zambian trade unionists' identity was intimately tied to a glorious (and imagined) union history, this was not the same for their Congolese counterparts. Yet trade unionists on both sides of the border engaged in similar activities and constructed similar identities. Both groups negotiated as thoroughly as possible, before being hamstrung by legal and structural realities. Ultimately, the political power of miners in Chambishi, which was linked to, but not solely derived from, their union's role in industrial paternalism, led to a better outcome to the strike than in Kolwezi.

The similarity between their actions encourages conceptualising trade unionists as brokers, policing the disconnect between workers and management (Cohen 2014). In doing so, one can see how differently positioned unionists, as opposed to unions, influence industrial outcomes. This chapter highlights the interplay between workers and unionists' dissatisfactions and the historic roots of unions' perceived power (see Chapter 1). In understanding the differences between Congolese and Zambian unionists' responses to industrial action, it is crucial to consider Zambia's imagined history of industrial action and the way this shapes politics and unionism today, as well as the actual bargaining power of each union.

These strikes and the tactical responses of unionists, politicians and industry were also influenced by dominant understandings of 'the Chinese'. Rumours about the Chinese as an undifferentiated emic construct shape the national political economy and influence social action in both countries (Alden 2007). While Chinese businesses, diaspora, capital and migrants are not a homogenous entity, national media, politics and gossip commonly conflate them, creating threatening narratives that can have a truly political effect (McNamara 2017). In both countries, worker mobilisation was intimately tied to the perception that their exploitation had uniquely Chinese characteristics. In Zambia nationwide discomfort about Chinese capital inspired an MP to quickly support striking workers (Fraser and Larmer 2010). In Congo too, despite the fact that the workers had praised the opposition leaders, provincial authorities intervened to find a solution favourable to them. Thus, whether Chinese companies are seen as close or opposed to government's interests, discourses about working conditions in these companies seem to have a certain political significance. They prompt state authorities to interfere in labour disputes, to remind foreign investors their sovereign power, to protect national citizens, and to restore order.

The findings of this chapter put into question the assumption that industrial action necessarily enhances union participation (McQuinn 2018). In both strikes, militancy encouraged workers to perceive a strong worker identity, it also enhanced workers' scepticism about union-based collective action. If strikes push management to restore and acknowledge trade unionists' formal power as workers' representatives, they also reveal that this power is increasingly empty from the point of view of those who are represented. In other words, strikes contribute to progressively erode the legitimacy of unions to the benefit of local political figures. This is especially the case in places such as the Central African Copperbelt, where political leaders regularly interfere in labour disputes.

Bibliography

Alden, C. (2007). *China in Africa*. London: Zed Books

Britwum, A. (2018). Power Resources and Organising Informal Economy Workers. *Global Labour Journal* 9(2): 249–53

Chen, F. (2003). Between the State and Labour: The Conflict of Chinese Trade Unions' Double Identity in Market Reform. *China Quarterly* 176: 1006–28

Cohen, S. (2014). Workers Organising Workers: Grass-Roots Struggle as the Past and Future of Trade Union Renewal. In Atzeni, M., ed., *Workers and Labour in a Globalised Capitalism: Contemporary Themes and Theoretical Issues*. Basingstoke: Palgrave Macmillan, pp. 139–60

Darlington, R. (2014). The Role of Trade Unions in Building Resistance: Theoretical, Historical and Comparative Perspectives. In Atzeni, M., ed., *Workers and Labour in a Globalised Capitalism: Contemporary Themes and Theoretical Issues*. Basingstoke: Palgrave Macmillan, pp. 111–38

Durrenberger, P. and Erem, S. (2005). *Class Acts: An Anthropology of Urban Workers and Their Union*. London: Routledge

Fraser, A. (2010). Introduction: Boom and Bust on the Zambian Copperbelt. In Fraser, A. and Larmer, M., eds, *Zambia, Mining, and Neoliberalism: Boom and Bust on the Globalized Copperbelt*. New York: Palgrave Macmillan, pp. 1–30

Fraser, A. (2017). Post-Populism in Zambia: Michael Sata's Rise, Demise and Legacy. *International Political Science Review* 38(4): 456–72

Fraser, A. and Larmer, M. (2007). Of Cabbages and King Cobra: Populist Politics and Zambia's 2006 Election. *African Affairs* 106(425): 611–37

Fraser A. and Larmer, M. (2010). *Zambia, Mining and Neoliberalism. Boom and Bust on the Globalized Copperbelt.* New York: Palgrave Macmillan

Fredricks, R. (2018). *Garbage Citizenship: Vital Infrastructures of Labor in Dakar, Senegal.* Durham, NC: Duke University Press

Hairong, Y. and Sautman, B. (2013). 'The Beginning of a World Empire?' Contesting the Discourse of Chinese Copper in Zambia. *Modern China* 39(2): 131–64

James, D. (2011). The Return of the Broker: Consensus, Hierarchy, and Choice in South African Land Reform. *Journal of the Royal Anthropology Institute* 17(2): 318–38

Jansson, J. (2013). The Sicomines Agreement Revisited: Prudent Chinese Banks and Risk-Taking Chinese Companies. *Review of African Political Economy* 40(135): 152–62

JCTR (2019). Basic Needs Basket for February 2019: Lifting of Mealie Meal Export Ban to Impact Negatively on the Poor. Statement of the Jesuit Centre for Theological Reflection. Available at: https://repository.jctr.org.zm/handle/123456789/36 (accessed 19 February 2021)

Kapesa, R. and McNamara, T. (2020). 'We Are not Just a Union, We Are a Family'. Class, Kinship and Tribe in Zambia's Mining Unions. *Dialectical Anthropology* 44: 153–72

Kasmir, S. (2014) The Saturn Automobile Plant and the Long Dispossession of US Autoworkers. In Kasmir, S. and Carbonella, A., eds, *Blood and Fire: Towards a Global Anthropology of Labour.* Oxford: Berghahn, pp. 203–49

Kesküla, E. and Sanchez, A. (2019). Everyday Barricades: Bureaucracy and the Affect of Struggle in Trade Unions. *Dialectical Anthropology* 43: 109–25

Kieran. A (2010). The Trade Unions: from Partnership to Crisis. *Irish Journal of Sociology* 18(2): 22–37

Kumwenda, Y. (2015). Casualization of Labour in the Zambian Mining Industry with Specific Reference to Mopani Copper Mines PLC. MA thesis, University of Witwatersrand

Landry, D.G. (2018). The Risks and Rewards of Resource-for-Infrastructure Deals: Lessons from the Congo's Sicomines Agreement. China-Africa Research Initiative Working Paper 16. Available at: https://foreignpolicy.com/wp-content/uploads/2018/06/01911-sicomines-workingpaper-landry-v6.pdf (accessed 19 February 2021)

Larmer, M. (2007). *Mineworkers in Zambia. Labour and Political Change in Post-Colonial Africa.* London: Tauris

Lazar, S. (2017). *The Social Life of Politics: Ethics, Kinship and Union Activism in Argentina.* Redwood, CA: Stanford University Press

Lee, C.K. (2010). Raw Encounters: Chinese Managers, African Workers, and the Politics of Casualization in Africa's Chinese Enclaves. In Fraser A. and Larmer, M., eds, *Zambia, Mining and Neoliberalism. Boom and Bust on the Globalized Copperbelt.* New York: Palgrave Macmillan, pp. 127–54

Lee, C. (2014). The Spectre of Global China. *New Left Review* 89: 29–64

Lee, C.K. (2017). *The Spectre of Global China. Politics, Labor, and Foreign Investment in Africa.* Chicago, IL: University of Chicago Press

Mawdsley, E. (2014). Human Rights and South-South Development Cooperation: Reflections on the 'Rising Powers' as International Development Actors. *Human Rights Quarterly* 36(3): 630–54

McNamara, T. (2017). Do the Chinese Bring *Chitukuko?* Rural Malawian Understandings of Chinese Development. *Journal of International Development* 29(8): 1149–65

McNamara, T. (2019). The Limits of Malawian Headmen's Agency in Co-constructed Development Practice and Narratives. *Journal of East African Studies* 13(3): 465–84

McNamara, T. (2021). A Reasonable Negotiation? Workplace-based Unionists' Subjectivities, Wage Negotiations and the Day-to-day Life of an Ethical-Political Project. *Journal of the Royal Anthropological Institute* 27(3): 617–37

McQuinn, M. (2018). Strengths and Weaknesses of African Trade Unions in the Neoliberal Period with a Sierra Leone Case Study. *Journal Africanan Studia* 28: 111–29

Mwanika, J. and Spooner, D. (2018). Transforming Transport Unions through Mass Organisation of Informal Workers: A Case Study of the ATGWU in Uganda. *Global Labour Journal* 9(2): 150–66

Rubbers, B. (2019). Mining boom, Labour Market Segmentation and Social Inequality in the Congolese Copperbelt. *Development and Change* 51(6): 1555–78

Uzar, E. (2017). Contested Labour and Political Leadership: Three Mineworkers' Unions after the Opposition Victory in Zambia. *Review of African Political Economy* 44(152): 292–311

Von Holdt, K. and Webster, E., eds (2005). *Beyond the Apartheid Workplace: Studies in Transition.* Scotsville: University of KwaZulu-Natal Press

Werbner, P. (2014). *The Making of an African Working Class. Politics, Law, and Cultural Protest in the Manual Workers' Union of Botswana.* London: Pluto Press

Zlolniski, C. (2019). Coping with Precarity: Subsistence, Labour and Community Politics Among Farmworkers in Northern Mexico. *Dialectical Anthropology* 43(1): 77–92

6

Human Resource Managers: Mediating Capital and Labour

EMMA LOCHERY AND BENJAMIN RUBBERS

Congolese and Zambian Human Resource (HR) managers employed by foreign-owned mining companies across the Central African Copperbelt work at the interface of capital and labour in a politically sensitive sector where foreign capital dominates. They run or work in departments responsible for overseeing a range of management techniques used to organise and control workers: processes including recruitment, promotion, discipline, industrial relations, organisational framework design and personnel administration, all central to the internal functioning of a firm. To fulfil these responsibilities, HR managers must mediate between mainly expatriate executive management teams and a largely national labour force, and represent the mine in dealings with government regulatory bodies and the wider society. In this chapter, we take a closer look at the professional backgrounds and work of HR managers and how they navigate the opportunities and risks inherent in their professional position. We situate their work as middle managers in the neoliberal labour regime that dominates both countries' mining sectors.

Although the work of HR managers, as company bureaucrats, mediators and brokers, is central to the 'how' of mining capitalism (Appel 2012), they rarely appear in anthropological studies of mining or in the social sciences literature more generally. Even in management studies, there is relatively little work on 'how the HR role is actually played by practitioners' (O'Brien and Linehan 2014). Undoubtedly, the neglect in studies of mining arises partly from the difficulty researchers have in securing access to company facilities. In Congo, Benjamin Rubbers was granted the opportunity to do an internship in one company's HR department, but only after being refused by five other companies. Nevertheless, even researchers who carried out ethnographic fieldwork inside mining companies – sometimes in the HR department – have used this access mainly to study other issues: the politics of personnel nationalisation (Burawoy 1972), the experience of workers (Gordon 1977), Corporate Social Responsibility (CSR) programmes (Rajak 2011; Welker 2014), or the specificity of Chinese capitalism (Lee 2010, 2014, 2017).

While these ethnographies provide detailed information on different aspects of the organisation of work, they do not take up HR management as a subject of analysis in its own right.

In this chapter then, we reflect on how HR staff themselves act in the power games surrounding the control of labour and worker welfare, reflecting on their position as middle managers facing pressures and tensions heightened by a political economy of precarious work. We begin by explaining how the broader structural changes outlined in Chapter 1 of this book have reshaped HR management in the context of privatisation and liberalisation. We then turn to examining the career paths and experiences of HR managers in the contemporary mining capitalism of the Central African Copperbelt. Finally, we situate their experiences in a broader terrain, tracing the political constellations that have emerged in the two countries around access to employment in foreign-owned mining companies. This chapter is based on the semi-structured and, at times, repeated interviews the two authors carried out with both senior and junior HR managers working in mining companies in Zambia and Congo between 2016 and 2019.

Managers in the Middle

The liberalisation and privatisation of the copper-mining sector in Zambia and Congo from the late 1990s to early 2000s reconfigured the role, career prospects and work of HR managers. Before the unbundling and privatisation of the mining conglomerates, in both countries' mining sectors personnel management had been run as a centralised operation. Personnel administration under Générale des Carrières et des Mines (Gécamines) and Zambian Consolidated Copper Mines (ZCCM) comprised a large bureaucracy, with head offices in Lubumbashi and Kitwe respectively overseeing manpower planning, training and management. These were coupled with a HR hierarchy in each of the mining company divisions, which dealt with industrial relations, manpower services and community services. Both companies employed tens of thousands. In Zambia, in the mid-1980s, ZCCM employed over 60,000 people, which had shrunk to just over 30,000 by 1997 (Nyamazana 1989; Matenga 2010: 2). Gécamines' personnel administration in Congo had more than 36,000 workers under its supervision in the 1980s, which had dropped to less than 25,000 by the second half of the 1990s (Gécamines 1969–99). These conglomerates, due to their size, overarching focus on training and indigenisation programmes, and general commitment to employment security until the 1990s, created large internal labour markets with a range of specific positions within the personnel management hierarchies.

In comparison, HR management in the mining sector today is inevitably organised on a company level and therefore involves much smaller bureaucracies. HR managers often move from one company to another, with only a few building a career in a single company. New private companies vary in size, with the largest having almost 7,000 direct employees (Konkola Copper Mines in Zambia), but most range from 1,000 to 2,000 workers. Nevertheless, while they oversee smaller teams, HR managers in the new mining projects have responsibilities that would previously have been carried out by the parastatals' centralised centres. These include recruiting workers, calculating wages, negotiating with trade unions and making organisational development plans.

Beyond the change in company structure and scale, as we outlined in Chapter 1, many labour practices that have been put in place by mining companies on both sides of the border since privatisation break with those upheld by Gécamines and ZCCM. In line with worldwide trends in the mining sector, new companies tend to be more capital-intensive, have a greater focus on their core business of mining and ore processing, and, especially in the case of Western multinationals, adapt the size of their operations to variations in the copper prices. As a result, they hire fewer workers, whom they prefer to pay in cash rather than through the provision of benefits in kind, such as housing or educational facilities. New investors also do not hesitate to cut labour costs or organise mass layoffs for economic reasons. In both countries, but especially in Zambia, the expansion of outsourcing has also meant an increase in employment by foreign and local contractor companies rather than direct employment in the mines. The position of HR managers in Congo and Zambia's copper-mining sector must be understood amidst the emergence of this neoliberal labour regime: they represent foreign companies that seek to cut labour costs in a region marked by the legacy of industrial paternalism during much of the twentieth century.

Generally speaking, HR managers are middle managers; professionals who are situated, both at work and in wider society, in an intermediate position between the owners of capital and much of the wage labour force (Peschanski 1985; Azambuja and Islam 2019). Literature on the sociology of work and organisational forms has historically highlighted the difficult position of managers in the middle (Dalton 1959; Jackall 1988; Kunda 1992; Watson 1994; Mills 2002; Whyte 2013). Recent work has additionally emphasised the increasing pressure facing these professionals due to frequent corporate restructuring. More qualitative and ethnographic studies of work are only now beginning to consider the human consequences of organisational changes, including downsizing, de-layering of hierarchies, outsourcing and the removal of employee entitlements, that have affected transnational corporations around the world, including in the mining sector (Barley and Kunda 2001; Hassard, McCann and Morris 2007, 2009; Foster *et al.* 2019). Accordingly, more attention is being paid to the roles of middle managers, the coordinating and mediating functions they fulfil, and the emotional labour involved in their job.

In their ethnography of a Brazilian accounting firm, for instance, Azambuja and Islam (2019) depict how middle managers coordinate between different parts of an organisation with conflicting roles and responsibilities. Depending on their relationship with top management, these managers can be 'boundary subjects', that is, 'agential and reflexive mediators between social positions' or 'boundary objects', 'interfacing and coordinating devices' (Azambuja and Islam 2019: 535). This 'boundary work' is a theme that runs through our study of HR managers as individuals situated as intermediaries between top management, the union and the workforce, as well as government and regulatory bodies. While charged with fulfilling certain responsibilities by management, HR managers' very position demands proficiency in managing relations across institutional and hierarchical boundaries. As boundary subjects, HR managers have space to act as brokers, mediating between different groups within 'a narrow band of flexibility' (James 2011: 335) to creatively shape outcomes; at other times, they are marginalised, have little room for manoeuvre, and are given the role of implementing policies over which they have little control.

As Jacoby (2007) argues, corporations are riven by struggles, both over the distribution of resources amongst different groups within the firm and 'internecine battles over which business unit or functional areas will dominate executive decisions' (Jacoby 2007: 3), a dynamic Welker (2014) captures in her ethnography of a mining company in Indonesia during the 2000s. HR departments are amongst the least powerful departments in mining corporations, and are often side-lined by production functions and finance, or maligned as self-important file pushers. However, like departments tasked with CSR or community development projects (see Jacoby 2007: 2; Welker 2014: 41), their profile rises in times of trouble, when their staff's expertise and knowledge becomes integral to solving a crisis or adjusting to conditions like increased unionisation or regulatory change. This position as problem-solvers in the middle, however, also risks making them the focus of blame and frustration from both above and below.

The HR managers we interviewed were empowered by their employers' need for their knowledge of and ability to navigate national institutions, particularly their legal expertise, their connections in various state administrations, and their capacity to act as mediators with political authorities. At the same time, HR managers owed their position of command to the often precarious trust of mainly expatriate executive teams. In the rest of this chapter, we examine how HR managers operated within the band of flexibility created by these opportunities and constraints as well as how they experienced the pressures of their job. We begin by examining the professional backgrounds of HR managers and the paths that led them to their positions as managers in the mining sector. We then look at the work they do within companies to ensure 'harmonious' industrial relations, focusing on their role as mediator within the company and their navigation of the micropolitics of work. Finally, we examine HR managers' work within a broader social and political arena, beyond the limits of the company. By doing so, we hope to shed more light on how mining capitalism becomes embedded in local contexts and, most especially, the people who are hired to manage that process.

Career Paths

The HR managers working for foreign mining companies across the Central African Copperbelt have similar profiles. In Congo, HR managers are all Congolese nationals: the position of personnel manager is on the list of occupations foreigners are forbidden by law from holding. In Zambia, it is stated on job advertisements and is widespread practice that HR managers must be members of the Zambian Institute of Human Resource Management (ZIHRM); plans are underway to renew the ZIHRM Act of 1997 which established this institute and enshrine the practice in law. It is thus an accepted norm that, right to the top of the hierarchy, HR managers should be Zambian. Companies that do not respect this practice have been publicly criticised by the minister of labour and even, at times, the president; the norm is also enforced by not granting work permits, preventing companies from hiring a foreigner for the position (*Lusaka Times* 2013a; Lee 2017: 62). Second, HR managers have a higher education degree from a university, usually a Congolese or Zambian institution, but sometimes also a foreign institution, especially in the cases of those who were headhunted for executive-level HR positions.

The gender profile differs on either side of the border, echoing dynamics discussed by Pugliese and Musonda in Chapter 3. In Congo, we found that the top HR managers were male, with only one exception: a woman who had been appointed by Gécamines as HR manager in a joint venture project with a Chinese State-Owned Enterprise (SOE). According to interviewees in Congo, if most HR managers are men, this is because the job requires managers to exercise authority over the workers, who are also predominantly men. Men, they explained, are more prepared to exercise such authority and are ascribed more legitimacy in the eyes of workers. In Zambia, however, both at junior and more senior ranks, women work as HR managers. At the time of our research, at the two largest mines in Copperbelt Province, women held the top HR positions: the chief services officer at Mopani Copper Mines and the vice-president of human resources at Konkola Copper Mines. Senior women working in HR in mining tend to have one of two profiles: they either entered HR through personnel management or education and training – including working as a teacher at a mine school – during the ZCCM era, or pursued a career as a consultant for multinational firms like PricewaterhouseCoopers and KPMG before taking on HR directorships at parastatals or multinational firms in Zambia.

There are three typical career paths or modes of access to the position of HR manager. First, the longest-serving HR managers built their careers in Gécamines and ZCCM before being reappointed by the new investors. When existing mines were privatised, the experience and knowledge of already employed HR personnel was important for the transfer to new management. In Zambia, for instance, new owners established recognition agreements with the same mineworkers' union and committed to taking non-unionised employees on the same conditions of service. The legacy of years of bargaining between ZCCM and the union and existing personnel officers' relations with the union were a useful inheritance for new investors interested in stable industrial relations (Bota 2001: 21). Even in greenfield projects or mines that have changed investors since privatisation, HR managers sometimes have experience from working at ZCCM or Gécamines, or were mentored by former ZCCM or Gécamines managers at other mines.

In Congo meanwhile, an additional dynamic is at play due to the lingering power of the SOE Gécamines. Most mining projects are based on joint venture agreements, which provide that appointments to certain managerial positions are the prerogative of Gécamines. Generally, Gécamines management identifies a candidate for a joint venture project from among its senior managers who are close to the end of their careers, who is then hired under a new contract by the joint venture. For example, one such manager, Mark, now over sixty years old, spent most of his career with Gécamines. In 2015, while he was the administrative manager of Gécamines' corporate offices in Likasi, he was offered the position of HR manager for a new project in Lubumbashi. Since the new position came with a raise, he accepted the job offer with enthusiasm, considering it a golden parachute that would allow him to save some money before retirement.

Second, a small number of the HR managers we interviewed had been recruited by mining companies shortly after graduating from university, sometimes on graduate training programmes, and progressively rose to the position of HR manager in the organisation. For HR managers interviewed in Congo, whether they had studied in Congo or abroad, none had been trained in HR but in another subject, such as law, economics or sociology. In Zambia, managers also held degrees from a range of disciplines, mainly in the social sciences, computer science or information systems, business or public administration. The background of HR managers below the top rank depends partly on the prerogatives of the senior HR staff. For one major underground mine in the Zambian copperbelt, for instance, a former senior recruitment manager, himself a graduate in computer science, explained he preferred computer science graduates for their discipline and commitment to problem-solving. As information technology and systems have become more central to HR departments, these skills are in in particular demand.

HR has developed as an area of study in its own right since the 1990s and is commonly offered at universities and colleges in both countries. In Congo, it was only just beginning to become popular at the time of the research; to the present day, employees with a degree in HR remain unusual in the mining sector. None of the HR managers whom one of the authors, Benjamin Rubbers, met had received specialised training on their job in a Congolese higher education institution. In Zambia, however, one of the top managers at a greenfield mine site had studied HR for his undergraduate degree and two others had continued to study HR at master's level, either through company sponsorship at South African or British universities, or through cheaper online options. Amongst more junior HR professionals in Zambia, it was more common to find people who had studied HR at undergraduate level; Evelyn Hone, a college in Lusaka known for its business courses, reported that a greenfield mine in North-Western Province had the previous year requested and hired eight of their HR graduates. In both countries, HR managers actively sought to build their CVs by continuing to study and attend trainings taught by Congolese or Zambian experts in labour law or HR. These trainings are organised by each country's national employers' association or, in Zambia, by ZIHRM. Conscious of gaps in their training and knowledge and the rising professionalisation of HR management, several interviewees in both countries disclosed their plans to secure a master's degree in HR management from an institution in South Africa, Europe or the United States.

Third, for top positions in HR management and executive positions, such as vice-president or chief services officer positions, if people have not built careers in ZCCM or Gécamines, they often have executive management experience in other multinational or major parastatal companies before being recruited or headhunted. In particular, those who built their careers during or after the liberalisation of the economy in both countries move from post to post and company to company, developing relationships with other business and political elites and building their profiles on the labour market. This increases their chances of being contacted by companies or headhunting agencies that find their CV on professional websites. In addition, in Congo, the experience of working in different companies also allows managers to improve their English, a skill necessary for working with most expatriate executives and taken for granted in professional circles in Zambia, where the official language is English.

Take for instance the career of Christopher, a Congolese HR manager in his late forties. After obtaining a degree in management mathematics, he was recruited by the chairman of the national railway company, first as the deputy manager of his private farm, and then as his secretary in the SOE. It was in this capacity that he first became familiar with HR management. In 2005, Christopher was recommended by a former schoolmate for a position as HR manager for a new mining project in Kolwezi. This was a formative moment in his career, he told us, as he was forced to learn the trade on the job, as a 'self-taught man'. Since then, he has strengthened this experience by working as HR manager for three other multinational companies. In 2014, he was unemployed for a few months but was then contacted by a headhunting agency based in London about a job opportunity as HR manager at another mining company near Lubumbashi. This is the job he currently holds.

No matter their degree or if they have worked in other sectors, when it comes to the practical work of HR management, the mining sector presents new challenges and managers learn many skills on the job. Organisational skills central to personnel management – mastering the rules and procedures for recruitment, the calculation of wages, disciplinary actions, dismissals, and communication and negotiation with trade unions – remain crucial and often involve the use of IT tools. HR managers also have to familiarise themselves with labour law covering employment contracts and relations with trade unions, and ensure their company follows the law; this is especially important in cases of dismissals or mass layoffs, to avoid former employees taking legal action. HR managers often have to appear in court to explain their companies' actions and at times represent their company. Finally, the most senior HR managers have to sit at the top table and, at some companies, take part in organisational development and planning.

Beyond all of this, HR managers have to master a range of social and cultural skills needed to tactfully manage the contradictory interests of executives, union representatives, workers and local state authorities. In particular, as senior as they may be in the HR hierarchy, the most successful managers emphasised that to do their job well, they had to know how to relate to workers working in the pit and at the rock face. To examine the work involved in this, we turn to the role of HR managers in managing industrial relations within the company.

Building a Harmonious Environment

Despite the challenges facing trade unions in both countries (see Chapters 4 and 5 in this book), they remain central to the tripartite organisation of work in the mining sector. In Zambia, the right to unionise is enshrined in law for employees working in an enterprise with at least twenty-five employees; in Congo, union representation is required by law in enterprises with ten or more employees.[1] In both countries, all major mining houses and, increasingly, many of the large contractor companies have recognition agreements with unions; negotiations are held annually or, in a few cases, every three years to determine wage increments and changes to other conditions of service. Last but not least, in both countries, for the government and many companies, union organisation helps make industrial relations more manageable.

[1] The union's approval is also required in Congo for certain internal organisational measures including the promulgation of staff regulations and the creation of a health and safety committee.

In Congo in particular, far from seeing trade unions as militant organisations struggling against capital, HR managers speak of unions as the company's 'partners' who can contribute to industrial peace. The unions themselves tend to emphasise their 'responsibility' as facilitators between capital and labour (see Chapter 4). For instance, there is nothing surprising to find on a calendar printed by the Alliance des Travailleurs Avertis et Consciencieux [Alliance of Informed and Conscientious Workers] union the slogan: '*Soyons performants et compétitifs. Produisons pour mieux revendiquer*' [Let us be efficient and competitive. We must produce to make more claims']. This way of thinking about trade unionism can be traced back to the Mobutu regime and the late colonial era (Poupart 1960; Banza n.d.; Mbili Kwa Mbili 1986). Since then, their role has primarily been to 'educate the working class'. To this day, both HR managers and union representatives continue to use this expression to mean sensitising unskilled workers to the requirements of industrial work and preventing the spread of false rumours amongst them. In their view, it is when they fail in fulfilling this mission that 'uneducated' workers go on strike.

In Zambia as well, management has a strong hand when it comes to dealing with unions. It is almost impossible to organise a legal strike in Zambia, and while militant workers still sometimes organise wildcat strikes or go-slows, these put workers at risk of being fired and so are usually discouraged by unions (Lee 2017: 81–83; Uzar 2017; McNamara 2021). Moreover, mines have fragmented their labour forces by contracting out work, causing membership to fall and decreasing trade unions' negotiation power and financial capacity. As they struggle to survive these challenges, unions remain dependent on mining companies in Zambia: they sell goods to workers on credit on company property and offer workers loans which are paid back through payroll in some mines, making the arrangement dependent on HR.[2] On a daily basis, union representatives are also dependent on their relationships with HR managers when pleading for clemency in disciplinary cases. Thus, in the (usually) annual negotiations over wages and conditions of service, HR managers are much better positioned to be able to convincingly argue the company's case, to obfuscate, and convince union branch executives that a minimal increase is all the company can afford and in the interest of all (see Chapter 5). The environment works to discipline branch union leaders, a dynamic one HR manager alluded to when remarking that the last decade had 'seen us move from confrontational union leaders to leaders that are… enlightened'.

However, focusing on the weakness of the unions in contemporary industrial relations hides the ongoing work that secures control over the workforce and maintains 'industrial peace'. What start as specific

[2] For a recent discussion between researchers and Zambian mining union leaders about the roles and responsibilities of trade unions in a neoliberal economy, see the blogpost by Thomas McNamara and James Musonda (2019), and the reply by George S. Mumba (2019), General Secretary of the Mineworkers Union of Zambia.

disagreements about conditions of service can spiral out of control if not managed well by HR professionals. Towards the end of our research in Zambia, a trade unionist remarked that the new HR manager at a mine in North-Western Province had ignored workers' demands for buses to take them home to Copperbelt Province, which led to riots. The trade unionist attributed the trouble to the fact that the HR manager was doing a poor job of 'listening' to the union. There is an art to industrial relations, old hands in HR management in the mines explained, intimating what they understand to be the typical psychology of miners, using phrases like 'a miner is a miner' or 'you know miners'. As one experienced HR manager put it, miners can feel 'they are really being used as tools', and to be effective, a manager must 'make them feel they are actually the most important capital in a company' while also maintaining his or her authority. They invoked a trope of a manual labourer as a 'simple person', averse to change and 'looking for fairness', who wants managers to 'walk the talk'. In particular, many HR managers emphasised the importance of appearing fair; they were aware that workers are watching their behaviour. They underlined the significance of small gestures, such as how they welcomed people to their offices, and the need to prevent accusations of favouritism; for one junior manager living on site at a remote mine, for instance, this meant limiting whom she allowed to visit her home.

Despite the importance of their work, the space given to HR managers to do their job varies, recalling Azambuja and Islam's (2019) distinction between managers as boundary subjects with space to build relationships and coalitions versus managers as boundary objects alienated from organisational decision-making. A range of factors matter: the size of the company, its experience in the mining sector and in Central Africa, the stage of the project, as well as the personality and management style of the top executive team, especially the general manager. In small mines and contractor companies, and large mining projects in the development phase, HR managers are usually employed as multipurpose local assistants who deal with all legal, administrative and social aspects of personnel management. As these projects are often autocratically managed by an expatriate general manager for whom personnel management is the least of his concerns, it is in these situations that violations of labour laws such as a lack of work contracts, unfair dismissals, or the refusal to recognise unions, commonly occur. No matter how skilful HR managers are, in the face of their boss's decisions, they cannot do much except attempt to find retroactive solutions to problems. As mining projects develop, however, and begin to have a larger permanent staff, HR managers have the opportunity to delegate responsibilities such as recruitment, discipline and industrial relations, and to establish better procedures for managing the HR function. Generally speaking, then, as midsized and large companies in the production phase have established rules and procedures in compliance with the law, they have much better organised HR management apparatuses than smaller companies, and HR managers can do their work with more ease.

In general, senior HR managers formally report directly to the general manager, have a seat on the board of the heads of department, and, in some cases, occasionally participate in meetings with the HR team at the headquarters of the parent mining company or majority joint venture partner. However, this does not mean they are considered full members of the senior management team. Even in better organised companies, HR departments are small, considered to be of minor importance, and often struggle to have their voices heard as priority is given to the needs of departments involved in production. The HR manager's 'band of flexibility' to mediate and broker can thus be limited as the heads of other departments tend to supervise their own staff and recruit, promote, or dismiss workers independently, relying on the HR department only as an implementation service. The power of the HR manager to intervene in or manage these processes depends on the prerogatives that a project's general manager is willing to give him or her.

Moreover, the power of HR managers vis-a-vis foreign or expatriate executive staff directly recruited by the operating company varies. Generally, in a *de facto* recreation of the colonial-era colour bar in the mines, national HR managers have limited power over the members of what often effectively becomes a sort of higher caste – unless foreign managers commit a serious offense against a Zambian or Congolese worker which is subject to disciplinary action by the HR department. As mentioned in the opening to this chapter, in many companies, including Western, Chinese and Indian mining companies operating on both sides of the border, an expatriate is appointed to supervise, sometimes informally, the Zambian or Congolese HR manager's work. The latter can find himself in a situation analogous to that of the black personnel officer described by Burawoy (1972) during Zambianisation in the 1960s, promoted to a senior position while simultaneously being undermined by having responsibilities taken away from him. In some mines, it is the expatriate supervisor, known by titles varying from consultant to support services or organisational development officer (ODO), who reports to the project's general manager, sits on the board of the heads of departments, and participates in strategic meetings at headquarters abroad. In other companies, the HR manager's powers are circumscribed in more informal ways. As described by a former HR manager in a Chinese company in Zambia, following meetings including Zambian managers, Chinese managers would simply review the decisions made amongst themselves while they had dinner together in camp, and return in subsequent meetings to pronounce decisions contrary to those previously decided with Zambian staff.

Thus, although Zambian and Congolese HR managers may have the title of a senior manager, and receive a relatively high salary, their actual role may be largely reduced to bureaucratic personnel administration and legal advice. This is, of course, a frustrating experience for managers who feel they are capable of contributing much more, as one Congolese manager supervised by an ODO complained:

> The ODO does not have any experience… You feel embarrassed when you talk to him, you must lower yourself to his level, and when you give him ideas, he takes them and then presents them as if they were his own ideas. This is very frustrating, you know. I'm the HR manager, but I'm not given any real value. They don't listen to me. They take me for a suspect person who'll give all the information to workers, or to state authorities.

Similarly, a HR manager working for a mining company in Zambia appeared frustrated as he discussed top-level appointments of Zambian managers: 'What kind of decision-making power do they have? How do you know they are not just a face?' He described his own workplace, where although a Zambian might hold the position of HR manager directly under the general manager of the mine, the Zambian manager's ability to exercise his authority was often undermined by an expatriate responsible for managing expatriate terms and services – an area, he explained wryly, that in the eyes of expatriate management a local cannot be trusted to manage. But then, he continued, that manager begins to take over HR tasks more generally, and the Zambian HR manager begins to lose his direct access to the general manager. As a result, senior Zambian HR managers don't really have the authority that their job is supposed to have, until there is a task that requires knowledge of the local context, such as an issue related to labour laws.

This situation is exacerbated by the way expatriate managers at mine sites usually occupy a social world from which Zambian and Congolese managers tend to be excluded – divisions that map onto deep legacies of colonialism and structural racism. Expatriate managers usually speak the same language, share interests, have similar life trajectories and are part of overlapping transnational social networks. Congolese and Zambian HR managers are, by contrast, *a priori* subjected to suspicion: are they able to do the job? Do they draw personal profits from their position? Are they on the employer's or the workers' side? Mistrust often lingers near the surface. When one author, Emma Lochery, explained her research questions to two white expatriate managers at a mine in Zambia, they immediately expressed frustration with HR staff: 'My challenge is getting people hired who have not paid a lot of money to HR managers. There are a few good staff, but time and time again, I find the people who have been hired are someone's brother or cousin…' The other manager replied that his strategy was to set up a committee and choose the candidate and then instruct HR to hire that person, or alternatively to run an internship scheme to judge candidates on their performance before offering them jobs. Either way, they bypassed the HR department. Being a senior Congolese or Zambian HR manager in this situation requires a great deal of skill and confidence; it may bring social prestige but can sometimes prove an alienating experience.

Beyond Company Walls

Beyond tensions and struggles within mining companies, HR managers working in the Central African Copperbelt must be situated in broader political arenas. As one top South African manager with experience of working in mines on both sides of the border with a Western multinational remarked simply, the position of HR manager is 'very political'. Top HR managers, often the most senior Congolese or Zambian managers in the company, tend to have a high profile and, as a consequence, face a variety of expectations at different political scales.

However, the ways in which HR managers are framed and positioned politically differs between the two countries. Zambia is a less populous country, with a smaller, more tightly networked elite. While trade unionists have historically been more prominent in the country's politics, there are also politicians with experience working or consulting in industrial relations or HR. The reverse relationship between politics and HR management is also important for some companies. It is helpful for companies if their senior HR manager, or another national executive manager, has links to the upper echelons of government.

The political framing of HR managers in Zambia is also affected by the significance of employment conditions as a political issue discussed not just locally, but at the national level. Mining communities have historically been integral to catalysing political change (Larmer 2006), and Copperbelt Province remains a significant electoral constituency, seen as a bellwether of political change. Concerns over the employment practices of foreign investors became an especially prominent political issue from the 2000s as public anger grew over austerity measures, increased unemployment, and the tax breaks and other benefits given to foreign-owned mining companies. As the Patriotic Front emerged with its slogan 'Zambia for Zambians', its leader Michael Sata focused his attention on the concerns of the urban working class and the unemployed, especially lambasting working conditions in Chinese-owned mining companies (Fraser 2010). In this context, the Zambian government made policy statements framing Zambian HR managers as potential bulwarks against the erosion of workers' rights. According to this line of thought, Zambian HR professionals would ensure that employment law is properly applied, thereby protecting workers' rights. After the Patriotic Front victory in 2011 in particular, minister of labour Fackson Shamenda called on HR managers to 'stand their ground' and correctly interpret labour laws for their employers. He portrayed HR managers as the crucial interface between management and workers, in a position to facilitate social dialogue, increase productivity, and by implication, national development (*Lusaka Times* 2013b). This discourse points to the high social status accorded HR managers and the corresponding opportunities for social and professional advancement. However, it also highlights the risks of being caught between competing pressures from a political economy of precarious employment and a government struggling to strengthen its regulatory power.

In Congo, by contrast, mining companies generally avoid hiring national executive managers with strong political connections. Their expatriate representatives – a shareholder, the project general manager, or an expatriate with long-standing experience in the country – prefer to make contact directly with influential political leaders and to protect the management of their business from political interference (see Rubbers 2009). If a position is offered to a politician, it is an honorary position as adviser or board member, with no real power over the functioning of the company. In only one case, we found that the position of HR manager was given to a member of the entourage of the presidency. But this occurred at the start of short-lived project funded by an infamous businessman with no experience in mining. As soon as the project was bought out by a mining company, the HR manager was replaced by senior managers from Gécamines.

Furthermore, the Congolese national government has not made policy statements about the protective role of HR managers in the mining sector, perhaps because of Gécamines' presence as a joint venture partner, and because the law is clear that HR managers must be Congolese. Policy statements emphasise rather the role of the labour inspector, who carries out control visits in mining companies and fines the employer in case of violation of the law. In Congo, political pressure is exerted more informally, at a more local level, in favour of smaller constituencies: it is the provincial authorities, the local ethnic associations or the customary chiefs who press HR managers to look after the interests of people considered autochthonous to the province, the tribe or the chiefdom. Such pressures are often intense. Far from only playing on the HR managers' loyalty to an imagined community, they may involve protests in front of the company, letters of complaint to management, or phone calls from political authorities that threaten the HR manager's job.

Besides these differences, however, in both countries HR managers' daily work and the challenges they face are shaped by the fact they are gatekeepers to the mine. They are in a position to affect the distribution of jobs and can face an array of requests and threats. In Zambia and Congo, jobs remain scarce while the number of higher education graduates constantly increases, and mining companies receive a large number of applications for each vacancy. Though it is organised slightly differently at each mining company, top-ranking HR managers oversee recruitment and are the main point of contact for applicants. Candidates send application files to the HR department which, at some mines, is responsible also for selecting the candidates who will make it to the second stage of the recruitment process, the tests and the interview. Although the head of the recruiting department makes the final choice, HR managers have the power to put CVs on top of the pile, making them prominent targets for recommendations especially since, while they are among the most senior Zambian and Congolese managers in the company, their phone numbers are easy to find, and they are able to gauge the importance of the candidate's sponsors.

The HR managers encountered during the research constantly fielded recommendations from all sides: relatives, neighbours, colleagues, church members, friends from university, customary chiefs, political parties and various state authorities, from the local to the national level. Faced with these multiple requests, their strategy was to routinely answer that the recommended candidate's CV would be taken into consideration and that the sponsor would be informed of the application's outcome. Even if they do not take recommendations into account, it is essential for HR managers to show goodwill to their interlocutor. To explicitly ignore recommendations would unnecessarily expose themselves to criticism, and, especially in Congo, potential threats from powerful people.

Indeed, in Congo, risks related to recruitment are higher for HR managers, especially those who are not *originaires*, autochthons of the territory or the province where the mine site is located. Most mining companies established in remote rural areas in both Zambia and Congo adopt 'local content' policies within the framework of their CSR programmes – another innovation that contrasts with the policies of ZCCM and Gécamines. In Congo, HR managers overseeing recruitment are expected to give priority to candidates from local communities and to pay particular attention to recommendations from local power figures. Even though this rule is only followed for unskilled jobs, which are rather limited in number once mining projects are in the production phase, HR managers who are not *originaires* are swiftly accused of favouring those from their own tribe or province to the detriment of local communities. With the support of customary chiefs, local ethnic associations such as Sempya (Bemba) or Lwanzo lwa Mikuba (Sanga) in Congo do not hesitate to send letters to the company to protest or ask for the support of the provincial authorities in demanding the dismissal of the HR manager. Although these efforts rarely achieve their goals, in Congo they lead mining companies to prefer to hire a candidate from the appropriate tribe or province when the HR manager position is vacant, in the hope of avoiding unnecessary tension with local communities.

In Zambia, the local political dynamics have less impact on the companies' choice of HR manager. The three large mines in North-Western Province have local recruitment systems for unskilled jobs which include databases developed in conjunction with local chiefs. However, pressure from local chiefdoms is often blunted by the compromised position of chiefs who, after facilitating mining investment by granting communal land to mining companies, are often accused of looking after their own personal and family interests rather than those of the wider community (Negi 2010; Kapesa 2019). Moreover, as mining projects move from the construction to the production phase and the available number of unskilled jobs falls, mining companies' interaction with chiefs is increasingly channelled through community development departments.

Beyond pressures over the distribution of jobs, however, the new political economy of precarious employment has consequences for

HR managers because they oversee dismissals and retrenchments. HR managers are responsible for charging and dismissing workers guilty of misconduct as well as for collating the list of those who will be impacted by a mass layoff. Although the number of dismissals for disciplinary reasons should not be overestimated, the number of punishable behaviours, the increased punishment for such behaviours, and the inflexible attitude of management contribute to fuelling workers' sense of precariousness. HR managers are suspected to have discretion in these procedures and are subjected to multiple pressures from within and outside the company. Those who fear losing their jobs do not hesitate to ask state authorities to exert pressure on the HR manager. While these pressures are present across many sectors, the numbers of workers, the foreign status of executive managers and the political prominence of the mining sector make it particularly likely that workers and trade unions will call for state intervention (see Chapter 5).

The challenge of HR managers' position at the interface between management and workers especially comes into focus during restructuring and 'rationalisation' exercises, when mining companies cut their workforces through mass layoffs, voluntary departure programmes, or technical leave procedures. These cuts have become more common since the sharp fall and then recovery of copper prices in 2008–09 following the global financial crisis, and the slower decline from 2011 into 2016. In Zambia, for instance, employment numbers rose as new investors pumped capital into the mines through the mid-2000s, from less than 20,000 workers in 2003, to around 40,000 in the mid-2000s. As the copper price rose to over US$ 8,000 per tonne in mid-2008, 63,151 people were employed in Zambia's mining sector (Fraser and Lungu 2007; Matenga 2010: 2). Once copper prices fell however, companies closed facilities, put mines on care and maintenance and carried out retrenchments: between June 2008 and May 2009 over 30 per cent of the labour force lost their jobs. The majority (62 per cent) of these job losses were from contractor companies, but the mining companies also retrenched over 7,300 direct employees (Matenga 2010). These job losses, and those that continue to occur periodically on both sides of the border, contrast greatly with the stability of employment provided by Gécamines and ZCCM in the past. As described in Chapter 2, while some workers may be rehired, in Zambia in particular many companies have increasingly shifted their labour force from directly to indirectly employed workers through contractor companies.

For HR managers, managing these complex and politically sensitive situations and organising and implementing restructuring is difficult and stressful. First, HR managers must often impose the decisions of management on workers. As they are confronted by similar difficulties – anxiety over the precarity of their own jobs, cost of living and family pressure, they are, unlike many expatriates, personally aware of the consequences these decisions have on workers' everyday lives. Thus, their work of translation between divergent interests is particularly difficult on a personal level. While expatriate managers suspect them of being on the side of workers, the workers regard them as expatriate managers' collaborators. As a result, they can end up isolated in the company. When a crisis occurs, such as a strike or a mass layoff, they may be the ones deemed responsible, especially if negotiations break down and the company turns to politicians and government officials to mediate between management and workers.

Lee (2017: 63, 146) has described how, in protests in Zambia, striking workers would hold placards calling for the dismissal of the Zambian HR manager. Similarly, both an HR manager and trade unionists in Zambia recounted the story of an HR manager at Lumwana Copper Mine in North-Western Province in 2015 who had to leave the site in a hurry after workers shut down the mine calling for his departure following a conflict over employee benefits. After government figures intervened, the general manager took responsibility for the policy changes which had been implemented as part of broader cost-cutting measures. Nevertheless, workers only agreed to return to work if the HR manager was dismissed. Protest actions calling for the dismissal of the HR manager also took place in several mines in Congo after the company decided to organise a mass layoff. In some cases, threats from retrenched workers led HR managers to take strong measures to protect themselves and their families. After some workers took their issues with the mining company out on his children, one HR manager decided to send them to school in South Africa, where they now live away from their parents. Another manager moved his family to Zambia after receiving a threatening letter.

At the same time, some viewed these difficult moments of change not only as a challenge but an opportunity to prove their skills and legitimise their position as a top-ranking manager, able to navigate relations with government and withstand the court of public opinion. In both Congo and Zambia, retrenchment is a costly and time-consuming exercise; companies are expected to notify unions and the labour officer a certain number of days before redundancies take place. According to these norms, mining companies should engage the ministry of labour, and sometimes, through negotiations with high officials in various national ministries, the number to be retrenched is reduced. Some HR managers took pride in the fact that they know how this political process works, are supported by their executive management team, and have good connections to enable them to help broker an agreement amongst partners. One of the professionally most successful young Zambian HR managers argued that those in his field can go even further and challenge norms around redundancy, ensuring companies have access to a more flexible workforce. Again, the position of HR managers remains ambivalent and dependent on their navigation of the boundary work that is inherent in their position.

Conclusion

The HR managers interviewed for this study have played a key role in the development of new mining projects funded by foreign investors in the Central African Copperbelt over the past twenty years. As part of their function, they have, among other tasks, recruited workers, negotiated with unions and organised mass layoffs. Through these various processes, their mission has been to keep labour costs low, maintain industrial peace, and ensure mining companies' employment practices comply with the law. Their work as HR managers has been central to mining companies' efforts to create the stable, efficient and flexible work environments deemed necessary for the development of mining capitalism in the twenty-first century.

To carry out their tasks as HR managers, the people we interviewed in Congo and Zambia used a range of legal, organisational and social skills that most had learned on the job while working for various mining companies. The boundary work carried out by HR managers requires them to interact strategically with a variety of actors: expatriate executives, union representatives, workers, state officials and politicians. Their job is to translate the specific and often contradictory interests of these different categories of actors and to find solutions that best benefit the company and its foreign shareholders. However, this work of mediation and brokerage often puts them in a difficult situation professionally and personally. While workers see them as collaborators in league with expatriate executives, the latter suspect them of drawing personal advantage from their position as the company's gatekeepers. Marginalised by both national workers and expatriate executives, they often find themselves isolated in the middle of the firm's social structure. This can have contradictory effects. On one hand, their power to effect change in the organisation can be limited by their position as a manager in the middle. On the other hand, when tensions rise over employment issues or industrial relations, they are at risk of being deemed responsible for the problems.

Beyond the company's organisational limits, the boundary work performed by HR managers highlights in a new way the various political constellations that have taken shape around access to employment in mining companies across the Central African Copperbelt. Considering the work of HR managers highlights significant similarities on either side of the border. Although trade unions are much larger and better organised in Zambia, they have not shaped the labour policies of mining companies more successfully than Congolese trade unions (for a study of how they deal with the constraints imposed by new mining investors, see this book's Chapters 4 and 5). Similarly, although Congolese labour inspectors have more formal powers than their counterparts in Zambia, their capacity to improve working conditions in the mining sector proves to be limited in practice, if only because employers can always appeal to political patrons to lift the fines levied by an overly punctilious labour inspector. As result, many small and midsized mining companies have deplorable working conditions without being troubled by the labour administration.

A significant difference between the two countries, however, is the way tensions over employment in the mining sector are expressed politically. As described above, in Zambia, the quality of employment in foreign-owned mining companies is a prominent issue, not just locally but also in national politics. Copperbelt Province has historically been important as an electoral constituency and a bellwether of political change. Moreover, mineworkers and their trade union, the Mineworkers' Union of Zambia (MUZ), have historically helped to drive political change in Zambia, particularly the fall of the one-party state under the United National Independence Party (UNIP) in 1991 and the rise of the Movement for Multiparty Democracy (Larmer 2006). As the Patriotic Front emerged during the 2000s, tensions around the behaviour of foreign investors and casualisation of employment took centre stage politically. Government statements urged HR managers to enforce Zambian labour laws, while companies in turn threatened to carry out redundancies in order to exact concessions from government.

In Congo, the constituency of the towns of the copperbelt does not dominate relative to other, more populous, provinces. Employment in the mining sector has thus been more a regional issue in Congo. To be sure, this is true in the rural areas of both Congo and Zambia, where greenfield mining projects have to navigate pressures from local power figures to prioritise local ethnic groups in access to employment (Rubbers 2019; Negi 2010). However, claims based on autochthony are arguably stronger in Congo, where they have been fuelled by a process of decentralisation and the creation of new provinces in 2015 (Gobbers 2016, 2019; Englebert, Calderon and Jene 2018).

Finally, our analysis suggests that across the Central African Copperbelt, the band of flexibility in which HR managers operate varies depending on investor strategy and management styles, but also over time, most especially in the case of new projects or greenfield sites. In the early 2000s, when new mining projects were in the development phase, HR managers' band of flexibility was relatively broad. Since foreign investors depended on them to recruit local workers, negotiate with trade unions, etc., they had considerable influence over the company's labour policies and from the outside, they were largely viewed as the company's gatekeepers. Everybody, including local power figures, went through them to get in touch with management or to access employment in the company. However, their band of flexibility was significantly reduced when mining projects entered the production phase, especially after the financial crisis in 2008. Indeed, HR managers have fewer and fewer jobs to distribute and, on the contrary, are increasingly asked to dismiss workers and cut labour costs. In addition, the parent company often seeks to take control of the organisational development of the mining project by imposing new organisational structures, tools and procedures from above. In some of these companies, the Congolese or Zambian HR manager is increasingly confined to bureaucratic tasks and legal advice while strategic decisions are taken by an expatriate manager who supervises his or her work. Nevertheless, it is the Zambian HR manager who is held responsible by workers, trade unions and local politicians for unpopular measures decided by management.

In a way, the HR manager in these mining companies is increasingly caught in a situation similar to that of the Zambian personnel manager described by Burawoy (1972; see also 2014) in the early 1970s, the target of blame and a symbol of frustration about 'window-dressing Zambianisation'. The main difference, however, is that managers in the twenty-first century no longer navigate the power games typical of state paternalism but rather the micropolitics of a neoliberal labour regime where precarious work dominates. In this study, we have situated HR managers within this transformation, showing how they have played a crucial role as gatekeepers and mediators while operating in an increasingly narrow space of possibility.

Bibliography

Appel, H.C. (2012). Walls and White Elephants: Oil Extraction, Responsibility, and Infrastructural Violence in Equatorial Guinea. *Ethnography* 13(4): 439–65

Azambuja, R. and Islam, G. (2019). Working at the Boundaries: Middle Managerial Work as a Source of Emancipation and Alienation. *Human Relations* 72(3): 534–64

Banza, M.N. (n.d.). *L'unification du mouvement syndical en République démocratique du Congo.* Bruxelles: De Clercq Monique

Barley, S.R. and Kunda, G. (2001). Bringing Work Back In. *Organization Science* 12(1): 76–95

Bota, K. (2001). The Impact of Liberalisation on the Worker: A Legal Perspective. Research Essay, University of Zambia

Burawoy, M. (1972). *The Colour of Class on the Copper Mines: From African Advancement to Zambianization.* Manchester: Manchester University Press

Burawoy, M. (2014). The Colour of Class Revisited: Four Decades of Postcolonialism in Zambia. *Journal of Southern African Studies* 40(5): 961–79

Dalton, M. (1959). *Men Who Manage. Fusions of Feeling and Theory in Administration.* New York: Wiley and Sons

Englebert, P., Calderon, A. and Jene, L. (2018). Provincial Tribalisation. The Transformation of Ethnic Representativeness under Decentralisation in the DRCongo. Secure Livelihood Research Consortium Working Paper 61. Available at: https://securelivelihoods.org/wp-content/uploads/SLRC-WorkingPaper-61-Provincial-tribalisation-DRC-final-online.pdf (accessed 19 February 2021)

Foster, W., Hassard, J., Morris, J. and Cox, J. (2019). The Changing Nature of Managerial Work: The Effects of Corporate Restructuring on Management Jobs and Careers. *Human Relations* 72(3): 473–504

Fraser, A. and Lungu, J. (2007). For Whom the Windfalls? Winners and Losers in the Privatisation of Zambia's Copper Mines. Report for the Civil Society Trade Network of Zambia (CSTNZ). Available at:
https://sarpn.org/documents/d0002403/1-Zambia_copper-mines_Lungu_Fraser.pdf (accessed 19 February 2021)

Fraser, A. (2010). Introduction: Boom and Bust on the Zambian Copperbelt. In Fraser, A. and Larmer, M., eds, *Zambia, Mining, and Neoliberalism: Boom and Bust on the Globalized Copperbelt.* New York: Palgrave Macmillan, pp. 1–30

Gécamines (1969–1999). Rapports annuels. Lubumbashi: Générale des Carrières et des Mines

Gobbers, E. (2016). Ethnic Associations in Katanga Province, the Democratic Republic of Congo: Multi-tier System, Shifting Identities and the Relativity of Autochthony. *Journal of Modern African Studies* 54(2): 211–36

Gobbers, E. (2019). Territorial Découpage and Issues of 'Autochthony' in Former Katanga Province, the Democratic Republic of Congo: The Role of Urban Ethnic Associations. *Ethnopolitics*. Available at: www.tandfonline.com/doi/pdf/10.1080/17449057.2019.1676523?needAccess=true (accessed 19 February 2021)

Gordon, R.J. (1977). *Mines, Masters and Migrants. Life in a Namibian Mine Compound*. Johannesburg: Ravan Press

Hassard, J., McCann, L. and Morris, J. (2007). At the Sharp End of New Organizational Ideologies. Ethnography and the Study of Multinationals. *Ethnography* 8(3): 324–44

Hassard, J., McCann, L. and Morris, J. (2009). *Managing in the Modern Corporation: The Intensification of Managerial Work in the USA, UK and Japan*. Cambridge: Cambridge University Press

Jackall, R. (1988). *Moral Mazes: The World of Corporate Managers*. New York: Oxford University Press

Jacoby, S.M. (2007). *The Embedded Corporation: Corporate Governance and Employment Relations in Japan and the United States*. Princeton, NJ: Princeton University Press

James, D. (2011). The Return of the Broker: Consensus, Hierarchy, and Choice in South African Land Reform. *Journal of the Royal Anthropology Institute* 17(2): 318–38

Kapesa, R. (2019). Perceptions of Horizontal Inequalities, Collective Grievances, and Ethic Mobilization in Emerging Mining Areas of North-Western Zambia. Unpublished PhD thesis, Copperbelt University Zambia

Kunda, G. (1992). *Engineering Culture: Control and Commitment in a High-Tech Corporation*. Philadelphia, PA: Temple University Press

Larmer, M. (2006). 'The Hour Has Come at the Pit': The Mineworkers' Union of Zambia and the Movement for Multi-Party Democracy, 1982–1991. *Journal of Southern African Studies* 32(2): 293–312

Lee, C.K. (2010). Raw Encounters: Chinese Managers, African Workers, and the Politics of Casualization in Africa's Chinese Enclaves. In Fraser, A. and Larmer, M., eds, *Zambia, Mining and Neoliberalism. Boom and Bust on the Globalized Copperbelt*. New York: Palgrave Macmillan, pp. 127–54

Lee, C. (2014). The Spectre of Global China. *New Left Review* 89

Lee, C.K. (2017). *The Spectre of Global China. Politics, Labor, and Foreign Investment in Africa*. Chicago, IL: University of Chicago Press

Lusaka Times (2013a). Human Resource Managers Urged to Enforce Labour Laws. Available at: www.lusakatimes.com/2013/06/01/human-resource-managers-urged-to-enforce-labour-laws/ (accessed 19 February 2021)

Lusaka Times (2013b). Shamenda Tells Human Resource Institute to Put in Place Measures Enforcing Ban on Foreigners in HR Management Positions. Available at: www.lusakatimes.com/2013/03/20/shamenda-tells-human-resource-institute-to-put-in-place-measures-enforcing-ban-on-foreigners-in-hr-management-postions/ (accessed 19 February 2021)

Matenga, C.R. (2010). The Impact of the Global Financial and Economic Crisis on Job Losses and Conditions of Work in the Mining Sector in Zambia. Report for the International Labour Organisation. Available at: http://citeseerx.ist.psu.edu/viewdoc/download?doi=10.1.1.233.124&rep=rep1&type=pdf (accessed 19 February 2020)

Mbili Kwa Mbili. (1986). Esquisse du syndicalisme au Zaïre: d'hier à aujourd'hui. *Africa* 41(2): 271–80

McNamara, T. (2021). A Reasonable Negotiation? Workplace-based Unionists' Subjectivities, Wage Negotiations and the Day-to-day Life of an Ethical-Political Project. *Journal of the Royal Anthropological Institute* 27(3): 617–37

McNamara, T. and Musonda, J. (2019). This is What a Neoliberal Trade Union Looks Like. Blogpost for Africa's a Country. Available at: https://africasacountry.com/2019/01/the-growth-and-stability-of-business-unionism-in-zambia (accessed 19 February 2021)

Mills, C.W. (2002). *White Collar: The American Middle Classes*. Oxford: Oxford University Press

Mumba, G.S. (2019). Mineworkers Union of Zambia's General Secretary Responds to 'This is What a Neoliberal Union Looks Like'. Blogpost for the WORKinMINING project. Available at: www.workinmining.ulg.ac.be/blog/mineworkers-union-of-zambias-general-secretary-responds-to-this-is-what-a-neoliberal-union-looks-like (accessed 19 February 2021)

Negi, R. (2010). The Mining Boom, Capital, and Chiefs in the 'New Copperbelt'. In Fraser, A. and Larmer, M., eds, *Zambia, Mining and Neoliberalism. Boom and Bust on the Globalized Copperbelt*. New York: Palgrave MacMillan, pp. 209–36

Nyamazana, M. (1989). Manpower Planning and Labour Shortages in an Underdeveloped Economy: An Empirical Analysis of Manpower Policies and Practices of the Industrial Development Corporation Limited (INDECO) of Zambia. PhD thesis, University of London. Available at: https://eprints.soas.ac.uk/28749/ (accessed 19 February 2021)

O'Brien, E. and Linehan, C. (2014). A Balancing Act: Emotional Challenges in the HR Role. *Journal of Management Studies* 51(8): 1257–85

Peschanski, V. (1985). Middle Managers in Contemporary Capitalism. *Acta Sociologica* 28(3): 243–55

Poupart, R. (1960). *Première esquisse de l'évolution du syndicalisme au Congo*. Bruxelles: Editions de l'Institut de Sociologie Solvay

Rajak, D. (2011). *In Good Company. An Anatomy of Corporate Social Responsibility*. Stanford, CA: Stanford University Press

Rubbers, B. (2009). *Faire fortune en Afrique. Anthropologie des derniers colons du Katanga*. Paris: Karthala

Rubbers, B. (2019). Mining boom, Labour Market Segmentation and Social Inequality in the Congolese Copperbelt. *Development and Change* 51(6): 1555–78

Uzar, E. (2017). Contested Labour and Political Leadership: Three Mineworkers' Unions after the Opposition Victory in Zambia. *Review of African Political Economy* 44(152): 292–311

Watson T. (1994). *In Search of Management. Culture, Chaos and Control in Managerial Work*. London: Routledge

Welker, M. (2014). *Enacting the Corporation. An American Mining Firm in Post-Authoritarian Indonesia*. Berkeley: University of California Press

Whyte, W.H. (2013). *The Organization Man*. Philadelphia, PA: University of Pennsylvania Press

Conclusion: Beyond the Neoliberal Labour Regime

BENJAMIN RUBBERS

This book has sought to study the power relations implicated in the labour practices that new mining investors have put in place in the Congolese and Zambian copperbelts since the early 2000s. These show certain general trends that contrast with the labour practices of Générale des Carrières et des Mines (Gécamines) and Zambian Consolidated Copper Mines (ZCCM) in the twentieth century: the new investors hire fewer workers, grant them with fewer benefits in kind; they do not hesitate to carry out mass layoffs in response to copper price reductions or tax increases; and a growing number of their activities are outsourced. As a result of these trends, the mining workforce in both countries has become smaller, more fragmented and more precarious than in the past.

As explained in the first chapter, these trends point to the emergence of a neoliberal labour regime, which can be associated with other general characteristics of mining projects in the twenty-first century, such as their tendency to operate within securitised enclaves and the development of Corporate Social Responsibility programmes. Far from being specific to the Central African Copperbelt, the characteristics of this labour regime can be found in most mining projects in the Global South. Indeed, this regime results from three main processes which have affected the mining sector as a whole. First, it is a response to the slow depletion of high-grade deposits since the nineteenth century, which has pushed mining corporations to search for ever larger and poorer deposits globally. Over the course of the twentieth century, mining and processing became increasingly mechanised, the number of workers in the industry was progressively reduced, and labour costs were cut all round – a process that primarily impacted the least skilled workers (Schmitz 2000). Secondly, because of the escalation of production costs, mining companies increasingly depended on financial markets to start or develop mining projects. Since the 1990s, the financial institutions willing to lend capital for risky mining ventures in the Global South have tended to demand high returns in the short term. The characteristic features of the neoliberal labour regime – starting with increasing job insecurity – can thus be associated with the rise of the shareholder value and lean management models among listed firms since the 1990s (Aglietta and Reberioux 2005; Ho 2009). Finally, this labour regime must be understood in the light of the neoliberal reforms that most countries in the Global South implemented under pressure from international financial institutions in the 1980s and 1990s. These reforms have provided foreign investors with favourable conditions for developing flexible labour practices: pro-employer laws, under-resourced labour administrations, weakened trade unions and, most importantly, a labour reserve army ready to work in the mining industry for low wages (see Standing 1997, 1999, 2001).

In many ways, this neoliberal labour regime breaks with the state paternalism characteristic of the heyday of Gécamines and ZCCM. The management of new mining companies do not hesitate to take credit for this break. In their view, paternalism was responsible for the decline of the two state-owned companies; in the neoliberal era, cutting labour costs is nothing less than a matter of survival. Although new mining investors develop CSR programmes, such programmes contrast with twentieth century paternalism in at least two respects. First, their main target is less the company's own workforce than local communities.[1] A striking example is the message that Mopani in Zambia sent to its employees in November 2015, announcing the dismissal of 4,300 workers. In the message, this dismissal is first presented as a necessary measure to ensure the company's viability, and as a measure that is comparatively favourable to the workers, since management had initially envisaged retrenching more than 6,500 workers. Later in the same message, however, the company provides the assurance that it will continue its CSR programme in local communities – a programme in which it claims to invest millions each year. Second, when it comes to workers, mining companies' CSR programmes focus almost exclusively on health and safety (Rajak 2011). As James Musonda and Francesca Pugliese suggest in Chapter 2, if mining companies continue to care for workers' lives, their care practices are largely reduced to biological life (*zoë*), to the exclusion of any consideration for workers' own conceptions of the good life (*bios*) (on this distinction, see Agamben 1998). This politics of life contrasts with the social policies developed by ZCCM and Gécamines in the second half of the twentieth century, which encompassed most aspects of the existence of workers. They did not simply aim to make workers live, but to reform their subjectivities – that is, the way they constitute themselves as ethical subjects in their relationship to others (Rubbers 2013). In doing so, although imperfectly, they allowed them to develop a 'modern' lifestyle, corresponding to what the workers themselves saw as a life worth living (Ferguson 1999).

* * *

[1] Of course, members of local communities may also be part of the workforce of mining companies. This is especially the case in remote rural areas, where mining companies' social programmes generally include the creation of jobs for the benefit of local communities. As mentioned in Chapter 1, however, these 'local' workers remain few in number, and most of them are at the bottom of the company hierarchy.

It is important, however, to recall that the concept of neoliberalism is used here as an ideal type in the Weberian sense of the word, that is, a methodological tool aimed at investigating further common trends and variations. The neoliberal narrative proposed above (i.e. the rise of a flexible labour regime superseding the paternalism of State-Owned Enterprises, or SOEs) should not lead us to neglect the diversity of mining projects characteristic of the recent boom. The comparison of new mining projects in the Central African Copperbelt suggests that their labour practices show a number of important variations, depending on the type of capital involved (state vs private), the type of mine being developed (underground vs surface) and the area where they are established (urban vs rural).

First, on the basis of research in the Zambian copperbelt, Lee (2017) shows that NFCA, a Chinese SOE, offers to its workers more stable jobs but lower wages than Konkola and Mopani, two global private companies. Moreover, instead of putting subcontractors in competition for operating the mine, it works on a long-term basis with a single subcontractor, who provides conditions of employment similar to the mining company. For Lee, this different 'labour bargain' is to be interpreted through the imperatives to which both types of companies are confronted. While global private capital is driven by the imperative of short-term shareholder value maximisation, Chinese state capital is subjected to various economic, strategic and diplomatic imperatives. Such imperatives lead NFCA to develop its activities in a longer-term perspective and to be more sensitive to political pressures. When confronted to (repeated) strikes and (strong) pressures from the government, it has been more willing to make concessions than Konkola and Mopani.

The comparison that Thomas McNamara and Kristien Geenen make between ChinMin, another CNMC's subsidiary, and Sino-Congolaise des Mines (Sicomines) in Chapter 5 supports this analysis, even though the Sicomines project in Congo entered into the production phase more recently and has been subjected to less political pressure than NFCA and ChinMin in Zambia. On the basis of a case study, I have highlighted elsewhere the existence of a third scenario in Congo, that of mining projects developed by global private companies, and then bought out by Chinese SOEs (Rubbers 2020a). Such projects seem to provide better employment conditions that those initially developed by global private or Chinese SOEs. As they take control of operational mines, the new Chinese owners retain the terms of employment established by their predecessor. The wages in these companies are thus within the range of those offered by global private companies, approximatively 30 per cent above those in projects run by Chinese SOEs. At the same time, as they benefit from state funding, they generally have the opportunity to provide more stable jobs than private global companies which strive to maximise short-term profits for their shareholders.

Second, the three companies studied by Lee (2017) operate (old) underground mines in Zambia's Copperbelt Province. From management's point of view, the best means to increase productivity in such mines is either to reduce workers' wages to the greatest extent possible (NFCA's choice), or to hire several subcontractors and to spark competition among them through a production bonus scheme (Konkola's and Mopani's choice). In contrast, most mining companies in Congo, as well as those established in North-Western Province of Zambia, operate opencast mines. Productivity in such mines is, above all, a function of the size of the fleet of mining vehicles, their loading capacity and the traffic flow in the pit. As a result, whether public or private, companies operating opencast mines tend to prefer working with a limited number of large, reliable, subcontracting firms that offer more or less equivalent conditions of employment to mining companies.

Third, and finally, the refusal to take over existing social infrastructure, or to develop new ones, does not only depend on capital's requirements, but also on the availability of housing and social infrastructure near the mines (Rubbers 2019a). When the mine is near a large urban centre, mining companies can pay their workers a housing allowance to arrange their own accommodation. Mining projects in remote rural areas, on the other hand, have to build camps to house their workers. The most striking case is perhaps Kalumbila, in North-Western Province (Zambia), where First Quantum has built a new 'company town' with hundreds of houses as well as schools and sport facilities. Like the mining companies of the colonial period, its aim was to attract skilled and experienced miners from Copperbelt Province, 300 km from Kalumbila, and to 'stabilise' them in this remote rural location by providing them with the necessary infrastructure to develop a 'modern' family life. In contrast to the mining companies of the past, however, First Quantum does not house the workers: the houses are for rent and purchase, which generates some dissatisfaction among workers who would have preferred to invest in the towns of Copperbelt Province. Consequently, it is they who, in their view, will eventually bear the cost of the new model town built by the company, as it is likely to become a 'ghost town' once First Quantum leaves the country.

* * *

The concept of the neoliberal labour regime should not lead us to neglect how new mining projects' labour practices are mediated, negotiated, or resisted by various categories of actors locally. The preceding chapters bring to light the agency of workers, trade unionists and Human Resource (HR) managers in the making of new mining projects' labour strategies and the complexity of the power games involved.

It is often these local actors who have to manage with the multiple contradictions generated by the new labour regime on a day-to-day basis: for mineworkers at the rock face, it is the contradiction between the pressure to increase production and compliance with safety rules; for women working in mining, the contradiction between the implementation of gender equality programmes and the various forms of everyday discrimination imposed upon them in the workplace; for trade unionists, the contradiction between their promise to obtain better employment conditions during elections and the importance to preserve workers' jobs during negotiations; for HR managers, the contradiction between the decisions made by expatriate management and their consequences for the national workforce of which they are part. In each of these cases, the practical solutions that local actors find to overcome contradictions have consequences on their life: some workers do not report minor injuries; some women have to walk kilometres wearing oversized shoes every day; some trade unionists lose their fellow workers' trust; some HR managers are the subject of slander in the community and receive threatening anonymous letters from workers. In many ways, however, this is a game these local actors cannot *not* play, at least if they do not want to end up losing their jobs (Finn 1998: 219).

Although it takes place in a field of significant constraints, the agency of workers, trade unionists and HR managers contributes to shape mining companies' labour strategies. They play a significant role in recruitment practices, the negotiation of wages and benefits, the improvement of working conditions, compliance of companies with labour laws, and the organisation of mass layoffs. However, the case studies we carried out show that the margin for negotiation of local actors not only varies from one domain to the next, but also from one mining project to another. The micropolitics of work do not take the same form or have the same effect in the different types of mining project identified above.

Such variations are well illustrated in the two chapters by Pugliese and Musonda. In the chapter on safety, they show that new rules and procedures have been imposed by foreign investors in this domain without leaving much room for workers to change them formally. But the way in which workers put them into practice differs between the two mines under study, one being an opencast mine and the other an underground mine. In the underground mine in Zambia, contract workers have to circumvent safety rules and procedures informally if they want to meet their production targets and get a bonus at the end of the month, while in the opencast mine in Congo, where the production bonus is less significant or non-existent, workers have no interest – except for their personal convenience – in deviating from safety rules and procedures. In the chapter on gender, on the other hand, Pugliese and Musonda's analysis suggests that gender equality initiatives by the parent company headquarters have had only a marginal effect locally. The main reason is that the people responsible for recruiting and promoting workers, who are generally Congolese or Zambian men, are still reluctant to hire women in the core departments of the mine – that is, mining, processing and maintenance. If the recent boom has represented a missed opportunity to introduce more gender equality in the mining sector, this is to a large extent due to the power games involved in the recruitment and promotion practices, the changes that have taken place in the contribution of women in household revenues, and the gender stereotypes prevailing in the two copperbelts.

Having said this, the negotiation margin of local actors also changes over time. Chapter 6 on HR managers suggests that, for various reasons, this 'band of flexibility' tends to shrink with the development of mining projects. Indeed, once a mining project starts production, it only has a limited number of skilled workers, and the parent company tends to exert tighter control over its operating costs. In the Central African Copperbelt, the development of new mining projects has been furthermore marked by two recent economic downturns – following the financial crisis in 2008–10, and during the decline in copper prices in 2011–16 – which led investors to rationalise the management of mining projects and to cut labour costs. This lean management strategy has considerably narrowed the room for manoeuvre available to HR managers, but also to other local actors (trade unionists, customary chiefs, workers, etc.) in the making of mining projects' labour practices.

* * *

The micropolitics of work in the mining sector has contributed to the transformation of various power constellations in Congo and Zambia. The evolution of the union power field provides in this respect intriguing similarities and differences. In both countries, the mining boom was accompanied by the creation of new unions which began to compete with more established unions to represent the workers in companies. Generally speaking, they are in a weak position with respect to their employers. The reasons for this weakness differ. In Congo, for instance, a large number of small unions compete to represent the workers in mining companies. As a result, they depend to a large extent on these companies' goodwill to organise union elections, to negotiate with the existing union delegation and to collect union dues, which are deducted from the pay of all employees by the employer. In Zambia, by contrast, unions are fewer and larger, and on the surface, because their presence in companies is guaranteed and union dues are paid directly by the workers, they have greater autonomy from employers. But, for various reasons, mining companies in Zambia show less hesitation than in Congo to use mass layoffs as a threat when negotiating wage increases with union representatives. For this reason, wages here are not higher than in Congo.[2] That said, unions in both copperbelts managed to obtain minor benefits for the workers in their

[2] To compensate for low wages and retain their members, the MUZ has started to offer various goods and services to workers with the financial support of mining companies. In doing so, it has created an unexpected situation in which some of the goods and services that were once provided by the companies with the framework of a paternalistic labour regime are now outsourced to unions, which operate as business ventures (McNamara 2021).

negotiations with employers. In the opinion of all the workers, their working conditions would be worse today had the unions not been there to defend their interests.

Outside of the union power field, various actors in the political arena have seized on the issue of employment in the mining sector (job and contract opportunities, access to managerial positions, wages and working conditions, mass layoffs, etc.) to extend their support base and impose themselves as essential interlocutors between local people and foreign investors. Such practices – which could be compared to what Benda-Beckman (1981) calls 'shopping forums' – have led in both countries to a resurgence of local, provincial and/or national identity politics in the past fifteen years. In Zambia, employment in the mining sector was one of the key electoral campaign issues that led to the rise of the governing party, Michael Sata's Patriotic Front, which found a strong support base in Copperbelt Province. Given the political weight of mineworkers in this province, the party leaders are sensitive to their demands and, as the chapter on strikes shows, do not hesitate to intervene in labour disputes on their behalf.

In Congo, mineworkers do not have comparable influence, whether in the provincial or in the national political arena, which are more strongly organised along ethnic/provincial lines. This does not mean, of course, that ethnic and provincial identities have no significance in Zambia, especially in North-Western Province, but they do not constitute a political resource as powerful as in Congo, where they have provided a basis for mass violence on several occasions since independence. Over the past twenty years, the establishment of new mining companies, and then the *découpage* (that is, the partition) of Katanga into four smaller provinces in 2015 has stirred growing ethnic competition for jobs and power positions in the mining sector and the state administration. In this context, new mining companies are under increasing pressure from all sides to provide jobs to the ethnic groups autochthonous to the area or province where they are established (Rubbers 2019b).

This growing political competition must be understood in the light of the inequalities that the establishment of new mining companies has helped engender and exacerbate in the two copperbelts. Contrary to what studies focusing on the dispossession of local communities by foreign corporations suggest, the recent boom of mining investments in the Central African Copperbelt has not resulted in a simple division between winners and losers. As in several other mining contexts in the Global South, the recruiting practices of foreign investors have resulted in what Hecht (2002: 699; see also Welker 2014: 81; Golub 2014: 5–6) has called an 'ethnotechnical hierarchy', with expatriate executives and specialised technicians at the top, skilled employees from the country's major cities in the middle, and the local unskilled workers at the bottom. At the same time, the development of subcontracting in the mining industry has led to the emergence of a class of small and midsized entrepreneurs and the formation of a large secondary labour market associated with precarious jobs and low wages. Finally, the consumption practices of these various categories of workers and entrepreneurs has had a significant effect on various sectors (construction, transport, food, schools, bars, etc.) with their own labour dynamics.

Labour can thus be fruitfully used as an entry point for analysing the class inequalities engendered by the mining boom (Wright 1997; see Rubbers 2019b). This analysis needs however to be complemented by a broader study of the social trajectories of various categories of people, which would examine in more detail their social mobility strategies and the role played by attributes such as age, gender, or ethnicity (Noret 2020; see Rubbers 2020b). Such an approach would enable a more comprehensive understanding of how new mining investments have transformed the social space of the two copperbelts.

* * *

In January 2018, and again in January 2019, we organised restitution seminars in Kitwe, Lubumbashi and Kolwezi to present the preliminary results of our research before a limited number of experts.[3] Depending on the situation, the audience numbered ten to forty people, and comprised HR managers, trade unionists, workers, consultants, university researchers and representatives of civil society organisations. On several occasions, in public or after the seminar, some participants asked me if we would make recommendations and, every time, my negative response aroused incomprehension: 'I can't believe that all this research will not lead to any recommendation', a trade unionist told me in Lubumbashi, and a civil society organisation representative immediately complemented this comment with a rhetorical question: 'If you, who have developed such an in-depth knowledge of the issue, do not make any recommendation, who will do it?'

My answer was not very original. I simply explained that our aim was to describe what is going on and try to understand why, not to tell people what should be done. There is no necessary link between the two, and it is the responsibility of Congolese and Zambian people to decide about their future. In other words, I gave the kind of answer that most social scientists give when confronted by such requests. The aim of social science research is to produce empirical and critical knowledge about historical processes. This knowledge can help people to better understand their situation, and in doing so, allow them to make informed decisions about their future, but it does not in itself grant the researcher the authority to make policy recommendations.

3 The seminars, which were part of the benefit-sharing arrangements of the project, had three practical aims. The first was to receive comments on our work, and test its acceptance by research participants. The second was to give voice to local researchers, and envisage research collaborations with them. The third was to create a dialogue between participants on labour in the mining industry, and to use these discussions to feed in our own reflections on the subject.

Since then, the dissatisfaction this flip answer aroused among my interlocutors has led me to reflect further on the issue. In one way or another, a social science researcher should respond to the concerns of research participants who wait for possible solutions to the problems they are confronted by in everyday life. Even without making recommendations, I could have opened up the debate on the range of possibilities offered to my interlocutors by sharing and discussing some of the ideas expressed by research participants in the course of our investigation: for instance, to organise the negotiation of a collective agreement at industry level, which would set minimum wages and benefits for different categories of workers, cost-of-living increases, maximum working hours, the number of permitted day leaves and so forth; to relax the procedures for organising legal strikes and empowering unions in wage negotiations; to tighten mass layoff procedures by conditioning such measures on an independent financial audit and the organisation of a social compensation plan; to set a minimum percentage for the permanent workforce and to impose strict rules regarding the employment of contract workers; to fight against various forms of discrimination by establishing a clear legal framework in favour of nationals, women and local communities; to make legal action against mining companies more accessible, fair and effective for workers and unions; to make the mining industry more transparent about their labour practices by forcing companies to provide information and authorise external controls; and to institute stiff penalties for non-compliance with established rules.

Even though they would not necessarily lead to a return of state paternalism similar to that of ZCCM or Gécamines in the past, all these ideas have in common a call for greater control of mining companies' labour practices by the state and better protections for mineworkers. Far from expressing fantasies disconnected from their everyday experience, they also call for practical solutions that lie within the reach of the Congolese and Zambian governments. After all, since the beginning of the mining boom in the 2000s, both states have taken initiatives to regain control over the distribution of mining revenues, and no longer hesitate to take radical measures to force the hand of foreign investors such as suspending their contracts, suing them in court, or withdrawing their mining licences. To be sure, these initiatives and measures were not taken on the sole initiative of governments (rather, they were taken in response to the pressure of civil society organisations and to gain the support of the electorate), and they gave rise to tough and lengthy negotiations. In some cases, political leaders gave in to the threats of mining companies; in others, they made unilateral decisions that turned out to have adverse consequences. Such jolts, however, should not hide the trend that is emerging. Since the financial crisis of 2008, there has been – to use Balandier's (1971 [1955]) expression – a 'resumption of initiative' (*reprise d'initiative*) by the Congolese and Zambian governments in the regulation of the mining sector.

For now, these political initiatives are limited to regaining control over the distribution of mining revenues. In the domain of labour, notwithstanding the superficial changes they have brought into the law, the only actions political leaders have taken are to intervene with mining companies conducting mass layoffs in an attempt to save jobs. Little has been done to sustainably improve conditions of employment that might align with the ideas above – i.e. to strengthen the bargaining power of unions, to tighten mass layoff procedures, to limit the negative effects of subcontracting practices, or to fight discrimination in the labour market. Yet, to escape the neoliberal labour regime that we have attempted to characterise in this book, it is necessary to move the debate on mining investments beyond tax issues, and to refocus it on labour and conditions of employment. If there is anything we have learned from our research, it is that, far from having become marginal, this issue remains at the heart of people's concerns in the Central African Copperbelt.

Bibliography

Agamben, G. (1998). *Homo Sacer: Sovereign Power and Bare Life*. Stanford, CA: Stanford University Press

Aglietta, M. and Reberioux, A. (2005). *Corporate Governance Adrift. A Critique of Shareholder Value*. Cheltenham: Edward Elgar Publishing

Balandier, G. (1971 [1955]). *Sociologie actuelle de l'Afrique noire. Dynamique sociale en Afrique Centrale*. Paris: Presses Universitaires de France

Benda-Beckman, K. (1981). Forum Shopping and Shopping Forums: Dispute Processing in a Minangkabau Village in West Sumatra. *Journal of Legal Pluralism and Unofficial Law* 13: 117–59

Ferguson, J. (1999). *Expectations of Modernity. Myths and Meanings of Urban Life on the Zambian Copperbelt*. Berkeley: University of California Press

Finn, J. (1998) *Tracing the Veins. Of Copper, Culture and Community from Butte to Chuquicamata*. Berkeley: University of California Press

Golub, A. (2014). *Leviathans at the Gold Mine. Creating Indigenous and Corporate Actors in Papua New Guinea*. Durham, NC: Duke University Press

Hecht, G. (2002) Rupture-talk in the Nuclear Age: Conjugating Colonial Power in Africa. *Social Studies of Science* 32(5–6): 691–727

Ho, K. (2009). *Liquidated. An Ethnography of Wall Street*. Durham, NC: Duke University Press

Lee, C.K. (2017). *The Spectre of Global China. Politics, Labor, and Foreign Investment in Africa*. Chicago, IL: University of Chicago Press

McNamara, T. (2021). A Reasonable Negotiation? Workplace-based Unionists' Subjectivities, Wage Negotiations and the Day-to-day Life of an Ethical-Political Project. *Journal of the Royal Anthropological Institute* 27(3): 617–37

Noret, J. (2020). Introduction. Theorizing Social Im/mobilities in Africa. In Noret, J., ed. *Social Im/Mobilities in Africa. Ethnographic Approaches*. Oxford: Berghahn, pp. 1–26

Rajak, D. (2011). *In Good Company. An Anatomy of Corporate Social Responsibility*. Stanford, CA: Stanford University Press

Rubbers, B. (2013). *Le paternalisme en question. Les anciens ouvriers de la Gécamines face à la libéralisation du secteur minier katangais (R.D.Congo).* Paris: L'Harmattan

Rubbers, B. (2019a). Mining Towns, Enclaves and Spaces: A Genealogy of Worker Camps in the Congolese Copperbelt. *Geoforum* 98: 88–96

Rubbers, B. (2019b). Mining boom, Labour Market Segmentation and Social Inequality in the Congolese Copperbelt. *Development and Change* 51(6): 1555–78

Rubbers, B. (2020a). Governing New Mining Projects. The View from the HR Department of a Chinese Company in the Congolese Copperbelt. *Extractive Industries and Society* 7(1): 191–98

Rubbers, B. (2020b). The Dynamics of Inequality in the Congolese Copperbelt: A Discussion of Bourdieu's Theory of Social Space. In Noret, J., ed., *Social Im/Mobilities in Africa. Ethnographic Approaches.* Oxford: Berghahn, pp. 132–54

Schmitz, C. (2000). The World Copper Industry: Geology, Mining Techniques and Corporate Growth, 1870–1939. *Journal of European Economic History* 29(1): 77–105

Standing, G. (1997). Globalization, Labour Flexibility and Insecurity: The Era of Market Regulation. *European Journal of Industrial Relations* 3(1): 7–37

Standing, G. (1999). *Global Labour Flexibility. Seeking Distributive Justice.* New York: Palgrave Macmillan

Standing, G. (2001). *Beyond the New Paternalism. Basic Security as Equality.* London: Verso

Welker, M. (2014). *Enacting the Corporation. An American Mining Firm in Post-Authoritarian Indonesia.* Berkeley: University of California Press

Wright, E.O. (1997). *Class Counts. Comparative Studies in Class Analysis.* Cambridge: Cambridge University Press

INDEX

Printed and bound by CPI Group (UK) Ltd, Croydon, CR0 4YY

09/06/2025

14685698-0001